BRINGING THEM UP ROYAL

BRINGING THEM UP ROYAL

How the royals raised their children from 1066 to the present day

DAVID COHEN

The Robson Press

First published in Great Britain in 2012 by
The Robson Press (an imprint of Biteback Publishing Ltd)
Westminster Tower
3 Albert Embankment
London SE1 7SP
Copyright © David Cohen 2012

ISBN 978-1-84954-369-9

10 9 8 7 6 5 4 3 2 1

A CIP catalogue record for this book is available from the British Library.

Set in Garamond

Printed and bound in Great Britain by
CPI Group (UK) Ltd, Croydon CRO 4YY

People talk about a normal upbringing. What is a normal upbring-ing? What you really mean – was I insisting that they go through all the disadvantages of being brought up in the way other children are brought up? Precisely that – disadvantages.

Prince Philip, on being a father

> If you prick us, do we not bleed?
> If you tickle us, do we not laugh?
> If you poison us, do we not die?
> And if you wrong us, do we not revenge?
> If we are like you in the rest
> We will resemble you in that.

William Shakespeare, The Merchant of Venice

I dedicate this book to Adele La Tourette, with love.

CONTENTS

1

THE THOUSAND-YEAR CASE HISTORY

'The Queen, like all young mothers, is *exigeante* and never thinks the baby makes progress enough or is good enough,' wrote Lady Sarah Lyttelton, the royal governess and great-great-grandmother of the late Princess Diana, on 6 October 1843. The inadequate infant was Queen Victoria and Prince Albert's first child, Princess Victoria.

When Lady Diana Spencer married Prince Charles on 29 July 1981, she was thought a suitable bride for the most medieval of reasons: she was a virgin. Her duty was to produce an irreproachable heir to the throne and, as she later put it, a 'back up'. No member of the royal family asked whether Diana would be a good mother. When it became clear she was a devoted and intelligent one, many were amazed. With some exceptions, the royals have not distinguished themselves as parents over the last 1,000 years.

A small example of imperfect parenting: when Prince William was hit by a golf club and badly injured just before his tenth birthday, Diana rushed to his school and took him to hospital for a brain scan. Prince Charles came too, but there was no question of him lingering by his son's bedside, as he was scheduled to attend an opera. The press pilloried the Prince of Wales, though through history royal fathers were often much crueller; they have imprisoned, beaten and in some cases even killed their sons.

Today, the ideal royal parent would be loving, intelligent and emotionally intelligent, and would bring up their children to possess all those qualities as well as being heroic, as kings have always been expected to be. Shakespeare understood that a Prince also needed the common touch. In his *Henry V*, the King wanders incognito among his troops on the eve of the battle of Agincourt to find out what they really think. To be ordinary, and yet also extraordinary, is asking a great deal. The royal 'child' who now best delivers both the 'common' and heroic is perhaps the 'back up': Prince Harry. He has served in Afghanistan, got plastered with his fellow soldiers, been snapped in the nude and risked his life on the front line; he has also become involved in charity work for Help for Heroes and Walking with the Wounded.

E. M. Forster wrote, 'How do I know what I think till I see what I say?' – and that has been true of my experience in writing this book. It was not until I was some way into my research that I realised the British royal family offers one of the longest, if not *the* longest, case history of an extended family. Using the phrase 'case history' does not imply that every individual royal since 1066 required the services of a therapist; however, some did, and many more might have benefited from such services.

On their father's side, the Princes William and Harry can trace their descent to William the Conqueror, who won the Battle of Hastings in 1066. On their mother's side, the DNA spools back to Charles II, who enjoyed at least twelve mistresses. Among others, the 'merry monarch' fathered Henry FitzRoy, Duke of Grafton, and Charles Lennox, Duke of Richmond. Beyond Charles II, Princes William and Harry can trace their maternal ancestry back to the Despenser family. Relations between that family and the monarchs were not always harmonious, though: in 1326, for example, Queen Isabella, the wife of Edward II, had Hugh Despenser executed for treason. When Lady Diana Spencer wed Prince Charles, she was marrying the descendant of a woman who had had one of her ancestors killed.

We cannot begin to construct a similar ten-centuries-long case history for the families of George Washington, Mozart, Einstein, Freud, Marx, Stalin or even the Kennedys – few details exist as to how they brought up their children. No one cared about the Mozarts in 1500 and no one knows where the Freuds lived, though many analytic zealots have tried to trace Sigmund's family back to Noah's Ark. We cannot begin to write a similar history for Mafia families, who, like the royals, fascinate because they are so different from normal families – and yet so similar.

Despite hundreds of biographies of kings and queens, which range through the obsequious to the considered to the gloriously bitchy, there does not seem to have been any attempt to study the ways in which royal parents have brought up their children, and to trace how these early experiences affected their later lives. In this book, I shall do just that, interweaving history with the infinitely younger discipline of child psychology, which is not even 150 years old. The discipline owes much to Charles Darwin. In 1877, he wrote *A Biographical Sketch of an Infant*, in which he recorded observations of his son. Darwin was not quite objective, referring to William as 'a prodigy of beauty & intellect', but the great naturalist was, as ever, an acute observer. In a daily diary, he noted William's gestures and facial expressions and compared his child's behaviour with that of the apes in London Zoo. Darwin's sketches inspired a number of psychologists to study their own children. Over the next fifty years, these often charming observations became more ambitious as psychologists tried to identify how the young were affected, even 'shaped', by early experiences. Some of those who tried – Freud, Jean Piaget, John B. Watson and B. F. Skinner – were among the most influential psychologists of the twentieth century.

There are a number of reasons that may explain the dearth of studies into royal upbringings. First, most historians know little psychology and most psychologists know even less history. Second, historians mainly study documents and, until the fifteenth century, there is usually insufficient evidence as to how any royal child was raised. There are some important exceptions, though, as we shall see in Chapter 2.

Then, F. A. Mumby's *The Girlhood of Queen Elizabeth* (1909) offers a wealth of information on the Virgin Queen from British, French and Venetian archives, while Queen Victoria's diary describes many aspects of her childhood and that of her children.

Prince Philip's grandmother, Princess Victoria, wrote 308 pages of recollections that have never been published. Marion Crawford's *The Little Princesses* deals with the childhood of the present Queen and her sister, Princess Margaret, and is peppered with astute observations. Precisely because the children of royals were expected to inherit the throne, material is also scattered in chronicles, letters and diaries. I have tried to make sense of this scatter, and this has led me to observe some profound changes in royal parenting over the last 1,000 years.

For four centuries after 1066, any would-be king had to be a good fighter, and parenting royal boys was an intensely physical business. Fathers often taught their sons how to handle swords, maces and even bows and arrows; they regularly fought side by side in battle. Every English king commanded forces in combat at some point in his life, and a few were even good generals.

By the mid-sixteenth century, monarchs had to be wily politicians rather than military leaders. Razor-sharp wit mattered more than rapiers and, for 150 years, royal parents ensured their offspring had the best teachers in Europe. These princes and princesses made the most of their stellar education and, without ghostwriters, produced a number of learned tracts, translations and even a few decent poems.

James I (and VI) had a superb education and was probably the best writer ever to sit on the throne. He admired his great-grandfather, James IV, who had conducted one of the first psychological experiments when he arranged for two children to live with a mute woman on a Scottish island to discover whether they had to hear language being spoken in order to speak themselves. The question posed by James I's great-grandfather – is language innate or learned? – is still debated. James wrote a number of decent poems and books, including a book for his eldest son, Prince Henry, giving him fatherly advice on how to be King.

After James I, there was much less emphasis on the education of royal sons and daughters, however. The intellectual calibre of the monarchy declined in 1714 when George I, the Elector of Hanover, took the throne. George I not only spoke dreadful English and lacked any intellectual curiosity, but also his appalling behaviour to his oldest son set the pattern for the next four generations. Between 1714 and 1820, royal fathers and their eldest sons were permanently hostile to each other. (Indeed, George III tried to kill his heir.) The next change in pattern concerns Queen Victoria, who was born in 1819 – a year before George III died. She was a victim of emotional abuse, the consequences of which are still with us.

Emotional abuse and Queen Victoria

Victoria's father died when she was still a baby. Her widowed mother, the Duchess of Kent, and her adviser, John Conroy, controlled every aspect of the Princess's life. This obsessive control left its mark. Victoria's granddaughter recalled her own mother saying that Queen Victoria once snapped, 'I detest this room', while in the tapestry room at Windsor Castle. When she was fifteen, Victoria's mother had scolded her furiously there, accusing her 'of making up to the King [William IV] at dinner'. The Duchess was furious because 'the King had drunk her [Victoria's] health and insulted her mother'. Though so many years had passed, Victoria remembered her mother's anger vividly.

Conroy encouraged the writing of a pamphlet to explain what he grandly called 'The Kensington System', after the family's Kensington Palace residence. The System had rigid rules. One was that Victoria was not allowed to meet anyone without her mother, Conroy or her governess present. There were endless confrontations between the Duchess and King William IV because she would not let him see his niece very often. As a result, Victoria felt bullied and unloved. When she became Queen, she turned against her mother and Conroy, but those who have been abused often abuse in turn. Victoria tried to control her own children, but she felt their experiences would be very different because she loved them, as did her husband, Prince Albert.

Victoria and Albert were so neurotic about their eldest son,

Bertie, that they became the first royal parents to seek professional psychiatric help for one of their offspring. They tried to improve their unsatisfactory son by having his skull analysed by George Combe, Britain's leading authority on phrenology – a then fashionable theory which claimed one could understand a person's character by mapping the bumps on their skull. Combe devised a programme of remedial education for Bertie, whose bumps left much to be desired. The child loathed the whole humiliating business and reacted against it when he himself became a father in 1864. He tried not to repeat the mistakes that he felt his parents had made with him. His second son – the future George V – saw that his father's lenience had disastrous consequences, and in turn became as demanding a parent as Prince Albert and Queen Victoria had ever been. George's eldest son, David, the future Edward VIII, was the victim of this severity and wrote that he was 'in unconscious rebellion against my father'. It would seem someone had introduced David to Freud's writings. And Freud figures more in recent royal history than one might imagine. It is no accident that, when the Freud Museum was opened in London, Princess Alexandra performed the ceremony.

Freud and the ambitions of psychohistory

Since the mid-nineteenth century, many brilliant historians have concentrated on political, social and economic history. At school, I had two distinguished teachers: Peter Brooks, who went on to become Dean of Peterhouse, Cambridge, and T. E. B. Howarth, later Master of Trinity College, Oxford. They taught us to look at the reasons why we won the Battle of Agincourt, why we defeated the Spanish Armada and how George III lost America. As a schoolboy, I had to master the arguments between Catholics, Lutherans, Calvinists and the God-fearing, sex-crazed Anabaptists, who seized the town of Munster in 1534 and declared the Kingdom of God on Earth had materialised in the town. The cage in which the tortured remains of their leader, John of Leiden, was exhibited still hangs from the steeple of

St Lambert's Church. The closest we came to discussing any psychological 'causes' of history was the thesis put forward by Max Weber, who argued that the rise of capitalism was helped by the Reformation. Protestants were more motivated to achieve, if only to convince themselves that they were among the elect who would be on a flight path to Heaven.

In a number of his writings after 1910, Freud attempts to use psychoanalytic insights to understand historical personalities. He first examined da Vinci's 'The Virgin and Child with St Anne' and offered an analytic interpretation. Look at the Virgin's garment sideways and you see a vulture, he claimed, arguing that this was a manifestation of a 'passive homosexual' childhood fantasy. In the *Codex Atlanticus*, da Vinci describes being attacked in his crib by a vulture. Freud translated the passage as follows: 'I recall as one of my very earliest memories that while I was in my cradle a vulture came down to me, and opened my mouth with its tail, and struck me many times with its tail against my lips.'

The tail in the mouth symbolises fellatio. Freud believed da Vinci's fantasy was based on the memory of sucking his mother's nipple. Freud had a surrealist imagination and produced a theory to match. Da Vinci's fantasy, he claimed, was connected to Egyptian hieroglyphs that represented the mother as a vulture because the Egyptians believed male vultures did not exist. Unfortunately, the word 'vulture' was a mistranslation. The bird that da Vinci imagined was, in fact, a kite, which rather destroyed Freud's thesis, as there are male kites – and the Egyptians knew that.

Freud's mistake enabled many historians to belittle his ideas but the Pentagon either did not know or did not care about these academic squabbles. In 1943, the American military contacted a young psychiatrist, Walter Langer, who had studied psychoanalysis in Vienna before the start of the war. He was asked to collaborate on a top-secret psychological profile of Hitler. The Allies hoped Langer's analysis would reveal Hitler's weaknesses and offer suggestions on how to defeat him. However, the study was cautious and did not draw far-reaching conclusions from limited facts.

Any hope that historians would employ psychology seriously was destroyed in 1958, when the well-known psychoanalyst Erik Erikson published *Young Man Luther*. Luther rebelled against the Church because he had unresolved issues with his father, Erikson argued. The youngish monk, who pinned his ninety-five theses to the door of the church at Wittenberg, was furious with the Pope because he had never dealt with his anger towards his own father. Many historians were unimpressed, particularly as Erikson made a number of factual errors and relied far too much on three remarks allegedly made by Luther in old age. Erikson's book sparked much controversy but he chose to stay aloof and refused to respond to criticism.

In 1967, nearly thirty years after he died, Freud 'published' his last book. It was a biography of President Woodrow Wilson, co-authored with William Bullitt, a former patient of Freud, who became the first American ambassador to the Soviet Union. The work was a devastating attack on Wilson, who never began to understand his neuroses. As a result of never having seen a therapist, he lacked insight and was subsequently out-manoeuvred by Clemenceau and Lloyd George in the negotiations for the Treaty of Versailles. As Bullitt knew Wilson well and Freud's nephew, Edward Bernays, had also worked for the President, the book was formidably well-researched, though marred by the contempt both authors had for their subject. The President suffered from subconscious cannibalism, they bitched, and wanted to eat his father, whom he pretended to adore.

In general, historians remain wary of descending into what many see as a pit of psychobabble. In her biography of Charles II, for example, Lady Antonia Fraser snipes that 'in his case blood was evidently less important than those early formative years rated so highly by the Jesuits and modern psychology', dumping Freud and Ignatius Loyola in the same unsatisfactory pot. But Charles II and Elizabeth I are among the most intriguing British monarchs – in childhood, each had to cope with severe traumas, but they survived and did not spiral into psychopaths, often behaving generously to their enemies.

Oldest children rarely succeed

Monarchy is very much a family business. According to the law of primogeniture, the eldest son should follow his father on to the throne. The statistics are surprising, however. I include some forgotten figures among the forty-eight who have been proclaimed King or Queen of England. The unhappy Lady Jane Grey reigned for only nine days – at fifteen, she was pushed on to the throne by her father-in-law. Other largely forgotten reigns are those of Henry the Younger, who ruled jointly with his father Henry II between 1170 and 1183 and that of Louis, heir to the King of France, also proclaimed King of England in 1216. For six months, he ruled the lands south of the Wash.

Henry VI confuses the statistics as he managed two reigns or, according to Shakespeare, two parts. In 1461, the King was deposed and replaced by Edward IV and so concluded his first part. Unusually, Henry was not filleted, beheaded, drowned in Malmsey wine, nor disposed of in any of the ways so popular in medieval times. This concession allowed him to return for a final flourish. (I have counted Henry as only one monarch, though.) A crowned king could not be crowned again and so Henry had to be 'readopted', a curiously modern term; he was eventually murdered by his cousin.

Seven Lord Protectors also ruled but only two did so in their own right. When Oliver Cromwell died in 1658, the belief that the son should succeed the father was so ingrained that the council of state named Oliver's son, Richard, as the next Lord Protector. England was 300 years ahead of North Korea in trying to establish a hereditary republic. Richard Cromwell was a true survivor and outlived Charles II, James II, William III and Mary II. In 1712, Richard died peacefully in his own bed, fifty-three years after he had given up trying to rule Britain.

The surprise is that only nine of the forty-eight rulers to succeed were the eldest child of the previous monarch. In 1272, Henry III was succeeded by his first son – Edward I – and, for the next 105 years, eldest sons followed their fathers. This is the longest period of orderly succession in the ten centuries. In 1307, Edward I was succeeded by his eldest son, Edward II. Then, in January 1327,

Edward II abdicated, to be succeeded by his eldest son, Edward III. Edward II was murdered at the end of the year to prevent any comeback on his part.

When he died in 1422, Henry V was succeeded by his son, Henry VI. It would be another 125 years until a first son again followed his father on to the throne. In 1547, Edward VI succeeded the flamboyant Henry VIII. The year 1727 saw the next 'correct' succession when George II became King after the death of his father, George I. The next father-to-eldest-son succession took place in 1820, when George IV took over from his 'mad' father, George III. It would be eighty years before another first-born inherited: Edward VII, in 1901. In 1936, Edward VIII, the first son of George V, was crowned but abdicated. Then, in 1952, George VI's eldest daughter, Elizabeth, followed her father.

The eldest child did not succeed for many reasons; the catalogue of mishaps and tragedies included shipwreck, murder, epidemics, appalling medical care, conspiracies, exile, execution, a wayward cricket ball and many other slings and arrows of outrageous fortune. Of the first-born who got there in the end, six were called Edward. Often there was rivalry between and within the generations. Since 1066, sons have plotted against their fathers, especially when the monarch lived a ludicrously long time in the opinion of his child. To date, no British monarch has reigned into their nineties. George III died at eighty-one; Queen Victoria lived to eighty-one. The present Queen, Elizabeth II, turned eighty-six in 2012 – the oldest person ever to occupy the throne.

Some royals have not been able to cope with the pressures. George III was not the first to have some sort of breakdown. The long history reveals a number of monarchs were psychologically fragile. Around 1370, Edward III suffered some such episode, as did Henry VI on a number of occasions – most dramatically around 1453 – and Henry VII in 1503.

The royals, childcare and therapy
In *The King's Speech* (2010), the speech therapist Lionel Logue

'saves' George VI. The film never mentions the fact that George was treated for depression years before he met Logue. He was seen by Sir Frederick Treves, who looked after the so-called 'Elephant Man', and by leading psychiatrist Sir Maurice Craig, whose patients included many upper-class winter sports enthusiasts who developed 'nervous exhaustion' on the slopes. George's father, King George V, was so concerned that he attached a doctor, Louis Greig, to his son's permanent staff. The king could see the boy was nervous and stammered, but never seems to have acknowledged that his own behaviour as a father might have helped cause those problems.

It is also impossible to understand the royal family today without looking at the childhood of Queen Elizabeth II and that of Prince Philip. Chapter 10 deals with the Queen's rather happy childhood; Prince Philip had a very different experience. He grew up in a family which included Princess Marie Bonaparte, a famous analyst who was close to Freud. His aunt by marriage, Edwina Mountbatten, was the granddaughter of Sir Ernest Cassell, who set up a psychiatric hospital for soldiers who suffered shell shock in the First World War. Cassell asked the psychiatrist Sir Maurice Craig to help plan the hospital. Together they appointed as its first director Thomas Ross. Both Ross and Craig treated members of the royal family, including Prince Philip's mother, Princess Alice, and George VI.

A year after Philip was born, his father faced an extreme life event: Prince Andrew of Greece and Denmark was court-martialled for losing a battle against the Turks and forced to flee his own country. Soon afterwards, Philip's mother began to behave in a very disturbed manner. The family consulted Thomas Ross, who diagnosed schizophrenia – a reasonable conclusion as Princess Alice claimed she was often in conversation with Christ and the Buddha.

Only those who have managed to cope with a severely disturbed person in their family can truly understand the constant stress it causes. Prince Philip's father could not handle it when his wife 'went mad' and he left for the South of France. In contrast, Princess

Alice's mother was distraught but practical. She arranged for her daughter to attend the Tegel Clinic in Berlin, which was run by Ernst Simmel, a close colleague of Freud's. Princess Alice then went to a Swiss asylum run by Ludwig Binswanger, another follower of Freud's. Binswanger also described her condition as paranoid schizophrenia.

Prince Philip's mother is not the only royal to have been incarcerated in an asylum in the last sixty years. The Bowes-Lyons family, the family of Elizabeth II's mother, had to place two first cousins and three second cousins of the current Queen in Banstead Hospital in Surrey; their presence there was revealed in the 1980s by *The Sun* and the royal family was shamed into providing for them. One reason this was kept secret is that at least two other royals have received psychiatric help – and these episodes almost certainly affected their performance as parents.

George VI and Elizabeth Bowes-Lyon knew this troubled history and made heroic attempts to give the current Queen and Princess Margaret a normal, loving childhood. The girls saw their parents every day, hugs and kisses were routine and the family played games together. When she became Queen in 1952, however, Elizabeth II was beset by pressures: she was just twenty-five years old and forced to cope with enormous responsibilities, as well as dealing with the loss of her beloved father. Official duties took her away from her family. Young children whose parents have recently been bereaved often absorb their depression.

As a toddler, Prince Charles faced another problem. His father had survived a traumatic childhood and survivors often find it hard to be sympathetic to those less robust than themselves. It seems Prince Philip was unable to see why his son could not 'get on with it', as he himself had done (Philip's own words to describe his reaction to his chaotic childhood). Prince Charles's sons, of course, have had to deal with the death of their mother, when the Mercedes in which she was travelling crashed in Paris on the night of 31 August 1997.

One of my aims is to use contemporary psychological research to make sense of the relationships between royal children and their parents. Authors do not always know what their readers are already familiar with, so it seems prudent to explain some concepts. Freud argued that all boys go through an Oedipal stage when they unconsciously want to sleep with their mothers and kill their fathers. He made much of sibling rivalry. In 1914, he wrote the paper 'On Narcissism', and the long case history shows that a number of kings, including Henry VIII and George IV, have been deeply narcissistic.

Life events – and their effect on parenting

As well as sibling rivalry, the Oedipus complex and narcissism, a fourth concept must be considered: 'life events'. In 1967, Thomas H. Holmes and Dr Richard H. Rahe suggested that individuals might be more vulnerable to illness had they suffered too many 'life events'. After some years, they compiled a chart of forty-three life events that provoked stress. The Life Events Scale has become a staple of psychological research and it is now clear there is a link between life events and the way parents behave. Key life events include:

- Death of a spouse
- Divorce
- Death of a close family member
- Pregnancy
- Sexual difficulties
- Success in work
- Trouble with in-laws
- Changes in living conditions

Any analysis of royal family history also has to include the grotesquely improbable. Holmes and Rahe did not have many subjects who had lived through murders in their immediate family, let alone instances when one family member ordered the execution of another. They did not imagine 'changes in living conditions' would include being removed by soldiers from a palace where they had been pampered only to be flung into the rat-infested Tower of London, knowing many of their relatives had not emerged from there alive. Holmes and Rahe also neglected the question of kidnapping. In 1786, George Washington encouraged a plot to seize Prince William, George III's third son, who liked to wander around New York without an escort. Princess Anne was also the subject of a kidnap attempt in 1974.

Assassination does not figure in the scale as a separate category. The royals have been targeted more than most. Two lunatics tried to kill 'mad' King George III. Six men attempted to kill Queen Victoria, and one of them tried twice to do so. There has also been at least one attempt to kill Prince Charles. A surprising number of royals and their close associates have died in accidents. Prince Philip's sister, Cecilie, her husband and two of their children died in an air accident in Ostend in 1937. She was pregnant and her stillborn child was found in the wreckage. George V's fourth son, George, died in an air crash in Scotland in 1942. The Duke of Gloucester destroyed his Rolls-Royce driving back from Churchill's funeral. He survived, but in 1972 his son died in an air crash. In 1979, Philip's 'honorary grandfather', Lord Mountbatten, was killed by the IRA, as was Lady Brabourne, mother-in-law of Mountbatten's eldest daughter.

Some of the research based on the Life Events Scale highlights the way life events affect parenting. One study of 451 families in Iowa, for example, found that when parents suffer 'stressful life events' many become depressed, 'which operates to disrupt skilful parenting practices'. This in turn makes it more likely their teenage children will become depressed. Overwhelmed parents tend to be harsher and more inconsistent, the study found. In *Parenting with Reason* (2010), Esther Strahan shows that depressed parents are less likely to interact with their offspring because they are obsessed with their own problems. She also offers evidence that depressed parents are more hostile to their children, sometimes without realising it. If parents are anxious as well as depressed, their children suffer even more disadvantages.

Good-enough parenting

Finally, we need to examine a concept developed by one of Princess Marie Bonaparte's friends, Donald Winnicott, one of the leading child therapists of the mid-twentieth century. Winnicott saw the dangers of great expectations and coined the phrase, 'spurious maturity'. It was neurotic to try to be a perfect parent, he argued. Mothers and fathers were fallible; the most loving parents should only hope to provide 'good-enough parenting', as he termed it. The 'ordinary devoted mother' did not have to be a paragon but need only – and indeed *can* only – provide 'ordinary loving care of her own baby'.

Winnicott stressed the baby's need for touch. He described 'the business of picking a baby up' and the way the 'mother's technique of holding, of bathing, of feeding, everything she did for the baby, added up to the child's first idea of the mother'. The 'child's ability to feel the body as the place where the psyche lives could not have been developed without a consistent technique of handling'. Royal children were often inconsistently handled. Nearly all of them had wet nurses, up until the end of the nineteenth century. Sometimes the wet nurse both fed and petted the baby; sometimes the biological mother did not breastfeed but was still very involved in caring for the baby.

In most cases, a well-fed, well-petted, well-potted baby becomes confident, while a child who is not held enough can easily lose what Winnicott called 'the sense of being' essential for developing 'a true self'. Winnicott contrasted this with a false sense of self, which in turn led to 'doing too much, being too little'.

Playing was also vital. Winnicott stated 'babies can be playful when they are cared for by people who respond to them warmly and playfully, like a mother who smiles and says, "Peek-a-boo!"' When children – and indeed adults – play, they feel real, spontaneous and alive. Only in playing are they entirely their true selves, according to Winnicott. The infant with a 'false-self disorder' cannot play properly, hides her or his own self and pretends to be whatever she or he thinks others want or need him or her to be. The mite wears the mask. Winnicott slapped down the false self as 'a rather ludicrous impersonation. Such incorporation of one person by another

can account for that spurious maturity that we often meet with.'
He insisted 'for maturity it is necessary the individuals shall not
mature early (and have) passed through all the immature stages, all
the stages of maturity at the younger ages'.

Children are always the future but only royal children are the
future of an entire country. Much is expected of them, and great
expectations can lead to great problems. Royal children have sometimes been what we might call 'trophy children' and have had to
perform – and not just to play the piano for doting aunts and
uncles. When she was four, for example, Mary Tudor was asked to
dance and sing for the Emperor Charles V. Her parents hoped she
would dazzle him, as they wanted her to marry Charles. The future
Queen Victoria was paraded by her mother in Kensington Gardens
so that the public could see the girl was happy, when she was, in
fact, a victim of emotional abuse.

Trophy children may be made to suffer if they fail to act the
way their parents expect them to. When he was just five years old,
Prince Charles was reunited with his mother, who had been away
for months touring the Empire and Commonwealth. Newsreels
show him waiting for her at Victoria station. Immaculately dressed,
as a trophy child should be, he was expected not to act his age.
When his mother gets off the train, she does not rush towards
him, kiss him or hug him. Instead, she shakes her son's hand. In
a nice display of 'spurious maturity', he shakes her hand back.
Achingly formal, it is an almost perfect example of protocol taking
precedence over love.

Parents who demand spurious maturity might be said to be lacking in emotional intelligence. One can hardly blame historians for
not using the concept, as psychologists did not 'discover' emotional
intelligence till 1990, when the term appears in a paper published
by Salovey and Mayer. For the next six years, only specialists knew
of it until Daniel Goleman published his bestseller *Emotional
Intelligence*. Princess Diana has sometimes been credited with being
the first royal to show any signs of emotional intelligence. Across
ten centuries, however, she is not unique. Eleanor of Aquitaine,

Charles II, the allegedly mad George III (except when it came to his eldest son), Adelaide, wife of William IV and Victoria (except when it came to her eldest son) all displayed elements of emotional intelligence. Queen Victoria, for example, stressed the need for boys to experience 'knocks' as they grew up and admitted royal lads were often too isolated.

Emotional intelligence suggests openness but British monarchs have usually been secretive and, when it comes to their behaviour as parents, with some reason. There has been much heartlessness and carelessness, precisely the kind of imperfections royals – who want to seem perfect – do not wish to reveal.

All the revelations and arguments in this book must be viewed in the light of a statement made by genius-clown psychiatrist R. D. Laing, who fizzed to fame in the 1960s and 1970s with *The Divided Self*, a wonderful book on schizophrenia, and *Knots*, a work of perhaps less wonderful 'poems'. Laing argued that schizophrenia was the result of dysfunctional parenting, but he was careful not to be judgemental. When one blames parents, he said, one should remember that they too had parents, who had parents themselves, and so on back down the generations to the Garden of Eden, which was, after all, rather dysfunctional. The Serpent seduced Eve and then, in the first recorded instance of sibling rivalry, Cain killed Abel.

Most children expect to inherit money and a house from their parents but royal offspring will inherit the throne, the trappings of power and a place in history. Princes-in-waiting have often tried to influence the political process in order to establish their own identity. Prince Charles's habit of bombarding ministers with memos against the 'carbuncles' of modern architecture and promoting alternative medicine is mild compared to the antics of previous Princes of Wales.

When I made a television programme, *The Madness of Prince Charles*, in 2006, opinion polls reported that many Britons did not want him to inherit the throne. They preferred to skip a generation and have Prince William succeed Queen Elizabeth. Latest polls claim only 39 per cent of Britons want Charles to inherit. No one has dared to ask Prince Charles, who has spent sixty years waiting to inherit the throne, what he thinks. If he does succeed, he will have done very well.

The Ten Commandments for Adults

Before examining the long case history, it seems necessary to ask just what one can, and should, expect of royal parents – and how that differs from what we ask of ordinary good-enough parents. In 1979, a German professor of comparative education, Leonhard Froeze of the University of Marburg, wrote Ten Commandments for Adults and especially for parents. They were:

- Thou shalt regard the child as the highest good entrusted to you.
- Thou shalt not form the child in thine own image.
- Children need free space for the unfolding of their physical and spiritual powers.
- Thou shalt respect the child's personality.
- Thou shalt not use force against the child.
- Thou shalt not destroy the confidence of the child.
- Thou shalt protect the child against death.
- Thou shalt not tempt the child to lie.
- Thou shalt recognise the child's needs.
- Thou shalt give the child his and her rights.

Since Froeze penned these 'commandments', child development has become a vibrant field of study. Psychiatrists, psychologists, doctors, nurses, nutritionists, social workers and teachers have all achieved some consensus on what parents should give children to be 'good enough'. Apart from providing food, shelter and regular baths, good-enough parents must play, talk and bond with their children. They must be given enough confidence from birth and this includes the confidence that their parents will not abandon or betray them. Love is not enough; love must be practical and the child must feel the love. These 'rules' mean, essentially, putting the child's needs first. The good-enough parent also eventually lets their child go, with love. That is not always easy in ordinary families, but it can be even harder in royal circles.

2

FOUR MEDIEVAL RELATIONSHIPS (1066–1400)

The relationships between four mothers and their sons had a major impact on British history. Adela, one of William the Conqueror's daughters, favoured her son Stephen and even allowed him to visit her when she retired to a nunnery. He became King in 1135. Stephen proved a less perfect parent and was willing to abandon his eldest son's claim to the throne in order to bring peace to England.

Eleanor of Aquitaine adored her third son, Richard, whom we know as 'the Lionheart'. In 1193, she looted the kingdom in order to pay the ransom demanded when her son was taken prisoner as he made his way back from the Holy Land after failing to capture Jerusalem.

The relationship of Edward III and his mother, Isabella, would have fascinated Freud, given his faith in the Oedipus complex. Isabella had her husband, Edward II, murdered in 1327. Though her son did briefly imprison her, he soon forgave her for her complicity in the killing. Freud would not have been surprised. Finally, the difficult childhood of Henry VII affected his behaviour for the rest of his life. One cannot understand the history of the early Tudors without taking into account how his mother's early abandonment of him impacted both Henry's personality and the upbringing of his son, Henry VIII. When she gave birth to him, Margaret was a child herself – only thirteen years old.

Before examining these relationships in detail, it is necessary to give a brief account of some of Freud's ideas. He was not only interested in history, but in pre-history too. Well before Oedipus, the ancients had an Oedipus complex, he argued. In his bizarre *Totem and Taboo* (1913), Freud claimed Stone Age sons killed their fathers because they wanted to sleep with their mothers. The lusty young men were then crippled with guilt so they turned their dead father into an object of veneration, stuck his head on a totem pole and worshipped him. They then punished themselves more by creating the incest taboo, which prevented them from sleeping with their mothers – which had been the object of the exercise in the first place.

Thirty years before he wrote *Totem and Taboo*, Freud won a school prize for translating some of Sophocles' play *Oedipus Rex*. Sophocles tells how Oedipus arrives in Thebes just after the murder of its ruler, King Laius. Plague is ravaging the city and will not cease until someone solves the riddle of the Sphinx, the oracles say. The question is: what walks on four legs, then on two, then on three? The answer is a human being. A baby crawls on all fours, an adult stands on two legs. When we are old, we use three legs because we need a stick. Oedipus solves the riddle, wins the crown and the King's widow, Jocasta. Twelve years later, the plague returns and the blind seer, Tiresias, reveals that it was Oedipus himself who killed Laius. Jocasta now admits to Oedipus that the oracles predicted her baby son would kill his father and have children by his mother. To avoid the curse-prophecy being fulfilled, Jocasta gave the baby to a shepherd and ordered him to kill the child, but the shepherd was soft-hearted and brought Oedipus up as his own son. So, when Oedipus killed his real biological father 'where three roads meet' on the way to the famous oracle at Delphi, he did not know what he was doing, any more than he knew that the woman he then married was his mother. The end is fearful: Jocasta hangs herself while Oedipus stabs out his eyes and goes into exile.

The start of the case history
In the Middle Ages, the history of the royal family was nearly as gruesome, though British kings did not usually wallow in guilt, being less advanced than Freud's imagined Neanderthals. To

understand the long case history, one must start at the familiar date of 1066, when William the Conqueror won the Battle of Hastings and conquered England. William had four sons and no one is sure quite how many daughters. One of them, Adela, turned out to be remarkably astute. William the Conqueror died in 1087 and split his lands between his two eldest sons, but it was the second son, William Rufus, who was given England. In August 1100, William Rufus became the first of a number of English kings who were probably murdered on the orders of a brother. There is, of course, no better example of sibling rivalry.

While hunting in the New Forest, William was killed by a stray arrow. The Normans hunted all the time; accidents did happen, but Walter Tirel was a good archer and unlikely to have fired a wild shot at his King by mistake. There is no evidence that Tirel was ever punished. William was childless. William's younger brother, Henry, was among the hunting party and had every interest in seeing his brother dead, as he would inherit the throne. Once he had made certain that his brother was dead, Henry rushed to secure the royal treasury and then went on to London, where he was crowned within days.

For a woman of her time, Henry I's sister Adela achieved an amazing amount of influence. She was instrumental in bringing about a treaty between her brother and the King of France. Adela had six sons by Count Stephen Henry of Blois, but the eldest was a disappointment as he was 'deficient in intelligence and second rate', according to the chronicler William of Newburgh. Her third son, Stephen, on the other hand, impressed her and became her favourite. She taught him to read, and saw that he had a good education. Stephen also showed proper manly prowess on the battlefield. After having helped conclude the treaty, Adela retired to a nunnery, where she allowed her favoured son to visit her. Stephen was a much-loved royal child, fortunate in that as in other things.

In 1120, Stephen was among 300 knights and soldiers who assembled at the port of Barfleur in Normandy to set sail for England in the *White Ship*. However, he decided not to travel. Two reasons are given for this: the first is that he thought the vessel was overcrowded, the second is that he was suffering from diarrhoea. Whichever of these was true, Stephen said he would travel some time later.

Soon after the *White Ship* set sail in the dark, its port side struck a submerged rock, which can still be seen today. The ship sank. It was said later that no one spotted the rock because the crew had been drinking and no priest had blessed the vessel. William of Nangis added the unlikely fantasy that all the men aboard were sodomites and God had decided to inflict a marine version of Sodom and Gomorrah. The only survivor was a butcher from Rouen, who wore thick ram skins that saved him when he fell into the freezing-cold water. This disaster decimated the Anglo-Norman nobility. William of Malmesbury listed the dead, who included some of Henry's illegitimate children, and lamented: 'No ship ever brought so much misery to England.'

Stephen's uncle, King Henry I, now had only one surviving child: his daughter Matilda. There had never been a queen who ruled alone, but Henry had seen over the years how capable his sister Adela was. There was no reason why his daughter could not rule, so long as she had loyal advisers. The King's strategy also depended on Stephen supporting her, so Henry heaped honours and huge estates on him. In return, Stephen seems to have promised to support Matilda in her attempt to become the first queen to reign in her own name.

When Henry died in 1135, however, Stephen ignored any promises he had made, and the sea once more came to his aid. Stephen was near Boulogne when he heard of the King's death, while Matilda was in southern France. He set sail at once, and within weeks had himself crowned at Winchester; usefully, his brother happened to be the local bishop. Matilda disputed Stephen's claim and a long civil war ensued between the two cousins. Chroniclers called it 'the Anarchy'. It lasted for eighteen years and exhausted everyone, as well as being ruinously expensive.

By rights, Stephen, who married Matilda, Countess of Boulogne in 1125, ought to have been succeeded by his eldest son. Eustace's

FOUR MEDIEVAL RELATIONSHIPS (1066–1400)   23

mother wanted him to inherit, but Stephen was willing to betray
his son in order to bring England the peace it desperately needed.
He put the interests of the state before those of his son and made
peace with Matilda and her son Henry. The terms were simple: the
war would cease and Stephen would remain King until he died, but
then Matilda's son would assume the throne.

Stephen tried to justify his decision to himself, to Eustace and
to Eustace's mother. He suggested Eustace was not fit to succeed,
claiming the young man was brutal and exacted excessive taxes.
Eustace did not survive his father's betrayal long and died in his
early twenties, apparently of natural causes. Stephen's sacrifice paid
off for the country: Henry II reigned for twenty years in relative
peace, which allowed him to organise the government of England
better than ever before.

Eleanor and Richard – an Oedipal relationship

Two years before Matilda's son, Henry II, was crowned, he
married Eleanor of Aquitaine, a lively woman who made a habit
of marrying monarchs. Her first royal husband was Louis VII of
France, though she did not find him very satisfactory. She
complained that she had thought she was marrying a king and
discovered she had married a monk. Louis was not entirely
monkish: he did manage to father two daughters. With a rare
degree of maturity, Louis and Eleanor ended their marriage relatively amicably, though Louis probably did not realise Eleanor
already had a second husband in mind. Two months after she
was free, she married Henry.

Contemporary sources praised Eleanor as *perpulchra* – more than
beautiful. When she was around thirty years old, the troubadour
Bernard de Ventadour called her 'gracious, lovely, the embodiment
of charm', as she had 'lovely eyes and noble countenance' and was
'one meet to crown the state of any king'. Even when she was old –
and she lived to be eighty-two – Richard of Devizes described her
as beautiful.

Eleanor bore Henry five sons and three daughters. Their marriage was passionate, and often passionately angry. They were fortunate in that all but one of their children lived. Henry also fathered children with other women but Eleanor could be tolerant. She raised one of his bastards at court, even though the child's mother was a prostitute.

Eleanor and Henry's second son (the first did not survive) was born in 1155. The King wanted his child to have a good education and so he fostered him out to his friend and Lord Chancellor, Thomas Becket. Henry and Becket saw each other often as they hunted deer and chased women together, so Henry also saw much of his son but the fostering would have unforeseen consequences.

Henry's third son was born in 1157. We have been left a nice detail about the future Richard Lionheart as a baby: he was wet-nursed by a certain Hodierna and remembered her fondly, as he gave her a generous pension. The wet nurse did not replace his mother in his affections and Eleanor did not hide that, of all her sons, Richard was her favourite. Their relationship became one of the most trusting and practical alliances in British history. Freud famously said that his mother's love had made him a conquistador. Eleanor's love also made Richard something of a conquistador, but she had to do rather more than Amalia Freud. Feisty though she was, Amalia did not take charge of Freud's kingdom when he was away, or raise one of the largest ransoms in history to save her son.

Eleanor took her beloved Richard to her native France when he was twelve. There, he witnessed a peculiar and, in some ways, peculiarly charming medieval institution. His mother created the 'Court of Love' in Poitiers and presided over this philosophical fancy with Marie of Champagne, one of her daughters by her first marriage. A contemporary book – *The Art of Courtly Love* – described how royal ladies would listen to lovers' quarrels and decide on questions of romance; altogether it recorded twenty-one cases in detail, including one that raised the perennial question of whether true love could exist in marriage. The married mother and married daughter did not think so.

In Poitiers, Richard grew up highly aware of the rules of chivalry. One of the oddities of the code was that knights had to obey their lord, but not necessarily their father. The events of the next few years would show that, just as medieval kings could betray their sons, princes could betray their fathers too.

Perhaps because of the confusions of the Civil War, Henry II tried to do something no other English king has done. He made his eldest son, who was known as Henry the Younger, joint king. By 1170, Henry II ruled England and a third of France as well as Ireland. It was not so strange to give his eldest son serious responsibilities but the scheme caused trouble for a variety of reasons. Kings never find it easy to give up power and, after eighteen years, the marriage of Eleanor and Henry had turned sour and the son wanted more power than his father would allow him to wield.

In 1171, his mother took fourteen-year-old Richard on a journey through Aquitaine in an attempt to placate troublesome local lords. The teenage Prince cut an imposing figure in the Middle Ages as he was 6ft 5in. tall – a veritable giant, given the average height at the time. Eleanor was proud that her son was brave and politically shrewd, given his youth.

Richard joined his brothers, Henry and Geoffrey, in a revolt against their father in 1173, when Henry the Younger finally tired of the limits his father imposed on his authority. There was also the sore of Becket's murder in Canterbury Cathedral in 1170. Some medieval chroniclers suggest that Henry the Younger found it hard to forgive his father for having had a man who often acted as his foster father killed. Richard's motives were simpler: he was furious that his father had abandoned his mother for a younger woman, Rosamund Clifford. He decided to avenge Eleanor and, according to the historian Jean Flori, she was only too ready to see her sons revolt against their father. The family battle now took a turn that echoes tensions and ploys in stepfamilies today. Eleanor's first husband, Louis VII, backed her three sons by her second husband in the war against their father. Louis even knighted Richard personally, which under the rules of chivalry obliged Richard to be loyal to him, rather than to his biological father.

Luck then favoured the older Henry. Some of his soldiers

captured Eleanor and Henry put his wife under arrest. Richard was left to lead his campaign against his father on his own. Then the two old and wily Kings, Henry II and Louis VII, agreed a truce in September 1174, which left Richard in a difficult position. Louis had abandoned him and his own father, whom he had betrayed, had a much larger army. Richard then did something magnificently dramatic and brave: he went to his father's court at Poitiers on 23 September 1174. There, he fell at Henry's feet, weeping, and begged for forgiveness. Medieval chroniclers are sometimes maddening; not one of them describes this scene in detail. All we know is that it ended with Henry giving his son the kiss of peace. The penitent Richard was also given two castles in Poitou, but Eleanor remained her husband's prisoner – the King knew Richard would obey him if his mother's life might be at risk.

In the way of many fraught marriages, Eleanor and Henry never seemed quite able to end their passionate love–hate relationship and, in the 1180s, Eleanor once more began appearing at Henry's side from time to time as she was still married to him.

When Henry II died in 1189, Richard became King. Mother and son shared in the triumph. Eleanor rode to Westminster and received oaths of fealty on behalf of her favourite son. He trusted her to rule and she did so in his name, signing herself as 'Eleanor, by the grace of God, Queen of England'.

On 13 August 1189, Richard landed at Portsmouth, but he did not stay very long in England. A few months later, he set off for the Holy Land on the Third Crusade. He placed Eleanor in charge of England as his Regent. Richard finally reached the Holy Land and took Acre, but he could not take Jerusalem. He and the Sultan Saladin finally agreed a three-year truce in September 1192. Richard then left for England, but, again, a shipwreck proved a turning point.

Richard's ship was forced aground on the coast of the Adriatic Sea, which was hostile territory. He got close to Vienna shortly before Christmas 1192, but was captured by soldiers of the army of Leopold V, the Duke of Austria. Capturing a king who had saved part of the Holy Land was an outrage to Christendom, however, and the Pope excommunicated Leopold. If he did not wish to burn in Hell for eternity, he was told to hand his prisoner over to Henry VI, the Holy Roman Emperor. Henry needed money to raise an army in southern Italy, so he demanded a ransom of 150,000 marks. Eleanor slaved to raise this vast sum, roughly twice the annual income of the English crown. She imposed new taxes, looted the gold and silver treasures of every church and slowly gathered the ransom. In February 1194, she paid it and Richard was released. The moment he was free, Philip of France sent a sharp message to Richard's youngest brother, John: 'Look to yourself; the devil is loose.' Philip clearly believed in sibling rivalry and expected one brother to kill the other. Eleanor, however, nagged her sons to make peace and persuaded Richard to name John as his heir.

Five years later, Richard was besieging the castle at Chalus in the evening. One soldier was standing on the walls, crossbow in one hand, clutching a frying pan in the other as a shield, and took a shot which missed. At the same moment, another crossbowman, who had some grudge against the King, also shot at the King. This second arrow pierced the King's left shoulder. Eventually, a surgeon removed the arrow but he did so clumsily, 'carelessly mangling' the King's arm in the process. Richard's wound became gangrenous.

Eleanor hurried to her son's side but even she could not cure him of gangrene. Richard died in her arms on 6 April 1199. It was a fitting Oedipal ending to their long romance.

The angry grandson
It is impossible not to mention the next part of the family saga because it is unique. The key player was Richard's nephew, Arthur of Brittany. Arthur's father was Geoffrey, Henry II's fourth son. In 1190, before Richard and John were reconciled, Richard named Arthur as his heir to the English throne. Around 1194, under pressure from his mother, Richard changed his mind and named his brother John as

his heir. Young Arthur refused to accept this betrayal, but his first reaction was to take refuge with his uncle. John treated his nephew kindly at first, but that soon changed. Fearing for his life, Arthur fled and did what any resourceful twelve-year-old would do: he raised an army. He knew Eleanor could still influence her one surviving son and trapped her in the town of Mirabeau. Arthur became the first grandson in recorded history to besiege his grandmother.

John sent troops against the delinquent teenage Prince and Arthur was captured. Sadly, no chronicler appears to have recorded the scene when Eleanor asked her grandson what he thought he was up to. Arthur then vanished mysteriously in April 1203. One rumour suggested his jailers were too frightened to kill him and so his uncle John had to murder him personally. The Margam Annals provide the macabre details:

> After dinner on the Thursday before Easter, when he [King John] was drunk and possessed by the devil, he slew him with his own hand, and tying a heavy stone to the body cast it into the Seine. It was discovered by a fisherman in his net, and being dragged to the bank and recognised, was taken for secret burial, in fear of the tyrant, to the priory of Bec called Notre Dame de Pres.

William de Braose, previously Arthur's jailer at Rouen, did well after the boy disappeared. John showered him with lands and titles, which made contemporaries very suspicious. Years later, de Braose's wife accused the King of murdering Arthur. The unwise Maud was imprisoned and starved to death in Corfe Castle in Dorset.

Having been rescued from her grandson's siege, Eleanor became a nun. She had had a life filled with 'life events': she had seen her sons wage war on her husband, her husband ensure that his Archbishop was murdered, one of her own sons killed and one grandson slaughtered by one of her sons. For the last three years of her life, she lived a more meditative existence and her tomb suggests she read the Bible a great deal. Violent as the Old Testament is in many places, it is somewhat more serene than Eleanor's own family history. It seems worth stressing the statistics: between 1066 and 1216 six kings ruled; one had a brother killed, another murdered his nephew.

One Oedipal fantasy fulfilled – Edward III and his mother

Over a century after King John died, the royal family enacted an almost perfect Oedipal drama. The four central characters were Edward II, his wife Isabella, their son Edward and Isabella's lover, Roger Mortimer.

As with Richard I, we have been left surprising details about Edward III's wet nurse, Margaret of Daventry. Edward gave her a pension and gave her daughter a gift of 100 marks when she got married. He even helped Margaret thirty years after she had nursed him, when she had to fight a case in court. One historian believes that Margaret was the only woman who had really loved Edward as a child.

In 1326, the French King Charles IV (Isabella's brother) demanded Edward II perform homage for the Duchy of Aquitaine. Edward did not want to leave England so Isabella went to France and agreed with the French King that her son Edward would perform the homage. As soon as she landed in France, Isabella conspired with her lover, Roger Mortimer, to have her husband deposed. She had been infuriated by Edward II's relationships with two men – first Piers Gaveston, and then Princess Diana's ancestor, Hugh Despenser. It was not just a question of sex; the besotted King had even given Piers his wife's jewels. To bolster her position, Isabella had her son Edward engaged to the twelve-year-old Philippa of Hainault. Isabella and Mortimer then invaded England. Edward II was so unpopular that his men deserted him and he had to give up the throne to his son.

Endless intrigues marked the start of Edward III's reign. His mother's lover, Roger Mortimer, now the de facto ruler of England, acquired estates and titles, while Isabella herself stole the huge sum of £20,000 from the Exchequer. Mortimer felt insecure, however, in relation to the King and humiliated Edward in public. Tensions in the family increased after Edward and Philippa had a son; but having a son gave Edward courage. With a few trusted men, he stormed into his mother's bedroom at Nottingham Castle and took her lover prisoner. Isabella pleaded for Mortimer's life and Edward did not have him killed there and then. Only too aware of Isabella's obsession with jewels, Edward seized all of them. Capturing Mortimer and humiliating his mother made it obvious that Edward had all the qualities a King needed.

Edward also knew how to wait: he kept Mortimer a prisoner and then had him indicted by Parliament. To no one's surprise, Mortimer was found guilty and sentenced to death. Perhaps for his mother's sake, Edward spared her lover being quartered and merely had him hanged at Tyburn. To kill the man who murdered your father is a variation on the Oedipus complex, of course. Edward then did something that Freud would have understood. To assuage his guilt it has been argued that he commissioned the poem *The Lament of Edward II*, which praised his father and even presented him as a virile heterosexual, whose evil wife conspired against him.

Having paid this literary homage to his dead father, Edward was able to mend his relationship with his mother. Isabella forgave him for having her lover killed and he in turn forgave her for having had his father murdered. By the time she died in 1358, her son had proved a capable ruler. However, Edward was not able to ensure that his children and their descendants did not fight each other, which led to the Wars of the Roses.

Sibling rivalry and the Wars of the Roses

The Wars of the Roses were a three-decades-long struggle between the House of York and the House of Lancaster, two royal houses that were, in fact, closely related. It was a textbook case of sibling rivalry. Everyone who played a significant part could trace their ancestry back to Edward III. The wars began because the descendants of Edward's third son wanted to make sure the descendants of his second son never sat on the throne. There was nothing especially Yorkist or Lancastrian about either side.

In 1902, J. M. Barrie, the author of *Peter Pan*, wrote a play, *The Admirable Crichton*, in which the butler rises to power and takes charge of the family he had initially served. Barrie never mentions that his fiction actually occurred over five centuries earlier.

3

THE HUMBLE ORIGINS OF HENRY VII (1400–1603)

The Bishop of Bangor had a butler. We know little of either the Bishop or his butler, except that the latter was ambitious for his family. Around 1415, he arranged for his son, Owen, to serve in the household of Henry V, hoping the lad would rise in service.

After the French were defeated at Agincourt, the King of France permitted his daughter, Catherine of Valois, to marry the all-conquering Henry V. In December 1421, she gave birth to a son: the future Henry VI. The father would never see his heir, because Henry was fighting in France again and did not bother to return to see his wife and child. At the end of August 1422, he fell ill and died. He was only thirty-five years old; his widow was not yet twenty-one.

Catherine doted on her young son, who was her constant companion and her comfort. The English nobles, however, were determined to keep her under control and passed an Act of Parliament to prevent her remarrying without the King's consent. They added an unpleasant rider: the one-year-old King could only give that consent when he was an adult. Facing seventeen years of loneliness, Catherine turned for consolation to the butler's son. Owen was so obscure that historians are unsure of his position in the royal household; one theory is that he was keeper of the Queen's wardrobe, or he might have been in charge of buttons. Still, he must have cut some dash because Catherine, daughter of the King of the France and widow of the King of England, fell in love with him. He clearly had the gift of advocacy, too, as he persuaded Parliament to grant him the rights of an Englishman (the Welsh had no rights at all in England at the time). Owen's family name was Tudor.

The evidence as to whether Catherine and Owen Tudor married is lost in the mists of time, but they had at least four children. After Catherine died in 1437, Owen managed to convince his stepson, Catherine's son Henry VI, to let him and his children come back to court. Pious Henry welcomed his stepfather, half-brothers and half-sisters back.

Owen had climbed high, so it was no surprise when his own son, Edmund, married Margaret Beaufort, the twelve-year-old daughter of the Duke of Somerset. Margaret became pregnant, but, two months before she gave birth, her husband died. Then her labour was particularly difficult: at one point, both she and the child nearly died because her body was so small. She never gave birth again.

Margaret and her son, the future Henry VII, remained in Pembroke Castle until the boy was three or four years old. She was still only sixteen and, for reasons that are not totally clear, she then abandoned him. Henry reacted in a way that would not surprise psychologists: he became anxious, and particularly anxious to please his mother. For the rest of his life, he tried to win Margaret's approval. For her part, she stayed in contact with him and encouraged him. She wrote to her son and very occasionally visited him, although these visits became less frequent after her marriage to the Duke of Buckingham's second son.

Margaret had left Henry in the care of a nobleman, Lord Herbert, who was not an ideal guardian as he managed to get himself executed. The boy then stayed with Herbert's widow, Blanche, in Pembroke Castle but the castle itself was soon under siege by men who were loyal not to Henry VI, but to his Yorkist rival Edward IV.

In 1470, the fortunes of war changed. For once, Henry VI got the upper hand and Edward had to flee to France. Henry VI summoned his half-brother and predicted he would one day be king. It did not seem likely when, a few months later, Edward returned with an army. London put up no resistance; Edward later took Henry VI prisoner and, within hours, Henry died. One chronicle claimed his death was due to 'melancholy', but many historians believe it had nothing to do with his state of mind. Rather, Edward ordered Henry's murder.

Henry Tudor managed to escape and set sail for Brittany. The Italian historian Polydore Virgil claimed Edward reacted 'very grievously' to the news that 'the only imp of Henry VI's brood has escaped'. The Duke of Brittany allowed the teenager to live at his court, but toyed with the idea of handing the boy over to King Edward. At one point, Henry was taken to the port of St Malo, but he managed to persuade the Duke not to put him on a ship bound for England. In Brittany, the boy learned how to plead for his life.

Henry Tudor's childhood might be compared to that of a twentieth-century refugee. His mother had left him, his guardian had been executed, he had to flee England; he had come back to England but then had to flee again. When he was about twelve, Henry's life became a little more settled and from the relative safety of France he had the pleasure of seeing nearly everyone else who might claim the English throne die. Murder, plague, illness and old age all took their toll. So Henry, the ambitious butler's great-grandson, became the main Lancastrian claimant to the throne. It had taken just over sixty-five years for the butler's progeny to become royal-in-waiting. The Life Events Scale does not contemplate such vertiginous upward mobility.

There were sibling rivalries between Richard III and his brother Clarence, and historians disagree on whether Richard conspired to have his brother tried for treason and executed. The King, Edward IV, had the ultimate responsibility, however. He died in 1483 without apparently having murdered any other members of his family. His son succeeded him, but Edward V was killed within a few months. Some traditions, fuelled by Shakespeare, claim that Richard ordered the murder and then took the precaution of having the murderers murdered so that they could never betray him. The Mafia could have learned a thing or two from the so-called hunch-back king.

Now twenty-six years old, Henry Tudor decided to try his luck, once he had made sure of his mother's support. He managed to raise a small army and landed in Wales. By then, Richard III was unpopular in the south of England. The two rivals met in battle at Bosworth in 1485. Lord Stanley, Henry's stepfather, was supposed to be fighting on Richard's side but he changed sides during the battle. This was decisive and, when Henry won, Stanley was quite happy to see Richard killed on the battlefield.

To bolster his uncertain claim to the throne, Henry Tudor married Elizabeth of York, Edward IV's daughter. In doing so, he united the Houses of York and Lancaster, which were not really so disunited, as we have seen. Their first child, Arthur, was born in 1486; Henry, their second son, arrived in 1491. Henry's childhood was deeply affected, not just by his father's persistent anxieties but also by deaths in his close family; his parents saw three of their children die in infancy.

Once he became King, Henry VII invited his mother Margaret to live at the court. She had survived a long time and was now something of an intellectual. Margaret was determined that her grandchildren should receive an excellent education. In his biography of Henry VIII, David Starkey argues that, unlike most princes, Henry VIII was 'not masculinised, not sent away. He was close to his mother, physically brought up with his sisters in a household dominated by women until he was well into his teens.' Starkey seems to downplay the fact that Henry was also taught the very masculine arts of fighting and jousting.

Margaret made certain that her grandson read every Greek and Latin author of any consequence and that he was schooled in the Bible. All this did not, however, prevent the future Henry VIII becoming the most pernicious narcissist ever to sit on the throne, and also one of the most tyrannical parents.

Henry VIII's narcissism

The way some royals have been brought up could easily make them prime candidates for Narcissistic Personality Disorder, which the *American Psychiatric Diagnostic Manual* describes as 'a pervasive disorder characterised by self-centeredness, constant need for attention, lack of empathy, and an exaggerated sense of self-importance'. The narcissist tends to believe he or she is unique and should only associate with others of the same status, dreams of success and power, and also expects special treatment. Henry VIII suffered from, or indeed revelled in, more extreme narcissism than any other British king. This would damage his own children and affect the history of England.

Margaret Beaufort recruited two teachers from Cambridge, William Home and John Skelton, for her grandson. Skelton was a decent poet, if rather vain. He had no qualms about making his own contribution to Henry's education clear:

> The honour of England I learned to spell
> I gave him to drink of the sugared well.

The self-inflating poet also fuelled Henry's narcissism by comparing him to Alexander the Great, which implied that he, Skelton, could be compared to Aristotle, who had been Alexander's tutor. More sensibly, Skelton was also influenced by Erasmus, the Dutch Renaissance scholar who came to England in 1499 and met the eight-year-old Henry; Erasmus tested him and helped plan his education.

Erasmus influenced the way children were brought up through three books: *On the Rules of Etiquette for the Young*, *On the Order of Study* and *On the Education of Children*. He had some sense of the balance children need between love and discipline and said, 'We learn with great willingness from those we love' – it's a good maxim.

Spare the rod and spoil the child was orthodoxy. 'Parents themselves cannot properly bring up their children if they only make themselves feared,' Erasmus noted, however. Mothers should be affectionate but fathers had an important role, too: they had to get to know their offspring. Children had to wash their faces every morning, though one should not encourage them to get obsessive because 'to repeat this exercise afterwards is nonsense'. They had to be pious as well as clean, he said. The fastidious Erasmus allowed them to wipe their nose with their fingers but condemned doing so with a cap or a sleeve. Then, children had to kiss a piece of bread if they dropped it and Erasmus was also very particular when it came to drinking. 'Morally speaking,' he warned, 'it is not proper to throw the head back when drinking in the way storks do in order to drain the last drop from the glass.'

Erasmus might have had his eccentricities but he was an astute observer, for he noted, 'Nature has equipped children with a unique urge to imitate whatever they hear or say; they do this with great enthusiasm,' but he did not think much of imitation as he added, 'as though they were monkeys and they are overjoyed if they think they have been successful'.

Children should also be taught 'tact in the conduct of social life', Erasmus said. When he was ten, Henry's first public engagement required him to show he had mastered tact and politeness. In a very grand ceremony, his older brother Arthur was married to Catherine of Aragon, the daughter of Ferdinand of Aragon and Isabella of Castile. As he walked around the palace corridors in the early morning after his wedding night, Arthur boasted that he had spent much of it 'in Spain' – in other words, they had consummated the marriage.

Five months later, Arthur and Catherine succumbed to the 'sweating sickness', a version of the plague. Arthur died on 2 April 1502; Catherine recovered only to find herself a widow. Henry VII's wife was thirty-six years old and decided, as many bereaved mothers do, that she should have a baby to replace the child who had died. In February 1503, she gave birth to a daughter but the child died, as did the mother. Within a year, Henry VII had lost his wife, the oldest son he adored and a baby daughter. He became depressed and for a month saw virtually no one. At this time, he also became very protective of his one surviving son, Henry, who became his heir at the age of eleven.

Once Henry VII had recovered from his acute depression, he decided it would make sense to marry Henry to Arthur's widow. Catherine's parents, Ferdinand of Aragon and Isabella of Castile, agreed in principle as they did not want to give up a useful match which would give them enormous influence in English politics. Henry VII, the butler's progeny, had no intention of giving up a glittering alliance. His son was told that he would now replace Arthur 'in Spain'.

After many arguments over Catherine's dowry, the soon-to-be crowned King Henry VIII married Catherine. He was seventeen years old and she was twenty-three. They were happy but failed to produce healthy children. Catherine was to be one of many queens and princesses who suffered a tragic number of miscarriages and stillbirths.

On 31 January 1510, Catherine gave birth prematurely to a still-born daughter. Henry VIII's first son – Henry, Duke of Cornwall – was born on 1 January 1511. He lived for just fifty-four days.

Henry's narcissism fuelled his ambitions too. In 1513, it was almost a century since Henry V had invaded France and Henry VIII wished to outshine his namesake. He sailed for France and appointed Catherine his Regent, though she was pregnant again. She coped with an invasion by the Scottish King and rode north in full armour to address the troops. When the Scots were defeated, she sent Henry a piece of the bloodied coat of King James IV of Scotland for her husband to use as a banner, a token of love and of the strength of their marriage. This token did not bring the couple luck, however: the obstetric tragedies continued.

Catherine lost another son when Henry returned from France and another one in December 1514. On 18 February 1516, she finally delivered a healthy girl, who was named Mary and christened three days later with great ceremony. In November 1518, Catherine gave birth to another daughter but the child died after a week.

Mary, the only child to have survived, was much loved by both her parents. Indeed, they were planning a splendid match and had their hearts set on the Holy Roman Emperor Charles V as a son-in-law; they also made sure she had a good education. They employed Juan Luis Vives, a pioneer in the education of Princesses who had taught in Paris, Oxford and Bruges, and edited Augustine's *City of God*. But the greatest teacher could not have prepared Mary for the problems she would face when her father became increasingly angry and worried when Catherine had not given him a son.

Henry's education allowed him to take part as an intellectual equal in the debates on religion that divided sixteenth-century Europe. In 1521, Pope Leo X gave him the grand title of Defender of the Faith in recognition of Henry's book, *Assertio Septem Sacramentorum* (*The Defence of the Seven Sacraments*). Henry defended the sacramental nature of marriage and the supremacy of the Pope against Martin Luther. The honour, of course, fuelled his narcissism.

As a more than competent Biblical scholar, Henry knew the Biblical texts were contradictory on the thorny subject of marrying one's brother's widow. Leviticus 20:21 said: 'And if a man shall take his brother's wife, it is an unclean thing: he hath uncovered his brother's nakedness; they shall be childless'. Genesis 38:8, however, was all for it, as Judah said to Onan: 'Lie with your brother's wife and fulfil your duty to her as a brother-in-law to produce offspring for your brother'. Deuteronomy 25:5 also ordered, if brothers are living together and one of them dies without a son, his widow must not marry outside the family. Moses had ruled where a brother died without children, a surviving brother must marry the man's widow; Arthur had died childless so Henry had apparently followed Scripture. Henry himself would have needed excellent self-knowledge to know whether he did really feel guilty, or was just desperate for a male heir, or if he was getting bored with Catherine who was becoming old and a bit podgy. If psychology has taught us anything, it is that motives are mixed.

A surprising gambler – Mary Tudor

Over the years, Catherine had tolerated Henry's many mistresses, including Mary Boleyn, sister of the more famous Anne. When she was fifteen, Mary had gone to live at the court of Francois I and, like Eleanor of Aquitaine, bedded the Kings of both France and England. Mary knew the King would never marry her and accepted the situation when Henry tired of her. Her sister Anne was different. When Henry became infatuated with her, she would not sleep with him and made the astonishing demand that the King marry her first. Even more astonishingly, Henry accepted Anne's terms, though he knew trying to divorce the daughter of one of the most powerful royal houses in Europe would cause mayhem. Catherine's nephew, Charles V, was not about to allow his aunt to be humiliated and was in a position to impose his will: he controlled Italy and could capture Rome and the Pope any time it pleased him. There were theological problems too as the Catholic Church did not allow divorce, though it often permitted annulments. Canon law also forbade men from marrying their brother's widow.

Henry's actions over the next ten years changed the course of English history. His narcissism made him believe he could persuade the Pope, the Emperor, the King of France, his soon-to-be abandoned wife and his daughter Mary to accept what he wanted. Henry's narcissism was so profound that he convinced himself that what he wanted was right for the country and probably for God, who he had recently assisted by attacking Luther.

Henry's daughter became one of the main victims of her father's narcissism. When the King's 'great matter' started, Mary was ten years old. She loved her father as well as her mother, but she believed her mother was right: their marriage had been proper, and properly consummated, and her father was now trying to weasel his way out of it. The subsequent battle would damage Mary's relationship with Henry for the next twenty years. He refused to see her and she had to suffer the humiliation of seeing her mother excluded from court while Anne Boleyn was showered with favours. The last time Henry saw Catherine was in July 1531.

After the Pope refused to grant his divorce, Henry seceded from Rome and announced royal supremacy over the church. He annulled his own marriage, in effect, and married Anne in May of 1533.

Mary was now in disfavour and her position became critical when Anne became pregnant. The new wife did not produce a male heir, however. Elizabeth was born on 7 September 1533. Two days later, Henry issued instructions that Mary was not to be called a true Princess, simply the Lady Mary. In a splendid show of pettiness, he also ordered her servants were to have their gold-embroidered coats taken away from them. Mary did not accept her demotion and wrote to her father, complaining one of his officials had written a letter to her in which he did not address her properly as a Princess.

Catherine realised Mary had to be careful, given her father's familiar temper. She wrote to her: 'Answer you with few words obeying the King your father in everything save only that you will not offend God or lose your soul.' The King refused to allow mother and daughter to see each other. Distraught Catherine recommended Mary prepare for her ordeal ahead by reading a Life of Christ and imagining the Stations of the Cross. It was pious and not very practical advice.

In November 1533, Henry inflicted a further insult on his eldest daughter: Mary was to be made a lady-in-waiting to Elizabeth, while her own ladies-in-waiting were to be sacked. Eustace Chapuys was the ambassador of Mary's cousin Charles, and kept making suggestions to her as to how she should behave so that no one could imagine she accepted these insults willingly. Mary was now separated from her mother, at war with her father and her cousin's ambassador was erratic; sometimes he urged Mary to defy her father, other times to obey him.

In December 1533, when the Duke of Norfolk asked Mary if she had a message for her father, she only said that she wanted his blessing, though she knew he would never give that until she accepted he was Supreme Head of the Church of England; Norfolk told her he dare not take such a message. 'Go away,' the teenage Mary apparently then told him before retiring to her chamber to weep. Henry subsequently accused Norfolk of having being too soft on his daughter and removed the last few servants Mary still had, leaving her with just one chambermaid.

During these quarrels, Anne Boleyn constantly nagged Henry to be tougher on his daughter. She promised to reduce 'the pride of the unruly Spanish blood line' and persuaded the King to confiscate most of Mary's jewels. Mary once had to be forced into a litter when she refused to travel as part of Elizabeth's entourage in her unwanted role as one of the ladies-in-waiting. But Henry also had moments of sentimentality when he softened towards his daughter and blamed her behaviour on her mother's Spanish stubbornness. He once saw Mary at a window and raised his cap in greeting. Anne Boleyn was livid when she found out and made sure her husband was never again near his eldest daughter.

For the next twenty-five years, the history of England would revolve around Henry's two daughters. The baby Elizabeth was 'as goodly a child as hath been seen'. At three months old, she was sent to live outside London because there was less plague in the countryside. We do not have a record of every visit her parents made to her but they certainly came to see her when she was six months old. Henry was enchanted by his bright little daughter.

On 30 March 1534, Mary was told to meet Elizabeth again. The Spanish ambassador, Eustace Chapuys, advised her to go and be polite 'for fear of irritating her father'. But Mary did not heed this advice, which infuriated Henry. A month later, he declared Elizabeth was his heir; Mary had been totally denied by her father.

Mary did not capitulate, however. When Elizabeth was about eighteen months old, someone referred to her as 'the Princess Elizabeth'. Mary snapped that she knew of no other Princesses in the realm but herself. She defied the King, writing, 'they were deceived if they thought her bad treatment' would make her change her attitude. A detail we have about Mary's habits may give a clue to her conduct: she has often been described as 'pathetic' but she adored gambling and her behaviour suggests she was indeed willing to risk everything. By the end of 1534, she was becoming nervous, however, and wrote to Chapuys because the King had again ordered her to see her little half-sister. She did not know what to do, she told the ambassador. Again, he urged her to go, and this time she did.

Sensing the King's hostility towards his daughter, some of Henry's nobles took liberties and were impertinent, even vicious. One told Mary that, if he had such an ungrateful child, he would either kill her or batter her head against a wall until it was 'as soft as a boiled apple'. Mary was often unwell and her mother kept begging the King to let them be together and offered to nurse her herself. Henry refused to allow it.

In late December 1535, sensing she would soon die, Catherine wrote to her nephew, Charles V, asking him to protect Mary. The jilted Queen then sent one final letter to Henry, addressing him as her 'most dear lord and husband', which she must have known would irritate him. She urged him to remember the health of his soul, which he should prefer 'before the care and pampering of thy body, for which thoust have cast me into many calamities'.

Catherine added: 'For my part, I pardon thou everything, and I desire to devoutly pray God that He will pardon thou also.' She begged her husband: 'For the rest, I commend unto thou our doughtere Mary, beseeching thou to be a good father unto her, as I have heretofore desired.' The phrase 'heretofore desired' implied Henry had failed in his duty. On 7 January 1536, Catherine died at Kimbolton Castle. Mary went into deep mourning as the rest of the court celebrated; tradition claims Anne Boleyn wore yellow the day that Catherine died. Chapuys reported it was actually the King who decked himself in colour to mark his ex-wife's death. Elizabeth was there with her parents, who made a great show of their two-year-old daughter.

Far from caring for Mary when she was distraught after her mother's death, Henry would not even let her attend the funeral.

But the human body can react in odd ways: on the very day of the funeral, Anne Boleyn had a miscarriage of a male child. The miscarriage sealed her fate.

A few weeks later, aware that Anne was losing influence, Chapuys suggested Mary should try to reconcile with her father. Mary finally wrote the letter Henry had wanted for so long in which she stifled her fury and humiliated herself before him. She humbly prostrated herself and begged him to forgive the daughter who had offended him so much and added:

> that my heavy and fearful heart dare not presume to call you father, deserving of nothing from your majesty, save that the kindness of your most blessed nature does surmount all evils, offences and trespasses, and is ever merciful and ready to accept the penitent calling for grace, at any fitting time.

Even at the last minute, however, Mary tried to defy her father, saying she accepted his authority under God Almighty, but this was not the wording the King wanted: his daughter had to give him total authority over her. Thomas Cromwell would not send that letter if it contained Mary's clever proviso. She capitulated and told her father she had not dared write to him before she knew he would forgive her for siding with her mother. In addition, she promised that she would never 'again offend your majesty by the denial or refusal of any such articles and commandments as it may please your highness to address to me'. She had 'most unkindly and unnaturally offended'. The penitent daughter begged Henry to forgive her for 'these things which I have before refused to condescend to'. She abased herself, saying, 'I wholly commit my body to your mercy and fatherly pity; desiring no state, no condition, nor no manner or degree of living but such as your grace shall appoint unto me.'

The end of the letter was equally abject as Mary signed herself 'Your Grace's most humble and obedient daughter and handmaid, Mary'. 'Handmaid' was both Biblical and unusual. Henry was not only interested in his daughter's obedience but also in her complete political submission, so Cromwell made her add:

> I do recognise, accept, take, repute and acknowledge the king's highness to be supreme head on earth, under Christ, of the church of England; and do utterly refuse the bishop of Rome's pretended authority, power and jurisdiction within this realm, formerly usurped, according to the laws and statutes made on that behalf, and by all the king's true subjects humbly received, admitted, obeyed, kept and observed.

She also denied her mother, saying she recognised 'that the marriage formerly had between his majesty and my mother, the late Princess dowager, was by God's law and man's law incestuous and unlawful'. This humiliation would affect Mary, her relationship with her younger sister and her attitude towards her people for the rest of her life.

After Anne lost her son, Henry became exasperated with his second wife. The cycle of stillbirths and deaths in infancy which had destroyed his first marriage must have seemed all too familiar. Within a few weeks, Anne was accused of adultery. Some historians believe the charges were trumped up and that Henry always knew they were; others disagree and argue Anne was unfaithful, though perhaps only in the hope of becoming pregnant again. She was put on trial for high treason, found guilty and beheaded in May 1536. Henry did not forgive Mary for defying him, but his attitude towards her became somewhat less hostile.

Princess Elizabeth's lack of underwear – and other vicissitudes
Elizabeth was only two years old when her mother was beheaded and the King proceeded to totally ignore his young daughter. Her governess, Lady Bryant, wrote to Cromwell to ask 'what degree she [Elizabeth] is of now I know not but by hearsay. Therefore I know not how to order her nor myself nor her women and grooms I have rule of.' There were problems of protocol and of basic necessities, such as underwear. Lady Bryant listed every item 'needful' for her

charge – kirtles or slips, petticoats, mufflers and the nicely named 'body stitchets' or corsets – and 'beseeched' Thomas Cromwell to give her clear orders – and the money to buy them.

Clothes were not the only issue as Sir John Shelton, who was in charge at Hunsdon, where Elizabeth was living, wanted the child to dine formally 'at the board of the estate every day'. Lady Bryant thought that absurd for such a young child and wanted the King's authority to provide a simple 'mess of meat' for Elizabeth in her own rooms. She ended her letter with a plea for sympathy for the Princess, whose teeth were hurting badly.

Children need physical and emotional security, modern psychologists agree, and find it hard to cope with separation from their parents or care givers. Nothing suggests they were any different in the sixteenth century, though there has been some debate among historians as to 'the invention of childhood', with some arguing that, as so many children died so young, parents did not invest as much emotion in them. A number of sixteenth-century diaries and memoirs suggest otherwise. The French writer Michel de Montaigne in his essay on fatherhood warned that men were all too often too reserved in showing their love for their sons. After his son died unexpectedly young, one of Montaigne's friends bitterly regretted never having told his son how much he loved him. Henry VIII tended only to pity himself, however. Once she was three, Elizabeth could not rely on the father who had so proudly showed her off the day Catherine died.

The letters that the Edwardian historian Mumby gathered – written by, to and about Elizabeth – unfortunately are silent on a number of key points. No one can be sure whether anyone made any effort to comfort her when she found out that her mother had been executed. Did her father ever explain why he had ordered that? How did her half-sister Mary, who was seventeen years older, behave towards her?

After Anne Boleyn, Henry fell in love with Jane Seymour, who was twenty-eight years old. He married her eleven days after Anne was beheaded. Jane was a good stepmother and tried to bring Henry and his daughters closer together. She became pregnant soon after the wedding, and that gave her more influence. Henry started to take more interest in his little daughter. When Elizabeth was four, Jane gave birth to a son, the future Edward VI. The Queen's efforts to reunite the family now bore fruit. Elizabeth was given a serious role at Edward's christening: she had to carry the baby's robe to the font, quite a task for a small girl. Mary was made one of Edward's godmothers, a sign of her coming back into favour.

Jane Seymour, however, died when her son was only twelve days old. Mary, who had not been allowed to attend her own mother's funeral, was given the honour of being the chief mourner at the Queen's funeral. She impressed Henry, who now granted Mary a household and allowed her to reinstate her favourite lady-in-waiting.

After Edward was born, Elizabeth's living conditions improved. She was sent with her baby brother to the palace at Hatfield and the two small children became friends. Henry also approved the appointment of Elizabeth's first governess, Kat Ashley, who took 'great labour and pain in bringing of me up in learning and honesty', Elizabeth wrote years later. She said nothing about love and warmth though she did add, 'We are more bound to them that bringeth us up well than to our parents.' Given that Elizabeth hardly knew her mother and that her father was erratic in his affections, her view is hardly surprising. It is arguable that the Princess, like a number of clever troubled children, buried herself in books, which gave her some security.

When she was five, Elizabeth started to learn languages, including French, Latin and Greek. Her abilities impressed. At the age of eleven, she could also speak Spanish and the native language of the Tudors: Welsh. She also had to acquire the then essential skills for a woman – how to sew, embroider and dance. Around this time, she became a competent horsewoman, could hunt deer and learned how to shoot well with a bow and arrow (archery was considered an acceptable sport for a woman).

In January 1540, Henry married for the fourth time. It was a diplomatic union and a total disaster. His new wife, Anne of Cleves, was nicknamed 'the mare of Flanders' because she was so unattractive; the King claimed he found it hard to have an erection with her. By July, he had divorced her.

A good illustration of Henry's erratic fathering was that, although Mary might no longer be out of favour, in 1541 he still had her old governess and godmother, Margaret Pole, the Countess of Salisbury, executed. She was accused of having been involved in a Catholic plot against the King, although the evidence was far from conclusive.

Even before Anne of Cleves had been divorced, Mary and Elizabeth saw their father fall in lust with a fifteen-year-old girl, Catherine Howard, who was nearly ten years younger than Mary herself. Perhaps for the first time in his reign, the narcissist made himself ridiculous. Catherine Howard was flighty and unfaithful, eventually paying for this with her life. For the second time in under ten years, a Queen of England was beheaded. This second execution seems to have reminded Henry of Anne Boleyn, as the angry and disappointed King now took his misery out on Elizabeth. She was exiled from court in the summer of 1542. A clever nine-year-old, Elizabeth was not just upset when her father yet again rejected her. She began to realise the implications too: if she was down, her half-sister was up. Once more, Mary was given an honoured place at court. After the execution of Catherine Howard, the temporarily unmarried King invited Mary to oversee the royal Christmas festivities 'in default of a Queen'. She did so with some elegance.

A sensible marriage

A year later, at the age of fifty-two, Henry finally made his second sensible marriage. Catherine Parr was thirty-one years old and had already been married twice, so Henry was her third husband and she was his sixth wife. Catherine was devout, well educated, intelligent and, perhaps crucially, had no children of her own. She was more than a good-enough stepmother and set about mending Henry's relationship with Mary and Elizabeth as Jane Seymour had briefly tried to do.

On 31 July 1544, Elizabeth wrote to Catherine Parr that she was finding a year away from her stepmother hard 'and in this my exile I well know that the clemency of your highness has had as much care and solicitude for my health as the king's majesty himself'. For the next five years, Catherine was a vital presence in the young Princess's life. She quickly persuaded Henry to allow Elizabeth to come back to court.

A number of letters between Catherine and Elizabeth have survived. Despite their ornate formalities, they show a girl of eleven trying to please and impress a stepmother she loves and admires. The first letter was written on the last day of 1544. After many expressions of love, Elizabeth wrote – and it is worth quoting for its sophistication in such a youngster – 'knowing also that pusillanimity and idleness are most repugnant unto a reasonable creature and that [as the philosopher says] even as an instrument of iron or of other metal waxes soon rusty unless it be continually occupied'.

Elizabeth wanted to prove to Catherine what she could achieve, so she had translated *The Mirror of the Sinful Soul* from the French. She was showing off and trying to please her learned stepmother, for, although she was sure her translation was 'all imperfect and uncorrect', Catherine, with her

> godly learning … shall rub out, polish, and mend (or else cause to mend) the words (or rather the order of my writing) the which I know in many places to be rude, and nothing done as it should be. But I hope, that after to have been in your grace's hands there shall be nothing in it worthy of reprehension and that in the mean while no other (but your highness only) shall read it or see it, less my faults be known of many.

She finished by wishing her stepmother a happy 1545.

Catherine was not just astute in dealings with her stepchildren but also canny as to the games married couples play – games that could be very dangerous with Henry. She was sympathetic to the 'New Faith', as Protestantism was called, and wrote two religious books. The second, *Lamentations of a Sinner*, argued there was truth in Luther's concept of justification by faith alone, a doctrine Henry had attacked when he denounced Luther as a heretic. Furious, the King had an arrest warrant drawn up for Catherine, but she was much smarter than Anne Boleyn. She insisted on seeing her husband and told him she had only argued about religion to take his mind off the atrocious pain his ulcerous leg was causing. The King must have loved her because he accepted what she said and they resumed married life. Meanwhile, the court and Henry's daughters knew of both the King's familiar fury and his unfamiliar willingness to kiss and make up with his wife.

Having no children of her own, Catherine persuaded Henry to revoke his earlier decisions and restore both Mary and Elizabeth to the line of succession three years before he died. By the end, it is likely he was suffering from syphilis and was so fat that he could not walk and had to be carried through his palaces in a chair.

Jane Seymour's son, Edward, succeeded Henry in 1547. The new King had a warm relationship with Elizabeth, but a much tenser one with Mary, who was twenty-one years older than he was. Many older sisters would have tried to mother their younger brother, but religious differences made that impossible. Edward had been brought up to be an uncompromising Protestant.

A case of royal child abuse

Soon after Henry died, Elizabeth had to adapt to yet another change. Before she married Henry, Catherine Parr had been in love with Sir Thomas Seymour, the brother of Jane Seymour. Thomas was an opportunist – he went to visit Elizabeth soon after her father died and proposed marriage. The letter she wrote in reply was very poised given that Elizabeth was just fourteen years old. She regarded the honour Seymour had paid her 'as an evidence of your natural courtesy' as well as respect for her late father, 'but I have been forced to perceive by the frequent visits which you have made to me that you have other intentions'. Elizabeth assured him that she had not 'refused you because I was thinking of someone else'. She promised that she did not have the slightest intention of being married and 'if ever I should think of it (which I do not believe is possible) you would be the first to whom I should make known my resolution'.

Having been turned down by the Princess, Seymour now proposed to Catherine Parr. She accepted her old flame, but it was only four months since the King had died. Given how short a time that was, Seymour went directly to his nephew, King Edward, and asked for permission to wed. At the end of May, Catherine was able to marry her old love but they had to do so in secret.

In early 1548, Catherine invited Elizabeth and her cousin Lady Jane Grey to live in the couple's household at Sudeley. She promised to provide education for both girls. Like Elizabeth, Lady Jane Grey was a precocious scholar. In March, Catherine Parr became pregnant for the first time at the age of thirty-five. But now something happened that would not surprise modern experts in stepfamilies and this was a very tangled one. Seymour was the brother of Henry's third wife, the husband of his sixth wife and a kind of stepfather to Edward, Mary and Elizabeth. He now began to take a great deal of interest in the young Princess who had refused to marry him. J. E. Neale, one of the great biographers of Elizabeth I, saw Seymour's flirting as quite innocent horseplay, but he was writing in the 1930s when child sexual abuse was ignored; Seymour was no innocent.

Today Seymour's behaviour would be seen as child abuse even if, as some evidence suggests, Elizabeth was flattered, intrigued and did not know how to say no to an older man. Her stepfather came into her bedchamber wearing only his night clothes. She would retreat on the bed away from him but sometimes let him catch her, it seems. The two were seen larking about on the bed together. Then Kat Ashley claimed Catherine had discovered her husband and stepdaughter embracing. Another source suggests Catherine did not just turn a blind eye to her husband's very physical flirtation but actually assisted him. There is evidence that Catherine held Elizabeth while Seymour cut her black dress to ribbons. Freud would have seen this as a very controlled display of sex and violence, particularly as it took place not in a bedroom but in an English country garden. Catherine would not have been the first wife to try to hold on to her husband by giving him latitude with a stepdaughter. Some historians suggest that Thomas Seymour was being even more opportunistic than usual: if Catherine died in childbirth, he would then marry the fifteen-year-old Elizabeth he had 'groomed'.

Her husband's all too sexual behaviour towards Elizabeth finally made Catherine angry. Two months after she had come to live with Catherine and Seymour, Elizabeth was sent away to live at Cheshunt. She never saw her beloved stepmother again, though the two corresponded. Seymour now demanded to be appointed governor 'of the King's person', which would give him great power. His brother, the Lord Protector, tried to buy Thomas off with a barony in appointing him Lord Admiral and giving him a seat on the Privy Council. All these honours did not satisfy Thomas, who began smuggling pocket money to King Edward, telling him that the Lord Protector was starving him of money and making him a 'beggarly king'.

After Elizabeth was sent away to Cheshunt, she acquired a new tutor: Roger Ascham, one of the best Greek scholars in the kingdom. Ascham was impressed with her as 'beside her perfect readiness in Latin, Italian, French and Spanish, she readeth here now at Windsor more Greek every day than some prebendary of this church doth read Latin in a whole week'. He also praised her 'beauty, stature, wisdom and industry ... she read with me almost all Cicero and great part of Titus Livius [the Roman historian, Livy]: for she drew all her knowledge of Latin from those two authors. She used to give the morning to the Greek Testament and afterwards read select orations of Isocrates and the tragedies of Sophocles. To these I added St Cyprian and Melanchthon's Commonplaces.' Ascham's approval of Elizabeth's style was 'because it is suitable and beautiful because it is clear' and 'it grows out of her subject'.

In September 1548, Catherine Parr died in childbirth. Elizabeth mourned the woman who had loved her. Ignoring the obvious decencies, Thomas Seymour promptly proposed marriage to Elizabeth once more. She told him sharply that she would not even entertain the question unless the Council approved his advances. Seymour had finally overplayed his hand. In January 1549, the Council had him arrested on a number of charges, including embezzlement and attempted kidnapping. The leader of the Council might have been his own brother, the Duke of Somerset, but he showed no mercy. Since there was insufficient evidence to convict him in court, Somerset had his brother condemned by an Act of Attainder, a procedure in which Parliament passed sentence on an accused person as if it were a court of law. Parliament turned itself into judge and jury. If Elizabeth had any feelings about Seymour's death, she kept them to herself when he was executed.

The triumphant Somerset now treated Elizabeth harshly. She was sent to Hatfield Palace but the conditions were very different from before. In many of the letters that she wrote from there she signed herself 'prisoner'. Six months before her sixteenth birthday, she had lived through the execution of her mother, the hostility of her half-sister, the death of her father, a few months when her stepmother's new husband tried to seduce her, the death of that once-loved stepmother and then the execution of Thomas Seymour, the step-father who had tried to seduce her. Such a hailstorm of life events should have crippled her, but she coped. Psychology can at least offer some explanation: her glittering intelligence probably allowed her to make some sense of the flow of events around her.

Perfect sibling rivalry: Edward and his sisters

As soon as Edward became King, Mary's fervent Catholicism again became problematic. She refused to submit to her brother's diktats on religion and for months retired to her estates in East Anglia. Edward's regency council then imposed its ideas through the Act of Uniformity of 1549, which required church services to follow Protestant rites. Catholic 'smells and bells' became illegal.

Edward could have allowed Mary to worship in the Roman Catholic way she liked in the privacy of her estates but he refused to do so. Nevertheless, brother and sister did make some attempt to mend their differences. The second Christmas of Edward's reign, the boy King invited Mary to join him and Elizabeth at court but the festivities became tense because of religious arguments. Edward embarrassed Mary, and reduced both girls to tears in front of the court by attacking Mary for ignoring the Act of Uniformity. She repeatedly refused to abandon her Catholic faith, though her brother put her under intense pressure. After Christmas, Edward had three members of Mary's household arrested. For her, it echoed the days when her father removed her servants – and their gold liveries.

The history of England would have been different if Edward had been healthy and had children. By February 1553, however, the Imperial ambassador, Scheyfve (who had succeeded Chapuys) reported: 'the King suffers a good deal when the fever is upon him, especially from a difficulty in drawing his breath, which is due to the compression of the organs on the right side ... I opine that this is a visitation and sign from God.'

Edward was determined that Mary should not succeed him. However, lawyers told him that he could not disinherit only one of his sisters and so he composed 'My devise for the succession', which excluded both girls. Instead, the boy King decreed his first cousin once removed, the sixteen-year-old Lady Jane Grey, should succeed him. Of course, it is perfect sibling rivalry to do your siblings out of their inheritance and Edward himself was being done out of life.

On 15 June 1548, Edward summoned judges to his sickbed to witness that he was changing his will so that Lady Jane Grey would inherit his throne. Two historians suggest the dying King was on a mission. Diarmaid MacCulloch has suggested Edward was motivated by 'teenage dreams of founding an evangelical realm of Christ'. That seems much like his father's narcissism. 'Edward had a couple of co-operators, but the driving will was his,' another leading historian, David Starkey, judges.

Finally exhausted by his illness, Edward died on 6 July 1553. His death provoked a political crisis that lasted a feverish month. Gambling as usual, Mary did not delay on her estates to mourn her brother, but gathered a small force. On 9 July, she wrote to the Privy Council, ordering it to proclaim her as Edward's successor. The next day, however, in accordance with Edward's will, Lady Jane Grey was proclaimed Queen. That very same day, Mary's letter reached the Privy Council. Two days later, she assembled soldiers at Framlingham Castle, less than 100 miles from London, and prepared to march into the city. Lady Jane Grey's father could not gather enough troops to fight against Henry's daughter and so his daughter, who had never been a very willing conspirator, was deposed a week later. There was now a delay of nearly two weeks. Finally, on 3 August, Mary rode triumphantly into London but she did not ride alone: Elizabeth was at her side.

Mary has often been portrayed as a hysterical and unattractive woman. When she became Queen, however, she made a good impression as even her enemy John Foxe, the author of *Foxe's Book of Martyrs*, admitted. Mary came to the Guildhall and addressed a crowd: 'When she had ended her oration, (which she seemed to have perfectly conned without book,) Winchester, standing by her, when the oration was done, with great admiration cried to the people, "Oh how happy are we, to whom God hath given such a wise and learned Prince!"' But Mary was not so wise nor so emotionally secure she could overcome her troubled past – and especially the rivalry often fuelled by Henry between herself and Elizabeth.

Again, it might be useful to compare the British royal family and that of Sigmund Freud. Soon after he was born, his mother became pregnant again. She and her husband called their second son Julius. At the age of two, Freud was too young to appreciate that his brother was named after the great Roman Emperor Julius Caesar. The baby was constantly ill, however, and died when he was eight months old. Freud 'discovered' forty years later when he started to analyse his own dreams that he had been delighted (unconsciously, as well as unconscionably) when Julius died: he did not want to compete for his parents' love with another boy. The stakes in royal families are even higher and can intensify such jealousies.

For the first sixteen years of her life, Mary was an only child but she then had to fight her half-sister for their father's favour, as well as her bastard half-brother, the Duke of Richmond. Henry was as inconstant a father as he was a husband. Once Mary became Queen, she found it hard to be kind or even sensible about Elizabeth. Mary's hatred of Protestantism was also an expression of her love for her mother, it might be argued. Her feelings were not just those of daughter. The detested Anne Boleyn was a Protestant and, in fact, far more Protestant than the King. During Mary's five-year reign, hundreds of Protestants were burned at the stake. Often Mary did not even attempt to prevent her Catholic advisers from trying to implicate Elizabeth in some of the rebellions against her, such as that of the poet Sir Thomas Wyatt. Instead, she encouraged a form of Inquisition.

From the start of her sister's reign, Elizabeth knew Mary was having her watched and that she was in danger. She was meticulously careful to worship in the now approved Roman way, but even that did not help their relationship much. Mary suspected Elizabeth – who was known as the hope of Protestant England – was being insincere.

In 1554, Mary married Philip of Spain but Elizabeth was not invited to the wedding. The Wyatt rebellion gave the new Spanish ambassador a perfect excuse to chivvy Philip to encourage Mary to execute Elizabeth. However, Elizabeth was saved by the fact that she was desirable. Mary was besotted with her husband, but Philip was far from besotted with her. In fact, the Spaniard, like Thomas Seymour, seems to have been attracted to Elizabeth and so he had every reason to make sure she lived, ready to marry him when her sister died. He persuaded his wife just to imprison her sister in the Tower. To please her husband, Mary agreed. Before Elizabeth was taken there, she begged her sister 'to remember your last promise and my last demand that I be not condemned without answer and due proof which it seems that now I am'. She would be ready to die 'the shamefullest death' if there was any truth in the allegations that she had conspired with Wyatt. Elizabeth begged to speak with her sister from the 'humbleness of my heart'.

When Mary received this letter she was furious. On Palm Sunday 1554, on the orders of the Queen, Elizabeth was rowed to the Tower.

'Here landeth as a true subject, being prisoner as ever landed at these stairs,' she protested. It does not take much imagination to guess at Elizabeth's anxieties when she entered the fortress where her mother had been executed. She told her household that she might never return.

In the Tower, Elizabeth came under the control of Sir John Williams, who was awed by her. When Mary discovered that he was being kind, she moved her sister out to Woodstock. The Queen gave the new jailer instructions that she did not wish 'hereafter to be molested with her disguised and colourable letters'. As much as possible, she wanted to forget Elizabeth even existed.

Elizabeth's new jailer, Sir Henry Benifield, 'showed himself more hard and strait unto her', Foxe said and concluded it was 'a singular miracle of God that she [Elizabeth] could or did escape, in such a multitude of enemies, and grudge of minds so greatly exasperated against her.' Foxe was being unfair. Benifield wrote letters to Mary and the Council, protesting as forcefully as he dared, about the restrictions placed on Elizabeth. His pleas did not sway the Queen. It is not surprising that in Woodstock Elizabeth wrote one sharp poem reflecting her predicament. It was inscribed in her French psalter:

> No crooked leg, no bleared eye,
> No part deformed out of kind,
> Nor yet so ugly half can be
> As is the inward, suspicious mind.

Throughout 1556 Mary refused to see Elizabeth when she begged for audience, but then, on 28 November, the sisters met. At first, Mary was angry when Elizabeth refused to beg for forgiveness, but they managed to compromise and get on. The reconciliation only lasted until Mary told her sister that she wanted her to marry the Duke of Savoy. Elizabeth had no intention of leaving England or of submitting to a husband. After she refused to even consider marrying Savoy, she was sent back to prison.

When Mary became seriously ill in 1558, her husband refused to return to England, though she implored him to do so. Feria, the

Spanish ambassador, did hurry back from France as he hoped to be able to influence Elizabeth, but she had no intention of being dominated by any man, having seen what her sister and most of her father's wives had suffered.

The survivor

After Mary's death, this time there was no hesitation about the succession. Robert Cecil, the Secretary of the Council, rode to Hatfield and the new Queen was acclaimed. She was just twenty-five years old – the same age, by a strange coincidence, as Elizabeth II when she succeeded.

The first Elizabeth had had many traumatic experiences, which should have made her insecure and vindictive. Her father had loved her when he loved Anne Boleyn, then abandoned her, then stripped her of her titles, then reinstated some of her titles and then become much warmer when he married Catherine Parr. Catherine had tolerated her next husband making sexual advances to her stepdaughter. Precisely because historians have tended to ignore psychology, they have not begun to explain why Elizabeth coped so well. It would be absurd to suggest there are clear answers, but the love of Catherine Parr was certainly a factor. The good stepmother was never as close to Mary as she was to Elizabeth. By the time Catherine married Henry, Mary was in her early twenties and set in her ways and her faith. The two women were also divided by religion: Catherine was not just a Protestant but a radical one.

A 'meta-study' that pools the results of a number of studies together offers some insight into Elizabeth's strength. There are methodological problems with the statistics involved but also a clear trend. Intelligent children who suffer cruelty, abuse and post-traumatic stress deal with this better than less intelligent youngsters. In sum, intelligent children tend to be more emotionally intelligent, too. One study of 718 children by Naomi Breslau found, for example, that those with a higher IQ were better able to deal with trauma and argued the reason is 'the way that people explain to themselves what happened to them, how it fits in with their lives and whether it is their fault or not their fault'. It may appear strange to use a study of 2006 to explain Elizabeth's reactions some 450 years earlier, but it seems a useful, if not especially surprising, explanation.

Some degree of religious tolerance would benefit the country, Elizabeth realised, and she saw the wisdom in not prying too deeply into the souls of her subjects. As long as they did not parade any disobedience, they could believe what they liked in private. Her tolerance did not extend to those who plotted against her, nearly all Catholics, but it did to her jailer, Sir Henry Benifield. Foxe noted 'the uncivil nature and disposition of that man', and compared it with the graciousness of the Queen. Elizabeth 'showed herself so far from revenge' that she did not restrict his liberty, though she banned him from court with 'scarce a nipping word; only bidding him to repair home, and saying, "If we have any prisoner, whom we would have sharply and straitly kept, then we will send for you."'

Like most educated people of her time, Elizabeth believed in astrology and asked the great scholar John Dee to cast a horoscope for her. She wanted him to pinpoint the best day for her Coronation, an auspicious time on an auspicious day. Dee picked well. On 15 January 1559, Elizabeth was crowned at Westminster Abbey. As she walked out, the Queen was greeted by a deafening cacophony: organs, fifes, trumpets, drums and bells all blasted out their joy. Elizabeth assumed the throne as a much-loved Princess and became a much-loved Queen. One of Britain's greatest monarchs, she reigned from 1558 to 1603 and saw off many plots against her, as well as defeating the Spanish Armada. Elizabeth chose not to marry, as seen. As a result, we will never know what kind of mother she might have been.

History books say that Elizabeth's death marked the end of the House of Tudor but her successor, James I, was in fact her second cousin. He could also trace his family back to Henry, the butler's great-grandson, who refused to call himself Tudor. James was the great-grandson of Henry VIII's rather forgotten sister, Margaret. How James I became a good father is one of the many mysteries of the long case history.

4

THE STUARTS (1603–1714)

Another traumatic childhood

Mary, Queen of Scots was extremely striking, being very tall for a woman. Since her death, she has inspired many plays and novels, including a masterpiece by the German dramatist Schiller. That is not surprising as her life was full of sex, intrigue and murder.

When she was five years old, Mary was betrothed to Francis, son of the French King. In 1548 she was sent to live in Paris. Though Francis was much shorter than she was, they liked each other. When Mary was fifteen, they married. Francis inherited the throne, but he died in December 1560. Eight months after that, Mary returned to Edinburgh. At the age of seventeen, she was already a widow – and a widow who liked and needed men.

In Scotland, Mary set about finding a new husband. She married her cousin Lord Darnley, who became the father of her only child, James. Darnley was very unstable and jealous, however. In 1565, when Mary was six months pregnant, he and some friends burst into her apartments and killed her secretary, an Italian called David Rizzio. Darnley believed the Italian was Mary's lover, which he may well have been. While Rizzio was being murdered, Darnley placed a pistol against Mary's belly; she claimed she was sure he was going to kill her too. Though she managed to calm him down, she never forgave him. She seems to have hated being without a lover and turned for consolation to James Hepburn, Earl of Bothwell. Together they plotted to kill her husband.

Darnley died dramatically. His house was destroyed in an

explosion and his body was found in an orchard together with that of
his valet. Different accounts claim he was smothered, stabbed or, in
an unlikely coincidence, died of smallpox at the very moment his residence was being blown up. Bothwell was put on trial for the murder
but not convicted; the fact that he was the Queen's lover helped.

The suspicion that Mary was guilty of murder caused outrage.
She was captured, imprisoned and forced to abdicate and flee south,
leaving her baby son with the Earl of Moray. The Scottish nobles
then forced her to abdicate in favour of the child. Mary expected
to return to Scotland quickly to reclaim her throne, but made the
mistake of throwing herself on the mercy of her cousin Elizabeth I.
Elizabeth was only too aware of the dangers of having a Catholic
female relative in the country who might plot against her and kept
Mary a prisoner for nineteen years. Mary never saw her son again.
James became an orphan boy, in effect.

The long case history makes it necessary to raise the question of
willpower. Many psychologists have found it hard to accept that we
are not conditioned or shaped by our early experiences. The Jesuits
claimed that, if they educated a child until he was seven years old,
he was theirs for life. Freud insisted our childhood experiences affect
us profoundly. The school known as behaviourists disagreed with
him on many points – they had little interest in dreams or our inner
life and instead concentrated on the objective study of behaviour
– but they too insisted every human being was made or marred
by what happened in their first years. If we are determined by our
early experiences, individual willpower does not matter – I am what
my experiences have made me. James I, like Elizabeth I and, much
later, Prince Philip, should have become a neurotic catastrophe after
a traumatic childhood. The truth would be very different.

James I became one of the most intellectual monarchs ever to sit
on any throne. In 1604, he commissioned the famous translation of
the Bible and took part in the debates surrounding this work as a
perfect equal with bishops and professors of divinity. He also wrote
four lively tracts – *Daemonologie*, *A Counterblaste to Tobacco* (he hated
the stuff), *Basilikon Doron* and *The True Laws of Free Monarchies*, as

well as two books on the art of poetry. The orthodox view has been that James defended the Divine Right of Kings and that his son, Charles I, provoked the Civil War because he clung stubbornly to his father's ideas. This is something of a misconception because James's ideas about kingship were more flexible than is usually admitted.

James managed to hand over a functioning kingdom when he died. He is also a fascinating subject, because his childhood should have made him bitter and vengeful. Once his mother was forced into exile in England, he had four different Regents and three died violent deaths.

James's first Regent, The Earl of Moray, was killed in January 1570. The following year, his new Regent – James's paternal grand-father, Matthew Stuart – was wounded during a raid by Mary's supporters and soon died. The next Regent was the Earl of Mar, who fared little better than his predecessors, though at least he did not die in battle but after a banquet, where he may or may not have been poisoned; forensic science was not very accurate in the 1570s. The Earl of Morton then became James's Regent.

In Schiller's great play, Mary and Elizabeth met, but, in truth, Elizabeth always refused to meet her unvirginal cousin. Mary was involved in a number of plots against her, and Elizabeth was wary that James himself might conspire to seize her throne. She insisted her ambassador in Edinburgh, Henry Killigrew, provide regular reports on the young King. When James was eight, Killigrew wrote that the boy was 'well grown', which was flattering, as James was weak, but, more to the point, that he was already an impressive scholar and 'was able *extempore* which he did before me to read a chapter of the Bible out of Latin into French and out of French into English as well as few men could have added anything to his translation'. The performance could not have been rehearsed because James's teacher, George Buchanan, allowed the ambassador to choose any portion of the Bible that he wished. The boy scholar rounded off his performance by doing a dance for Killigrew and then, conscious of his manners, asked him to convey his best wishes to Elizabeth.

Buchanan remained as James's tutor when the boy's fourth

Regent, the Earl of Morton, was jailed and charged with murdering James's father, Darnley. Morton, was executed on 2 June 1581. By then, the fourteen-year-old King had suffered enough life events for, well, a lifetime: he had seen his mother exiled, his father murdered and two of his Regents murdered and one executed. There was one constant presence in his life, though: his tutor, Buchanan. Most royal tutors have been teachers or clergymen, who were flattered when asked to teach a prince. Buchanan was in his own right a Member of the Scottish Parliament, a theologian of some repute and well-respected. He thought himself more than the equal of any of the Regents who kept on being killed. Not remotely deferential, he was determined to beat discipline and fear of God into the boy. This was not sadism, but duty: Buchanan wanted to make sure James became a good Protestant King.

The tutor also had a nice line in repartee. When James was twelve and fighting with one of his friends, Buchanan became so angry he yelled at the boys to 'hold your tongues or I shall come down and whip your breeks for you!' In their 1938 biography of James, the Steeholms tell the story not just with gusto, but as if repeating an eyewitness account.

> 'Come on,' James challenged his teacher.
>
> Incensed, Buchanan advanced on the boy and whipped James 'breeks' (or breeches) – so hard James that cried out. The royal wails brought Lady Mar rushing into the room. 'There, there,' she soothed and took the young King into her arms, 'Has Master George been hurting you? For shame. How dare you lay hands on the Lord's Anointed?'
>
> 'Madam I have whipped his arse, you can kiss it if you like,' Buchanan is said to have replied.

There is a flamboyant comparison to be made between the childhoods of James I and Stalin: both had childhoods marked by extreme violence (both were beaten by priests), both grew up in a time of political turmoil, both were extremely competent in theology, having been taught by priests, and both wrote decent poetry. Stalin became a paranoid monster. James only had Sir Walter Raleigh killed, and that only after something resembling due process.

Despite his almost gothic childhood, James turned out to be a reasonably successful and stable King. He married Anne of Denmark in 1589, having sailed to Oslo to claim his bride after her passage to Scotland was thwarted by a series of misadventures. The couple had three sons and four daughters. Their eldest, Henry, was born in 1594. His mother was deeply disappointed that she was expected to hand him to the Earl of Mar to be brought up. She told her husband that she wanted to stay with her baby, but the King refused her wish. When a daughter was born, the King let his wife see more of the child and, when another daughter was born, James personally ordered night caps and a cradle for the baby. He also had the sense to order dolls for his eldest daughter so she would not get too jealous of the new arrival. Household accounts from the sixteenth century have occasional entries recording payments for toys. As well as dolls, royal children played with toy soldiers and had pull toys, which they could drag after them.

Anne and James's second son was born in November 1600, but Charles was so weak he was not expected to live long. When his parents rode to England in 1603, the boy was left in the charge of Sir Robert and Lady Carey. Carey wrote that Charles 'was not able to go nor scant stand alone he was so weak in his joints and especially in his ankles as many feared they were out of joint'. Charles was also tongue-tied, which provoked a dispute between Lady Carey and the King. James wanted the tongue string cut for the Prince 'was so long beginning to speak as he thought would never have spoke, but my wife protested so much against them both as she got the victory and the King was fain to yield'. Charles's speech impediment stayed with him all his life. Carey and his wife looked after him until he was eleven years old, by which time he had grown 'in health and strength both of body and mind to the amazement of many that knew his weakness'.

James's eldest son, Henry, loved his adoring mother and showed it in a nice way: when he was nine years old, he wrote her a sweet letter of congratulation on giving birth to another child. Henry was also arrogant and lazy, however. James once warned that, if he did not mend his ways, he would leave the crown to Charles instead. The warning seems to have worked. So it was to Henry that James wrote *Basilikon Doron*, which is far from being a strident justification for the right of a monarch to be tyrannical, as it is often presented. As I read it, I came to admire James not just for his obvious love for his son but also for his style, which includes some well-crafted phrases such as the 'slipperiness of memory'. At the end of his time in the White House, the outgoing American President leaves a confidential memo for his successor and *Basilikon Doron* has something of that flavour. The book is a mix of personal history, reflections and political advice. I have quoted from it extensively because it deserves close attention. How many fathers write books for their sons?

Basilikon Doron – a father's gift to his son

James begins with a sonnet in traditional Elizabethan style:

> God gives not Kings the style of Gods in vain,
> For on his Throne his Scepter do they sway:
> And as their subjects ought them to obey,
> So Kings should fear and serve their God again
> If then ye would enjoy a happy reign,
> Observe the Statutes of your heavenly King.

As Henry's natural father, James had to 'be careful for your godly and virtuous education, as my eldest Son, and the first fruits of God's blessing towards me in thy posterity'. James's son had to beware 'failing, which God forbid, of the sadness of your fall, according to the proportion of that height' and so he had written a treatise to prepare him for the duties that a king owed to God and included some essentials no king should neglect. It was his own duty to keep his son on the straight and narrow, James felt – 'I ordain to be a resident faithful admonisher of you.' He charged Henry 'in the presence of GOD, and by the fatherly authority I have over you, that ye keep it ever with you, as carefully, as Alexander did the Iliads of Homer'. The book would provide 'just and impartial advice' and he begged his son to confer with it, 'when ye are at quiet as ever ye thinks to deserve my Fatherly blessing, to follow and put in practice, as far as lieth in you.' If Henry ignored his advice, James protested, 'before that Great GOD, I had rather not be a Father, and childless, then be a Father of wicked children.' He then begged God to make his son work hard to deserve his 'blessing, which here from my heart I bestow upon you'.

The 57-page book was distilled from James's own experience. He did not think it fitting that it should be made public because this was a manual for a future king written by his father and so he only let seven copies be printed. In some copies there is a Freudian slip and 'seven' has become 'semen'. The *Basilikon* was a gift, 'both of the honest integrity of my heart, and of my fatherly affection and our natural care'.

A sense of grievance about the past is a theme throughout, although James admitted he had made many mistakes. His son should learn from them as well as from the injustices that he himself had suffered. Given his own experiences with his mother, James told his son not to tolerate 'any unreverent speeches or books against any of his parents or progenitors'. He had noticed that those who were 'steadfastly true to me in all my troubles [had] constantly kept their allegiance to her in her time'. So his son should not allow 'any virulent detracting of his predecessors'.

James knew that 'a Prince so long as he is young, will be so carried away with some sort of delight or other, that he cannot patiently abide the reading of any large volume.' Then, once the Prince was older, 'he would be so busy he would have little time to think and read.' That was why James restricted himself to fifty-seven pages of advice.

A king had two obligations to God: 'First, for that he made you a man; and next, for that he made you a little GOD to sit on his

Throne, and rule over other men.' James put his phrase 'little God' in context: Henry should be grateful for his exalted position and strive to deserve it. He should be aware of his faults and not imagine he had a licence to sin because he was a king. A king should 'shine before their people, in all works of sanctification and righteousness, that their persons as bright lamps of godlinesse and virtue, may, going in and out before their people, give light to all their steps'.

Knowledge and fear of God would teach Henry all he needed to discharge his duties. James urged his son to read Scripture 'with a sanctified and chaste heart: and to pray to understand it properly'. He had to concentrate 'and study carefully to understand those that are somewhat difficile'.

James recommended the psalms of David, which had, after all, been written by a king. He himself was a sharp controversialist and told Henry so he should not merely parrot prayers out of books nor should he presume unlike many vain Puritans to be too 'homely' and talk to God as if He were their next-door neighbour. Prayers had to be for decent things, not for revenge or lust. 'Above all them, my Son, labour to keep sound this conscience, which many prattle of, but over few feel,' he advised.

Once every twenty-four hours, James wrote, 'when ye are at greatest quiet, to call your self to account of all your last day's actions, either wherein ye have committed things ye should not, or omitted the things ye should do, either in your Christian or Kingly calling.' Examining his conscience and behaviour was vital. 'Censure your self as sharply, as if ye were your own enemy. For if ye judge your self, ye shall not be judged.'

The Bible contained all that was necessary for salvation, but anything not precisely ordained by Scripture could be changed to cope with the necessities of time. His son should pay close attention when Churchmen claimed something was ordained in the Bible as priests often interpreted the Word of God in ways that suited them. James had plenty of experience of priestly vanity and warned if some 'deboshed' – the very word he used – priest 'or other urge you to embrace any of their fantasies in the place of

God's word', Henry should point out their vanity to them with all his authority.

James's failure to deal with the fantasies of fanatical priests had caused him problems and he begged his son to learn from 'my over-dear bought experience'. He had hoped that in being gracious he would 'win all men's hearts to a loving and willing obedience, I by the contrary found, the disorder of the country, and the loss of my thanks to be all my reward'. He also warned against vain astrologers and necromancers. Horoscopes were heresy and James was adamant that his son should 'Take no heed to any of your dreams, for all prophecies, visions, and prophetic dreams are accomplished and ceased in Christ'. It is perhaps surprising that he dismissed the role dreams played by those God-inspired interpreters Joseph and Daniel in the Bible.

In the Old Testament, the King was a judge. In that role, he had to be compassionate but there were some terrible sins he should never forgive, 'such as Witch-craft, willful murder, Incest, [especially within the degrees of consanguinity], Sodomy, poisoning, and false coin'. When the offence had been 'against your own person and authority, since the fault concerneth your self, I remit to your own choice to punish or pardon therein, as your heart serveth you, and according to the circumstances of the turn, and the quality of the committer'.

The king had to rule impartially on questions of property and James urged his son to neither love the rich nor pity the poor. In England, he would often have to deal with the greedy and dishonest, not to mention the bitchiness of the natives and their mania for novelties – the tobacco against which James counter-blasted being one of those.

James still revered his mother Mary and reminded his son, 'ye know the command in God's law, Honour your Father and Mother.' So the king should not let his parents to 'be dishonoured by any; especially, since the example also touches your self. For how can they love you, that hated them whom-of ye are come?' It was monstrous to 'see a man love the child, and hate the Parents: as on the other part, the infaming and making odious of the parents, is the readiest way to bring the son in contempt'. He reminded Henry again of his own experience – all those who were not faithful to his mother had not been faithful to him.

James urged his son to be on the side of the oppressed. The King should not spare 'any pains in your own person, to see their wrongs redressed'. He again reminded him of his own past and urged him to 'remember of the honourable style given to my grand-father of worthy memory, in being called the poor man's King'; he was refer-ring to James V of Scotland. A good king, however, should not swing to the other extreme and constantly condemn the nobles. He reminded his son how 'that error broke the King my grand-fathers heart'. James's grandfather had been kept prisoner by one of his nobles for three years.

He then returned to the question of loyalty and urged his son to show 'your constant love towards them that I loved [and] your constant hatred to them that I hated: I mean, bring not home, nor restore not such, as ye find standing banished or fore-faulted by me.'

When it came to the question of war, James was cynical. If his son went to war, he should 'hazard his safety once or twice' but, once he had acquired 'the fame of courage', Henry should be sensible and not expose 'rashly your person to every peril'.

Servants had to be watched carefully. James remembered that the first rebellion raised against him 'compelled me to make a great alteration among my servants'. A king had to be 'a daily watch-man over your servants'. If he could not ensure they obeyed him, why should the country obey him? The king also had to realise that his actions were constantly under scrutiny by his servants and subjects were always trying 'to interpret the inward disposition of the mind' of the monarch.

A king must choose his wife well

James warned Henry that if he married someone of a different faith, by which he meant a Catholic, 'inconvenients were like to ensue', but there were few Protestant Princesses in Europe. The question of succession was, of course, vital: Henry had to make sure that his bride was able to have children.

The strict religious education that James had received meant he did not hold with loose morals, on paper at least. As the bridegroom, 'ye must keep your body clean and unpolluted, till ye give it to your wife, whom-to only it belongeth. For how can ye justly crave to be joined with a pure virgin, if your body be polluted? why should the one half be clean, and the other defiled?' Of course, few kings have followed this moral code. A husband should treat his wife as 'the half of your self; and to make your body (which then is no more yours, but properly hers) common with none other. I trust I need not to insist here to dissuade you from the filthy vice of adultery.' He warned Henry to 'abstain from haunting before your marriage, the idle company of dames, which are nothing else, but *irritamenta libidinis*'. The sense of the Latin was that dames could provoke an itching of the loins.

Then again, he referred to his own unhappy family, telling his son to remember James's own grandfather, 'who by his adultery, bred the wreck of his lawful daughter and heir in begetting that bastard who unnaturally rebelled, and procured the ruin of his own Sovereign and sister'. The 'unnatural bastard' was the Earl of Moray, who had been one of James's Regents.

His son would have to be a vigilant father, keeping his children 'ever in a reverent love and fear of you'. Being a good king did not come naturally, though; it required study but a king could only hope to read in 'idle hours not interrupting therewith the discharge of your office'. He urged Henry to study the history of England and Scotland.

Then again James turned personal and counselled his son to be magnanimous – again, in turning 'empire' into the verb 'empiring', he showed a sweet stylistic touch. The king should treat these enemies as 'not worthy of your wrath, empiring over your own passion, and triumphing in the commanding your self to forgive'. Forgiving was Christian and kingly. Some attacks were however too serious, so 'where ye find a notable injury, spare not to give course to the torrents of your wrath'. He ended with a familiar image: 'The wrath of a King is like to the roaring of a lion.'

His own turbulent childhood had marked James deeply; he wrote: 'Neither deceive your self with many that say, they care not for their Parents curse, so they deserve it not. O invert not the order of nature, by judging your superiors, chiefly in your own particular! But assure your self, the blessing or curse of the Parents, hath almost ever a Prophetic power joined with it.'

He then turned to more mundane matters. People would always be watching the king and so his table manners must be impeccable as he should often eat in public but he should avoid the slightest suggestion of gluttony – he must not be seen scoffing anything too exotic, such as a peacock stuffed with pomegranates. Henry should also not be 'effeminate in your clothes, in perfuming, preening, or such like', and no king should make 'a fool of yourself in disguising or wearing long hair or nails, which are but excrements of nature'.

Shakespeare was writing his great tragedies when James became King of England. In *Hamlet*, the Player King tells the Prince to match the gesture to the word. As *Hamlet* was written before the *Basilikon*, it seems James made use not just of the Bard's ideas but almost his words. His son should pay attention 'framing ever your gesture according to your present actions'. The king should take care 'in your gesture; neither looking sillily, like a stupid pedant nor unsettledly, with an uncouth morgue, like a new-comeover Cavalier'. He had to be natural, grave and courteous or he would be accused of arrogance. In addition, he must be careful 'not to keep nodding at every step' to make himself popular, but he had – a question of image again – to look grave and 'with a majesty when ye sit in judgment, or give audience'.

As must be evident now, James wrote well. In the following extract, he compares the mind and body to an engine, instructing Henry that he

should use a plaine, short, but stately style, both in your Proclamations and missives, especially to foreign Princes. And if your engine spur you to write any works, either in verse or in prose, I cannot but allow you to practise it: but take no longsome works in hand, for distracting you from your calling.

He advised his son to write in English for there was nothing left to be said in Greek and Latin.

From the mind, James turned to the body. The king should engage in pastimes which could improve his abilities and health and he repeated his novel use of the word 'engine' – 'I grant it to be most requisite for a King to exercise his engine, which surely with idleness will rust and become blunt.' But a king also needed to relax and could play cards, though James warned against chess 'because it is over-wise and Philosophicke a folly'. At cards, the king's son must 'play always fair, that ye come not in use of tricking and lying in least: otherwise, if ye cannot keep these rules, my counsel is that ye all utterly abstain from these plays.'

He ended by urging Henry to remember his duty to God and to ensure that his deeds reflected 'the inward uprightness of your heart' and showed 'your virtuous disposition; and in respect of the greatness and weight of your burden, to be patient in hearing, keeping your heart free from preoccupation, ripe in concluding, and constant in your resolution'.

It was better to take time to make decisions than to be hasty and then change one's mind. James urged his son 'to digest ever your passion, before ye determine upon anything'. Henry should judge every man according to his own offence and not punish or blame the father for the son, nor the brother for the brother. He should always judge the virtue of those he was dealing with and never seek excuses to take revenge.

James's finale to his son was florid, but heartfelt:

I will for end of all, require you my Son, as ever ye think to deserve my fatherly blessing, to keep continually before the eyes of your mind, the greatness of your charge: And being content to let others excel in other things, let it be your chiefest earthly glory, to excel in your own craft.

It was, among other things, a beautiful love letter. James, however, turned out to be as unlucky a parent as he had been a child.

Prince Henry's sickness

In 1607, Queen Anne fell ill and asked Sir Walter Raleigh for a dose of some potion with which he had returned from the Americas (probably quinine). It was generous of Raleigh to send some, since he was her husband's prisoner in the Tower – though his life there was none too harsh. His wife sometimes came to stay and they were allowed to share a bed. Raleigh was permitted to garden and he started writing his *History of the World*.

After the quinine had helped her, the Queen started to visit Raleigh. James did not stop these visits, and the Queen once took her eldest son with her. Henry became fascinated by Raleigh and could not understand why he should be imprisoned. He is rumoured to have said: 'No one but my father would keep such a bird in a cage.' Henry now started to champion the idea of releasing a man who had been found guilty of plotting against his father, though James refused to countenance the idea.

The summer of 1612 was unusually hot. Prince Henry seems to have enjoyed it, playing tennis and then ending the day with a swim in the Thames.

On 10 October, Henry developed a fever. Over the next ten days, he seemed to improve, though he often had headaches. He was well enough by 25 October to dine with his father. Within twenty-four hours, Henry had sharp pinched faeces, which, James noted a little pedantically, Hippocrates considered a sign of serious illness. From that point on, he became more and more concerned about his son's health.

Two nights after he ate with his father, Henry suffered new symptoms: irregular breathing and twitching movements. The next day, when the fever was worse and Henry's abdomen badly swollen, the best doctors could offer was senna and rhubarb. Henry then began to show symptoms of delirium. At one point, he jumped out of bed, babbling like a lunatic. He also started to defecate in his clothes as he stumbled about the room. Again, Raleigh's elixir was sent for, but this time the quinine did not work. Henry finally died on 6 November 1612. James was distraught, and it was after his son's death that he became infatuated with at least one younger man.

Tongue-tied Charles now became James's heir. He had recovered from his sickly childhood but seems to have been unable or unwilling to follow the subtle advice James had given Henry. It is tempting to suggest that Charles needed to prove he was strong because he had been weak as a boy, could not speak clearly and was the victim of persistent teasing by his brother. James never produced a second version of the *Basilikon* dedicated to his second son, Charles.

The death of James I in 1625 signalled the end of over a century when British kings and queens had been determined to have well-educated children. Their offspring were unusually intellectual and even produced some serious writing – Henry VIII's attack on Luther, Catherine Parr's two books on theology, Elizabeth's translations and the four tracts written by James I. His *True Laws of Free Monarchies* is also not quite the crude statement of the Divine Right of Kings many historians have assumed – the King had duties to God but also to the people. The fact that God had anointed him did not mean that he could ignore questions of justice and morality; there was a tripartite contract between ruler, the ruled and God.

Charles I – the King who asked too much of his son

Charles I does not seem to have grasped his father's subtleties; after a disastrous attempt to marry a Spanish Princess, he married Henrietta Maria, the sister of the French King Louis XIII, in 1625. She was only fifteen years old, nine years younger than Charles. Their first son died when he was just a day old. Henrietta said she intended to forget the loss, while her mother blamed the midwife. But the Queen was soon pregnant again and, this time, her mother Marie de Medici sent for a French midwife and a 'useful chair' to make sure nothing went wrong (she also insisted the curtains around the royal bed should be a soothing green).

Around 4 a.m. on 29 May 1630, Henrietta went into labour, and she was delivered of a very large and obviously healthy boy eight hours later. Charles I was so pleased that he gave the midwife £1,000 – a truly fabulous sum then. The baby was named Charles after his father, but was largely brought up in the care of the Protestant Countess of Dorset to make sure he did not become a Catholic. The young Charles learned his lessons well, as an extraordinary incident reveals.

By 1639, when relations between Charles and Parliament were at breaking point, the nine-year-old Prince of Wales was made to attend seven weeks of debate in Parliament. The boy sat in the House of Lords at one side of the empty throne. Charles said he would not attend these debates and then promptly did so, but 'incognito'. He had a special box made and sat in it, sometimes with the Queen and sometimes with his daughter, Mary. The Chamber was not large and so the idea that the King could hide in a box without Members of Parliament realising his whereabouts was absurd. His father's bizarre behaviour must have convinced many in Parliament that the King was not fit to rule.

A year or so later, the King made another even more peculiar demand of his son. Thomas Wentworth, the Earl of Strafford, was Charles's most able minister. When he convened a new Parliament in November 1640, the Commons impeached the Archbishop of Canterbury and started to sniff for Strafford's head. John Pym, who was famous for his hostility to the divine rights of Kings, loathed Strafford. Strafford went on trial for high treason but the trial collapsed for lack of evidence. Pym now dredged up the tactic used against Thomas Seymour. He moved a Bill of Attainder, which simply stated Strafford was guilty and should be executed. Like any other Act, the Bill needed the Royal Assent. Charles promised Strafford that he would not sign. On 13 April 1641, the Commons passed the Bill with a huge majority of 204 to 59 and the Lords passed it, too, in early May.

Charles believed he could save Strafford from execution at the very last minute, but he did not have the courage to refuse the Royal Assent and so he signed the Bill on 10 May. A scene must have followed of which sadly there is no known record. Charles summoned his son and told him that he relied on him to pull off an astonishing political coup: it would be up to the boy to persuade Parliament to spare Strafford. The next morning, the Prince of Wales attended the House of Lords to read out a desperate message. This time, his father was not hiding in his ludicrous box to hear his son beg the Lords. Now that Strafford had been condemned, would not Parliament be satisfied with just keeping him in prison to 'fulfil the natural course of his life'? If Parliament conceded that, it would afford His Majesty 'unspeakable contentment'. The boy read the message no doubt more eloquently than his tongue-tied father might have done, but there was no reprieve and on the 12 May Strafford was executed.

As a result perhaps of seeing the Prince of Wales so often in the Chamber, Parliament tried to intervene in Charles's education. With his mother a Catholic, the Commons wanted to ensure the Prince received a proper Protestant grounding and one of the most distinguished of the King's enemies, John Hampden, suggested he be appointed as tutor. In a politically unwise move, the King refused.

The dispute between King and Parliament grew worse and Charles was eventually forced to leave London in January. After some time trying to gather troops, he raised the royal standard in Nottingham on 22 August 1642. Both sides then recruited armies. The Civil War that followed brought the Prince of Wales, his younger brother James and their father very close. Henry VII, Henry VIII and James I had not taken their children into battle with them. Charles I's son had to grow up faster than any British monarch for centuries.

The King took both his sons to the Battle of Edgehill in 1642. Three years later, when he was only fourteen years old, Charles was made commander of the English forces in the West Country. The teenager did not have true charge but took part in some fighting. He spent three years on the campaign with his father, sharing a few successes and mostly failures, because Cromwell had better generals, more money and more resources. By spring 1646, the King

was losing the war and decided that his sons should leave England
for the relative safety of France, just as Henry Tudor had done 175
years earlier.

The teenage Charles first made for the Isles of Scilly, where he and
his tiny court had to live in a castle whose roof leaked badly. They
then set sail for Jersey, where their lodgings were more comfortable. Charles finally reached France, where his mother was already
living in exile and his first cousin, eight-year-old Louis XIV, was
undisputed King.

While Cromwell and Parliament controlled England, the situation in Scotland was more confused. The Scots would support King
Charles as his father, James, had also been King of Scotland. They,
however, insisted Charles I accept some harsh conditions. The Civil
War unleashed a flood of preachers, prophets and men of God, who
squabbled about such important theological issues as whether Christ
had owned his own clothes. The most powerful group in Scotland
was the Covenanters, who had bound themselves to keep Presbyterian
doctrine. In 1640, the Scottish Parliament adopted the Covenant and
the Covenanters became, in effect, the government of Scotland.

The Scottish Parliament was deeply suspicious of the English
Parliament so Charles I fled north. He thought, as he so often did,
that he could control events but the Scots insisted he first accept
the Covenant. The King refused and eventually the Covenanters
lost patience. They handed him over to the commissioners
of the English Parliament in early 1647.

Charles's sons were safe in Europe but no one was prepared
to help them much – the boys even had trouble raising money to
survive. After Paris, Charles moved to The Hague, where his sister
Mary and brother-in-law, William II, Prince of Orange, seemed
more likely to assist the royalist cause but they too did very little.

Charles was far more loyal than many Princes of Wales – he
was desperate to know just what was happening to his father.
He wrote to General Thomas Fairfax, who effectively ruled with
Cromwell, that: 'we have no sources of information regarding the
health and present condition of the King our father.' They were

forced to rely on 'the common gazettes', which reached Holland. Charles told Fairfax that he had sent a servant to present his humble respects to His Majesty but Parliament had prevented the man from seeing the King. Charles had reasons to believe that his father had been moved from the Isle of Wight, 'with some intention of proceeding against himself with more rigour or of deposing him from the royal dignity given him by God alone or even of taking his life, the mere thought of which seems so horrible and incredible'. Charles acknowledged his father was in Fairfax's power and begged him to consider 'the choice you make'.

Some historians claim Charles attached to the letter a blank piece of paper on which Parliament could write the conditions under which it would release the King, but, in her biography of Charles II, Antonia Fraser claims this to be a myth. Whatever the truth, Charles made it clear that Parliament could make considerable demands of him so long as his father was safe.

Cromwell then tempted the young man and offered Charles his father's throne if he would agree to the constitutional safeguards the King had already refused to accept. But Charles did not allow himself to be tempted. After some soul-searching by Parliament, the King was put on trial. The prospect of the trial provoked much reaction in the courts of Europe: there was no doubt that Charles I would be found guilty, but his son still hoped that he would be saved the block. Charles I's youngest son and daughter were allowed to see their father the day before he was beheaded in 1649. The King embraced them and told them to maintain the dignity of the Stuarts. However, Cromwell did not allow them to send a letter to their brother. The Prince of Wales only found out that his father had been beheaded while he was playing tennis. One of his small band of courtiers read the dreadful news in a gazette and hurried to inform the Prince. Charles was devastated – the boy who had failed to save Strafford had also failed to save his own father. Biographies tend to gloss over his sense of loss and his attempts to console his mother and siblings. At the age of eighteen, Charles was head of a family which had lost its power, position and virtually all sources of income.

When Charles I was executed, the English and Scottish crowns were still united. The Covenanters might have been politically radical but they also believed in the literal truth of the Bible, and the Old Testament is mostly the story of the kings of Israel. The Scottish Parliament was willing to allow Charles to take the Scottish throne so long as he did what his father had refused to do and signed the Covenant. As soon as Charles reached Scotland on 24 June 1650, he agreed, even though he disliked its doctrines and disliked many of the Covenanters even more. He had seen the dangers of his father's stubborn defiance.

Charles was crowned King of Scotland on 1 January 1651, but Cromwell had no intention of allowing a threat to develop in the North. He defeated Charles at the Battle of Worcester in September 1651. With his father dead and his inheritance lost, Charles was forced to flee again.

Cromwell offered a reward of £1,000 for Charles's head and warned that anyone who helped him would be guilty of treason and put to death. Posters proclaiming this were put up all over England. Charles had grown into a very tall man, which made it difficult for him to disguise himself. Nevertheless, he managed to get to Normandy. It was the start of a further nine years of exile.

While Charles waited and waited with little money, and seemingly little hope, Cromwell invaded Ireland, fought the Dutch (in case William of Orange was tempted to help Charles) and even sent the Navy to the West Indies to remind the world of how powerful the English Commonwealth was; the very word 'Commonwealth' was, of course, a provocation to any royalty. As it established itself, however, Europe's kings betrayed not just their own class, as a Marxist historian might have put it, but also their own family. The French were especially perfidious.

Far from helping her son, Henrietta made things more difficult because she allowed her religious adviser to encourage Charles's brother, James, to become a Catholic. In November 1654, Charles wrote to his mother, begging her to put the interests of her son above her faith: 'I must conclude that if your Majesty does continue to proceed in the change of my brother's religion I cannot believe Her Majesty does either believe or wish my return to England.' If his mother 'had any kindness towards him', she would not persist, as no one in England would believe that Charles did not condone his brother abandoning the Protestant faith. That was folly at a time when he needed as much support in England as he could muster. Charles even invoked the memory of his father who, he claimed, had told James never to change his religion. Henrietta was more interested in her soul and that of James than in her oldest son's political future, however.

The Lord Protector – and his son

The new Constitution gave Cromwell the right to appoint a successor and he turned to his third – and eldest surviving – son, Richard Cromwell, even though he had been disappointed in him when Richard was a young man. Until he was thirty, Richard's great achievements were to marry a rich country girl and be appointed a Justice of the Peace for Hampshire. Cromwell had great expectations and, like many fathers, was disappointed. He wrote acidly to Richard's father-in-law: 'I would have him mind and understand business, read a little history, study the mathematics and cosmography: these are good, with subordination to the things of God. Better than idleness, or mere outward worldly contents. These fit for public services, for which a man is born.'

The lazy son was not allowed to sit in Parliament until 1654, but then his father's attitude changed and Cromwell made sure Richard became the Member of Parliament for Cambridge University, though he had never been a student there. Cromwell then involved Richard in the administration of the country. In July 1657, his son was appointed Chancellor of Oxford University, although he had not studied there either. Richard was promoted again in December and made a member of the powerful Council of State. Nine months later, when his father died on 3 September 1658, Richard was informed that he was to succeed him.

When he heard that Cromwell was dead, Charles was cautious.

The next eighteen months saw a game of cat and mouse being played by the son of the brilliant dictator and that of the failed King. Ironically, Cromwell probably would have been prouder of his son than Charles I might have been of his: Charles II was more willing to compromise than the father he loved had ever been.

The new Lord Protector faced two problems – the country was £2 million in debt and the army questioned his authority because Richard had not fought even one skirmish in the Civil War. Politically, however, Richard was quite skilful. He called a new Parliament, which was divided between moderate Presbyterians, crypto-royalists and a few determined republicans. Richard managed these differences reasonably well but the army proved less pliable. In April 1659, the army's General Council met to demand higher taxation to pay for what the military always want: more men and more equipment. They sent a petition to the new Lord Protector, who sent it on to Parliament, which refused to be bullied. In response to the army, the Commons then banned all meetings of army officers unless they had the permission of the Lord Protector and Parliament. Parliament capped its defiance by passing a resolution that all officers should swear an oath that they would not use force to subvert the sitting of Parliament. The army was outraged and demanded Richard dissolve Parliament.

Richard refused, so, to show who really controlled the country, the generals gathered in St James's Palace. He now gave in and dissolved Parliament. There were no new elections but the surviving members of the Rump Parliament were summoned back to Westminster. Sitting began on 7 May 1659.

As the crisis developed, the French ambassador approached Richard with an extraordinary proposition, given that France was a monarchy: France would provide troops to fight the army on behalf of Parliament. The King of France, Louis XIV, was uninhibited by the fact that Charles happened to be his cousin. Perhaps unwisely, Richard refused the French offer. On 25 May, after the Rump agreed to pay his debts and give him a pension, he resigned. Richard was never formally deposed or arrested, but simply allowed to fade away. Of course, royalists rejoiced at his fall and he became the butt of many satires, which mocked him with nicknames such as 'Tumble Down Dick' and 'Queen Dick'.

In Holland, Charles was being courted for the first time since his father had been beheaded. Here, there is a parallel with Elizabeth I: Charles had had a traumatic childhood, just as Elizabeth had experienced a century earlier. He wanted revenge because he loved his father but, like Elizabeth, he was highly intelligent and saw the need for forgiveness. Charles agreed to the Declaration of Breda, which promised a general pardon for crimes committed during the Civil War and the Protectorate for everyone who now recognised him as the lawful King. On 2 May 1660, Parliament passed a resolution that 'government ought to be by King, Lords and Commons'. Charles was invited to return and, on 8 May, he was proclaimed King.

Relatively few of Cromwell's allies were punished, but Charles did pursue those who had personally condemned his father to death. Nine were hanged, drawn and quartered, including Gregory Clement and Thomas Harrison, both of whom had signed the King's death warrant. Two unrepentant republicans and around another twenty people were forbidden to sit in Parliament or to hold any public office. Meanwhile, Richard Cromwell had the good sense to disappear.

There are some nice parallels between Richard Cromwell's fate and that of Charles: both had to be enterprising, devious and to appear not to support their fathers in order to stay alive. After July 1660, Richard travelled to Europe using a number of pseudonyms, though there is little evidence that he was being actively hunted. He was once invited to dine with the Prince of Conti, who did not know his true identity and observed, 'Well that Oliver, tho' he was a traitor and a villain, was a brave man, had great parts, great courage, and was worthy to command; but that Richard, that coxcomb and poltroon, was surely the basest fellow alive; what is become of that fool?' Richard replied: 'He was betrayed by those he most trusted, and who had been most obliged by his father.' The next morning, he left the Count's house and he did not return to England until twenty years after the Restoration.

'Six bastard Dukes survive his luscious reign'
– Daniel Defoe on Charles II

Charles had learned from his father's failures and, once he was King, enjoyed the kind of popularity that had always eluded the first Charles. But, where Henrietta had delivered a succession of healthy babies, her son was less lucky – and the country paid for it. Charles married Catherine of Braganza but they had no children, though he had at least twelve by seven of his mistresses. Princess Diana could include in her own ancestry two of Charles's illegitimate sons: Henry FitzRoy, whom Charles made Duke of Grafton, and Charles Lennox, who became the first Duke of Richmond. The King seems to have been rather fond of his children. Royal accounts often mention sums for cradles, rattles and other toys. He was also proud of the two sons that he had by Nell Gwyn. In April 1684, Lady Mary Tudor (Charles's daughter by Moll Davis) was given money to pay her chamber-maid, laundry maid, page and footman. The King even paid for the weddings of all these children. The poet Andrew Marvell put it nicely:

> The misses take place, each advanced to be duchess
> With pomp as great as queens in their coach and six horses
> The bastards made dukes, earls, viscounts and lords
> With all the title that honour affords.

Charles got on well with his daughters too, especially Charlotte. He sent her notes, signing himself as her loving and kind father. There is a picture of her tickling the King's bald head as he dozes after lunch, a gesture he was delighted by.

It has been reckoned that over half the hereditary peers in the House of Lords can trace their ancestry to the merry and promiscuous Charles II.

Charles's brother James was more fertile in wedlock. His eldest daughter, Mary, was born on 30 April 1662 and named after Mary, Queen of Scots. James's wife, Anne Hyde, gave birth to seven more children, but only Mary and her younger sister Anne survived. Mary became second in line to the throne and Anne third.

To the dismay of his mother Henrietta, Charles ordered his nieces to be brought up as Protestants. They were moved to Richmond Palace, where they were raised by Lady Frances Villiers, with only occasional visits to see their parents. The marriage between James and Lady Anne Hyde was never an easy one and it became increasingly unhappy as James had at least as many mistresses as his brother. Though a bad husband, James also seems, as Samuel Pepys noted, to have been a devoted father. Anne Hyde, made wretched by her husband's infidelities, died on 31 March 1671.

Two years after his wife died, James remarried. He tried to charm his daughters into accepting his second wife, Mary of Modena. 'I have brought you a new playfellow,' he wrote to his eldest daughter, Mary. She was eleven years old while her stepmother was only four years older. The age difference mattered far less than the fact that her father had married a Catholic and, worse still, one who had wanted to be a nun. Mary of Modena had been persuaded to marry James by her priests, who convinced her that she might help return England to the Catholic Church. For both his daughters, James was now an apostate.

James's eldest daughter, Mary, started to behave very strangely: she wrote passionate letters to an older girl, Frances Apsley; the letters delivered by a drawing teacher who happened to be a dwarf, just to add a baroque touch. The correspondence lasted for seventeen years. In it, Mary addressed Frances usually as 'dear husband'. Gossipy, but also full of endearments, the letters read like love letters; they were a conceit but conceits can conceal true feelings, especially perhaps when one girl calls another girl her 'husband'.

'You have no reason to challenge me with unkindness to my husband,' Mary wrote early on, after she and Frances had had a tiff. 'I should be very base to be so to one from whom I have received so much kindness. Clorine is so much Aurelia's servant that she shall ever be your obedient wife.' In this fantasy, Mary styled herself as Clorine and Frances as Aurelia.

Again, Freud comes to mind. While a teenager, he and his friend Eduard Silberstein wrote letters to each other as if they were dogs who for some reason lived at a hospital in Seville. Some biographers have suggested the correspondence was the first of a number of indications that Freud had some homosexual leanings. The passionate letters between Clorine and Aurelia also suggest some homoerotic undercurrent between Mary and Frances, though they may not have been aware of it.

The next crucial moment in the family history came when Mary was fifteen and was betrothed to her cousin, the Protestant Stadtholder of Holland, William of Orange. Charles II pressured his brother to agree to the marriage, which he hoped would make James more popular with Protestants. But Mary was not thrilled. When her father told her that she was to marry William, 'she wept all that afternoon and all the following day'. Though extremely cool to her husband-to-be when William came to London for a month, she was given no choice. As soon as they were married, William took his reluctant bride off to Holland – and, miraculously, everything changed. They spent two weeks more or less alone in a small Dutch town. From then on, Mary was a devoted wife. It seems likely that William introduced her to the physical pleasures of marriage.

By 1684, James II's wife, Mary of Modena, had been pregnant many times but only four babies lived for any length of time: Isabella, who survived almost five years before dying of a fever, Catherine Laura, Charlotte Maria and a boy, who was christened Charles to please the King. The infant got smallpox when he was just five weeks old, however, and was dead within a matter of days. Mary's ordeals would pale into comparison with those of her stepdaughters, however.

The marriage of Mary's sister Anne to the Protestant Prince, George of Denmark, was also arranged by Charles II and turned out to be a strong one. They were faithful and devoted, though forced to bear a succession of tragedies. Within months, Anne was pregnant but the baby was stillborn. Her second child was stillborn, too. On 2 June 1685, Anne had a second daughter, who seemed to be healthy but, when she was twenty months old, died of smallpox.

When Anne's fourth child lived, James unwisely tried to persuade her to baptise her daughter as a Catholic. At this, Anne burst into tears. 'The Church of Rome is wicked and dangerous,' she wrote to her sister, 'their ceremonies – most of them – plain downright idolatry.'

When Charles II died in 1685, James became King. The differences between him and his daughters now assumed huge political importance. He knew that he could not make Britain a Catholic country again and so he settled on a more modest ambition – stopping discrimination against Catholics. As a result of his religious ambitions, he paid little attention to Anne, who gave birth to a third daughter in May 1686 (that baby also died in infancy). A decent father would have realised his daughter needed help. Her sister was in Holland, but James was obsessed with making England at the very least possible for Catholics to live in.

In April 1687, James issued a Declaration of Indulgence which would allow Catholics to worship according to their rites. The following year he ordered this Declaration be read in every church in the land, but seven bishops objected, including the Archbishop of Canterbury. James now gave up any pretence of being tolerant; he had the bishops arrested and tried for seditious libel.

And unto us a child is given – possibly in a warming pan

James had been married for eleven years to Mary of Modena when he became King. She was twenty-six years old and he was fifty-one. Mary now did something curious: with her stepdaughter Anne, she travelled to Tunbridge Wells to take the healing waters. It was assumed she was trying to get pregnant but nothing happened. Two years later, Mary decided to visit that other royal spa, Bath. She believed its waters had helped her conceive her son, Charles, back in 1677. The Queen's most trusted physician, Dr Waldegrave, thought the trip to Bath an excellent idea. On 16 August, the King joined his wife there and stayed for five days. He then left for Wales, stopping at the famous Well of St Winifred to pray for a son. Today, the Well has a shop that sells holy water, as well as a variety of what a former monk and a former nun (both my friends) describe as 'Catholic kitsch'.

While her husband prayed at the Well, the Queen bathed in the Cross Bath where a cross was placed in memory of her son, Charles. Bathing was a grand public spectacle: the Queen wore a stiff yellow canvas with large sleeves so that no one could begin to guess the shape of her body. The holiday turned into a spectacle, though: whenever she set any part of the royal body in the water, the ever-present Italian string orchestra would start to play.

In early 1687, Anne needed her family again and James should have been consoling his daughter. She miscarried once and, a few days later, her husband caught smallpox. Their two young daughters were infected and died, though their father survived. George and Anne had 'taken [the deaths] very heavily ... Sometimes they wept, sometimes they mourned in words; then sat silent, hand in hand; he sick in bed, and she the carefullest nurse to him that can be imagined,' wrote Rachel Wriothesley, daughter of the Earl of Southampton, previously one of Charles II's ministers.

In the circumstances, the King needed to be tactful when informing his daughters that his wife was expecting another child, but he seemed to have expected them to simply be glad for him. Callously, he appears to have forgotten that both his daughters had suffered the death of one child after another. By 1688, they had lived through at least eight pregnancies and neither sister had a child who was still alive. Now an older woman might give birth and possibly give birth to a boy. A son of James II would not only bolt onto the throne ahead of the sisters but would try to make the kingdom Catholic again. The precedent, Mary Tudor's reign, was not a happy one.

Three months before the Queen's child was born, Anne wrote to her sister: 'I cannot help feeling that the Queen's belly is a little suspicious. It is true indeed that she is very big but she looks better than she ever did which is not usual for people when they are far gone for in the most part they look very ill.' In her book on the Queens of England, Agnes Strickland admitted that she was surprised the sisters did not insist on staying with the Queen to make sure she was really carrying a child (Anne, in fact, went to Bath). Strickland concluded that Anne left London because the Queen 'had given her indisputable proofs that she was about to become a mother and Anne went purposely out of her way that she might not be a witness of the birth of a brother whose rights she intended to dispute'.

Few pregnancies have been the subject of so much scandal and speculation as Mary of Modena's. James's daughters were convinced that this was not so much a phantom pregnancy as a fraudulent one. In return, James felt he had to prove his wife truly did give birth.

Soon after her labour pains began, the Queen was attended by her midwife – Judith Wilkes – and a nurse; next up was Mrs Dawson, who had to be summoned from church as it was Trinity Sunday. Mrs Dawson was a woman of the Bedchamber and a Protestant, so she was supposed to be an impeccable witness. The Queen seemed rather distressed and was sitting on a stool when Mrs Dawson reached the great 'bed chamber'. She urged Her Majesty to get back into bed – the bed was apparently still warm as the royal couple had spent the night together, a cosy touch.

Neither of James's daughters was present when the Queen went into labour. Nevertheless, from the first, Mary was certain that her half-brother was 'suppositious'. This is, of course, a perfect example of sibling rivalry: to believe your brother or sister is a fiction and does not really exist. The fact that the sisters were absent by their own choice did not prevent them from suggesting a baby had somehow been smuggled into the royal bedroom. The Protestants seized on one incident at 8.15 a.m. when a servant – no doubt a papist – was instructed to get a warming pan for the Queen's bed.

During the next hour, more and more people – men as well as women – crowded into the bedchamber. The audience included the Countess of Sunderland, the Lord Chancellor, almost the entire Privy Council and Catherine of Braganza, Charles II's widow. Forty-two witnesses were named but there were also pages, servants and priests. If the *Guinness World Records* had an entry for the most people ever present at a birth, Mary of Modena's delivery would surely be a contender.

At 8.15 a.m., the warming pan arrived.

By 10 a.m., the Queen's labour was reaching its end. 'I die, oh you kill me, you kill me!' she yelled.

The midwife, Mrs Wilkes, encouraged the Queen to push and, with the third push, the child was born.

'I don't hear the child cry,' the Queen observed anxiously but just at that moment the baby did so.

Madame de Labadie, one of the Queen's other bed women, took the baby from Mrs Wilkes and was about to carry the infant into another room when the King stopped her. James II called on the Privy Council to witness the Queen had given birth to a child.

'What is it?' he asked Madame de Labadie, eager to know if he had finally fathered a boy.

'What Your Majesty desires,' she replied.

The Earl of Faversham got the point and shouted patriotically to the horde in the bedchamber to 'make room for the Prince!'

An ecstatic James knighted the Queen's physician, Dr Waldegrave, on the spot and gave Judith Wilkes 500 guineas, apparently for her breakfast. On 12 June 1688, he wrote to tell Mary that she now had a brother. Of course, the unhappy sisters did not share their father's joy: they could only see their baby half-brother as a religious and political threat. It would have been polite to congratulate their father and his wife. Instead, Mary sent an extraordinary missive to her sister, days after the birth. In an obsessive inquisition, she set out eighteen questions about the birth, numbering them as Q1 to Q18. The letter reeks of suspicion and malice; it also feels like a daughter's cry for help after her relationship with her father had forever soured.

Mary's first question was: 'Had the Queen asked any of her ladies to feel her belly since she thought herself quick or late?'

Anne replied that she had never heard anyone say they felt the child stir, though the Protestant Mrs Dawson said she had seen it stir.

Mary then asked: 'Was the milk that was in the Queen's breasts seen by many or conducted in a mystery?' Anne replied that she had never seen any milk expressed but again Mrs Dawson said that she had seen 'it upon her smock and that it began to run at the same time as it used to do of her children'.

The next question requires some knowledge of seventeenth-century medicines. Mary enquired as to whether the Queen had openly taken astringents or 'whether a mystery was made of that?' Anne replied that she had seen the Queen use what she described as 'restringing draughts', a term whose precise meaning is uncertain.

The fourth question returned to the Queen's breasts. Mary wanted to know: 'Was the treating of the Queen's breasts for drawing back the milk managed openly or mysteriously?' Anne replied that one lady-in-waiting had come into the room when the Queen was putting off her clouts and she was very angry 'because she did not care to be seen when she was shifting [excreting]'. Mary of Modena was hardly being unreasonable.

Q5 wanted Anne to specify at what time the Queen went into labour. 'It was 8 a.m. and the King was sent for at once,' she answered.

Mary then asked if 'the notice [of the Queen's labour] was sent secretly or let fly all over Whitehall and St James's.' Anne replied that the Privy Council had been told as soon as the King knew – there was nothing secret about the message.

'At what time the Privy Councillors came into the bedchamber?' Mary asked next. She was particularly interested in 'whether a screen was erected at the foot of the bed or not'. There was no screen, Anne replied, and the Queen gave birth in the bed she had slept in all night and 'in the great bed chamber as she was with her last child'.

Mary suspected former would-be nun, Mary of Modena, was in fact the best actress of her time. 'Did anyone other than the Queen's confidantes see the Queen's face when she was in labour and whether she had the looks of a woman in labour?' she asked. The additional questions resembled those that a prosecutor might have asked: 'Who was in the room and how close did they stand to the woman giving birth?'

Anne said the foot curtains were drawn and the two sides were open. She reported, almost as if it were strange, that the Queen minded so many men being present while she was giving birth. The Queen then asked the King to hide her face with his head and peri-wig, which he duly did. Poor Mary of Modena's body was clearly not her own to control. Anne added that when the Queen 'was in great pain, the King called in haste for my Lord Chamberlain, who came up to the bedside to show he was there; upon which the rest of the Privy Council did the same thing'.

Q12 concerned timing – Mary insisted on knowing to the minute how long the King had spent talking to Privy Councillors before the child was carried into the next room. Anne replied that the midwife had cut the navel-string at once but that the afterbirth did not follow quickly. The midwife had handed the baby to Madame de Labadie; the King stopped Madame de Labadie and told the Privy Councillors that they were witnesses that a child had been born. He asked them to come into the next room and see what it was, 'which they all did'. Anne managed to inject one doubt: 'for till after they came out again it was not declared what it was but the midwife had only given a sign that it was a son'. The baby might have been a girl, she implied, who was swapped for a boy baby, who just happened to be present. Even for conspiracy theories, this was extreme and would have required the King to have on tap a spare male infant, as well as possessing the skills of a fine magician.

At her sister's request, Anne then listed all those present, starting with the Lord Chancellor but added that only the King held his wife while 'the child was parted'.

Q14 asked if the Queen had ever given birth 'so mysteriously, so suddenly and so few being called for'. 'Few' was hardly appropriate. Mary's previous question had elicited a list of twenty-four men, as well as unnamed pages and priests and eighteen women – 'All these stood as near as they could.'

Mary then asked whether anyone had noticed that the child's limbs were 'slender at first' and then miraculously blossomed 'to be round and full'. Her next question again harped on the possibility that a boy had been substituted for whatever the Queen had produced: 'Was everyone permitted to see the child at all hours dressed and undressed?' she wanted to know.

Anne replied that she had never heard of the change in the limbs, but they did avoid the child being seen. One reason, all too familiar to her, was that they did not want people to know that the child was extremely sick. 'All of the servants,' she sniped, 'were papists so they would conceal anything.'

Mary then asked, 'Is the Queen fond of it?' Anne could offer some hope here as she had dined at the Palace soon after the birth and 'they said it had been very ill of a looseness and it really looked so' (the 'looseness' was presumably of the bowels). Yet the uncaring Queen came in from her prayers and sat down to eat without seeing her child. Afterwards, she 'played at Comet and did not go to it till she was put out of the pool' – in effect, until she was out of the game. If the child was truly hers, what kind of mother did that make her?

Finally, Mary wanted to know which of the women of the Bedchamber were in favour and when Charles II's widow, Catherine of Braganza, had been sent for.

Mary and Anne were never going to accept that the child was really their half-brother. Their stepmother noticed and complained in a letter to Mary:

> You are not as kind as you used to be and the reason I have begun to
> think is that since I have been brought to bed you have never once
> in your letters to me taken the least notice of my son, no more than
> if he had never been born.

The Queen had also discovered that Mary did not pray for her brother and berated her for this. Mary replied stiffly: 'All the King's children shall ever find as much affection and kindness as can be expected of children of the same father.' She continued to believe that the child was not her natural brother and that her father was conspiring to secure a Catholic succession.

The baby who provoked a revolution

The birth of a male heir to James made possible a permanent Catholic dynasty. Several Protestants echoed Mary and Anne's doubts that the baby had been smuggled into the bedchamber in the warming pan in front of over forty witnesses – not all of whom were 'papists'. In order to prevent a Catholic succession, seven Protestant nobles invited the Prince of Orange to invade the country. Mary backed her husband against her father.

When William invaded, James had the larger army, but though he had much military experience – in 1650 he had served in the French army with General Turenne – he lost his nerve. On 11 December, he threw the Great Seal of the Realm into the Thames and attempted to flee to France but was captured in Kent. William had no intention of executing his father-in-law and allowed him to escape to Paris, where Louis XIV offered him a palace and a pension.

Despite her eighteen questions, Mary was upset by the circumstances surrounding the deposition of her father and was torn between concern for him and duty to her husband, but she was convinced that William was working to 'save the Church and State'. She travelled to England and wrote of her 'secret joy' at returning to her homeland, 'but that was soon checked with the consideration of my father's misfortunes'. William noted her conflicted state and instructed her to look cheerful when they arrived in London. As a result, she was criticised for appearing cold to her father's plight. James felt betrayed and savaged Mary in a diatribe, criticising her disloyalty. For her part, she was deeply hurt by his attack.

William and Mary took the throne jointly in 1689 and agreed to a political compromise, which was the final resolution of the Civil War. The Bill of Rights laid out basic rights for all Englishmen and there would be no royal interference with the law; the sovereign remained the fount of justice but could not unilaterally establish new courts or act as a judge. Parliament had to agree to any new taxes. Any subject could petition the monarch without fear of retribution and there was to be no standing army unless Parliament agreed. The monarch would not interfere in the election of Members of Parliament. Freedom of speech in Parliament was also guaranteed.

The Bill of Rights barred Roman Catholics from the throne as 'it hath been found by experience that it is inconsistent with the safety and welfare of this Protestant kingdom to be governed by a papist Prince'. Now the monarch would have to swear a Coronation oath to uphold the Protestant religion. British democracy slowly evolved from the Bill of Rights to the system we now have.

Almost miraculously, Anne now gave birth to a boy, who managed to outlive her previous children. William, Duke of Gloucester was born on 24 July 1689 at Hampton Court. Much of what we know about him comes from a memoir written by a royal servant – Jenkin Lewis – who spent seven years with him.

When William was born, he seemed to be 'a very weakly child' and few believed that he would live long. His wet nurse had too large a nipple so a new nurse was found and, for the next six weeks, the baby thrived. 'All people now began to conceive hopes of the Duke living,' Lewis wrote, 'when Lo he was taken with convulsion fits.' In despair, Anne summoned physicians from London, who recommended an age-old remedy: change the wet nurse. This decision led to a comic parade as mothers of young babies flocked to Hampton Court, hoping to be chosen as the breast fit for royalty; the infant Duke was then passed from breast to breast, testing each potential wet nurse.

The final choice was pure accident. The baby's father was passing through the room where the would-be wet nurses were lined up, their breasts on display, and spotted a Mrs Pack. The wife of a respectable Quaker from Kingston, one can only imagine her breasts inspired confidence. Prince George at once ordered Mrs Pack into bed with his ailing son, 'who sucked well and mended that night'.

Mrs Pack was, according to Lewis, however, an unpleasant woman who traded on her sudden fame and was 'fitter to go to a pigsty than to a Prince's bed'. There was some mystery as to the nature of the illness that William had been suffering from, which caused 'an issue from his pole', according to Lewis. Some historians of medicine have assumed this to mean some kind of fluid coming out of his head.

After that, William seems to have grown up fairly normally. He began to walk and talk, though his walking was never perfectly normal. In some ways, he was a very active boy, although he could not go up or down steps without help. Lewis was not sure whether this was a real infirmity or due to 'the overcare of the ladies about him'. The issue came to a head one day when William's father believed the boy was shamming and, for the first time in his life, beat him with a birch rod. Following this, the child conceded he might go downstairs just leaning on one person's arm. 'He was whipped again and went ever well after,' Lewis noted.

As pious Protestants, William's parents felt the boy needed a tutor who would concentrate on religion. Dr Pratt was aptly named, as he did not think the boy should have much fun or play games. For his part, William liked games, especially military ones, and the memoir records him studying the Norman Conquest and planning an invasion of France. A smart tactician, William told Lewis: 'I go to conquer France but I will burn my shipping so that my men may not desert me by coming back.'

Instead of discussing famous battles, Dr Pratt larded on conventional morality. He asked the boy how he could be a Prince and not be tempted by 'the pomps and vanities of this world'.

'I will walk in God's commandments and keep his ways,' William replied smartly. (I like to imagine he sniggered the moment he was out of Pratt's way.)

In 1695, William asked Lewis to help him compose a battle song for his troops. At this, Lewis dashed off eight rhyming couplets starting:

> Hark Hark the hostile drum alarms
> Let ours too beat a call to arms.

After Mary died in 1694, William of Orange ruled alone and visited the boy every month. The Prince once made Lewis prepare complex toy fortifications so that he could impress his uncle. William now read the reports in *The London Gazette* and worked out that they had implications for his own position. When he saw that both Houses had issued a declaration of loyalty, he decided to compose one of his own. It ran: 'I Your Majesty's most dutiful subject had rather lose my life in Your Majesty's cause than in any man else's and I hope it will not be long ere you conquer France.'

William had no more intention of invading France than going to visit the Pope but his soldier-mad nephew was obviously itching for action. The note continued: 'We Your Majesty's dutiful subjects will stand by you as long as we have a drop of blood.'

The boy Prince needed courage as he pluckily endured a succession of illnesses. In the spring of 1696, his eyes swelled and became bloodshot. The Queen sent for Dr John Radcliffe, who prescribed a horrid medicine, which William promptly spat out. Radcliffe then applied blisters to the boy's back, which made him scream out in pain.

The most serious problem, however, was that William seems to have had a bizarrely large head. Some medical historians, like Jack Dewhurst, claim he suffered a mild form of hydrocephalus (water on the brain), but that condition is usually associated with low intelligence. William was certainly not backward, though. Lewis's memoir makes it clear that he was quick-witted and could learn about the great generals of the past, their tactics and technologies. Fortifications particularly fascinated the boy.

The Prince's games with soldiers

In 1937, the future Queen Elizabeth II became involved in a Girl Guide troop, which meant that she could work and play with normal children. The project was seen as novel and democratic. In fact, it wasn't at all novel, but it seems royals can forget their own family history.

William was good friends with George Lawrence, an enterprising boy who organised a troop of twenty boy soldiers, which included many children of the royal servants. Lawrence drilled them. William joined in the fun and then organised a troop of his own, recruiting more children of the household and its servants. Anne and her husband were delighted their boy was bright and busy, but it was too good to last.

The year 1700 would turn out to be one of calamities. On 25 January 1700, Anne miscarried yet again. Jack Dewhurst, who analysed her obstetric history, argued she had been pregnant at least seventeen times. Twelve of these pregnancies ended in a miscarriage or stillbirth. Four of the five children who were born alive died before the age of two. Few women have undergone such ordeals and it says much about Anne's strength of character that she was not continuously depressed.

In July 1700, the son on whom she doted suddenly became very ill. Four days after he first started running a fever, William died. He was just eleven years old. Devastated, Anne ordered her household to observe a day of mourning every year on the anniversary of his death. The personal tragedy had huge political implications, too. When her son died, Anne was the only individual remaining in the line of succession established by the Bill of Rights. To avoid a Catholic restoration, the English Parliament passed the Act of Settlement in 1701. If neither William III nor Anne had children, the crown would go to one of James I's granddaughters: Sophia, Electress of Hanover. She was formidably clever. More crucially, she was a Protestant and she even had a son.

The news that Sophia would inherit infuriated James II. He died in 1701, with none of the conflicts with his one surviving daughter resolved. His widow wrote to Anne to inform her that her father forgave her, but also as a reminder of her promise to seek the restoration of his line. But Anne had no intention of ceding her rights to the Catholic child who had been at the centre of the warming-pan episode.

John Locke, one of the first experts on childcare
During the penultimate decade of the House of Stuart, John Locke (1632–1704) was developing a very modern philosophy of

childcare. Had Sophia, her sons and her grandsons followed his advice, the history of England would probably have witnessed fewer family disasters in the next century.

Today, John Locke is best known as a philosopher but he was also a fellow of the Royal Society and twice served on its council. He trained as a doctor and helped develop some techniques to prevent spontaneous abortions so it is perhaps surprising that Anne and Mary never consulted him. By 1690, Locke was seen as an expert on children and often was asked by aristocrats to advise them on how to bring up their young. He stressed it was the duty of parents to educate their children well as the nation's future depended on this. It was his ambition to provide 'a helping hand to promote everywhere that way of training up youth … which is the easiest, shortest, and likeliest to produce virtuous, useful, and able men in their distinct callings'.

We are born without innate ideas, Locke argued, so everything depends on experience. Parents had to start educating their children from birth and should learn to observe their offspring meticulously. The attentive parent would get a sense of the abilities and inclinations of their child and could therefore sensibly plan their education. According to Locke, they should pay great attention to the child 'in those seasons of perfect freedom' when the child played.

Parents should answer questions patiently and never mock or embarrass a child as 'children are strangers to all we are acquainted with, and all the things they meet with are at first unknown to them, as they were to us'. Locke was a realist, however, and concluded, 'in many cases, all that we can do or should aim at is to make the best of what nature has given.' Great expectations were not always sensible.

Like Winnicott two-and-a-half centuries later, Locke stressed the value of play. For him it was a question of freedom. Children loved to play games not just because they excite their imagination, he claimed, but that it is 'liberty alone which gives the true relish and delight to their ordinary play-games'. If children were forced to play, they would soon tire of the games imposed on them, which would be no fun at all. He claimed that children wanted to be treated rationally and parents should realise 'earlier perhaps than we think' that they become 'sensible of praise and commendation'. Anticipating modern psychologists such as John B. Watson, B. F. Skinner and Hans Eysenck, Locke argued it was better to reward a child for doing something well than to punish him for doing something badly. Parents should 'double the reward' of praise by commending their children in front of others. If they had to criticise or punish, they should do so in private.

Locke suggested parents discuss a child's mistakes and misdemeanours and deal with them 'as a strange monstrous matter that it could not be imagined he would have done and so shame him out of it'. He was utterly opposed to beatings.

Locke also turned his attention to the duties of the upper class. Gentlemen had to serve their country. Parents were duty-bound to train their children (who would, after all, be running the country) in moral and political knowledge, as well as 'the arts of government'. A gentleman had to know some law, some history and how to behave on the battlefield.

When King William III died in 1702, Anne took the throne. By now, it was obvious that she would not have any more children, so Sophia of Hanover would inherit. Sophia's son George became second in line. He was forty-one years old, knew nothing of England and could not even speak the language well.

Ironically, there was still living a man who had ruled England and could speak perfect English. Richard Cromwell had returned to England in 1680 and lived quietly off the income from his estate in Hursley. Of course, there was no possibility of restoring the Cromwell 'dynasty'. One of the last survivors of the Civil War, Richard died peacefully in his bed on 12 July 1712 at the age of eighty-five.

When Sophia of Hanover died, her son George became Queen Anne's heir. He was probably the last English king, though perhaps not the last heir, to arrange a murder – and get away with it.

5

THE HANOVERIANS (1714–1821)

Four generations of hatred between fathers and sons

The Tudors and the Stuarts are, in effect, ancient history. In 2014, we shall celebrate the 300th anniversary of the Coronation of George I, Sophia of Hanover's son. There is a direct line of descent between George and the current Queen. Elizabeth II is the great-great-granddaughter of Queen Victoria, who was herself the great-great-great-granddaughter of George I. We can now trace a very direct case history – and one which shows how an often troubled family managed to hang on to the throne.

For all their political failures, the Stuarts had been generally loyal to each other until the quarrels over James II's Catholic faith. The Hanoverians were more successful as monarchs, but, as a family, they were spectacularly dysfunctional. From 1714 to 1820, the kings of England often wanted to throttle their sons, especially the eldest. In his authoritative book on the first four Georges, J. H. Plumb argued that the eighteenth century was marked by extraordinary aggression in every social class and suggests the kings were somehow infected by this mood. It seems a rather vague explanation that ignores the question of what caused individual monarchs to be such destructive fathers.

Sophia of Hanover left her son, the future George I, for almost a year when he was five because she had to convalesce in Italy, but she corresponded regularly with his governess. In her letters, George's mother described him as a responsible, conscientious child, who set a good example to his younger brothers and sisters. Her son either changed as he grew up or she had very little sense of his real personality.

By the time George was a teenager, he was at odds with his domineering father, who ordered him to marry his first cousin, Sophia Dorothea of Celle. The consequences of this marriage would be considerable for the royals so it must be put in context. Politically, it made sense: the marriage would make Hanover richer and could lead to joining the territories of Hanover and Celle. George's mother opposed the match because she looked down on Sophia Dorothea's mother; the minor German aristocracy were major snobs. She wrote: 'the marriage is repugnant to the boy' and suggested they insist on a vast dowry if he was to be forced to tie the knot with a social inferior. For her part, Sophia Dorothea's mother implored her husband not to send their daughter to Hanover, which she seemed to view as an outer circle of Hell. However, the political advantages were so great that both mothers were overruled. Sophia Dorothea may have been a provincial nobody but the philosopher Leibniz called her 'a divine beauty'.

In 1683, Sophia Dorothea bore a son, who was christened George Augustus. The following year, George's father made a decision which was typically divisive. He adopted the law of primogeniture for Hanover so that his eldest son would inherit Hanover and Celle, while his younger son would not even inherit one acre. The two boys, who had once been close, became very hostile towards each other. It was the first of the many cruelties Hanoverian fathers inflicted on their sons.

George's marriage to Sophia Dorothea began to disintegrate soon after she bore him a daughter in 1687. He neglected her in favour of his mistress. It was partly a question of bulk: George liked his women plump and complacent. Sophia Dorothea begged George to return to her, but he refused. The too-thin Sophia Dorothea became embittered and began to dally with a Swedish aristocrat, Count Philip Christoph von Königsmarck. He was twenty-three years old, a good soldier and often at court. Seeing how unhappy she was, Königsmarck declared his undying love and Sophia decided to elope with him. Perhaps because she was a provincial, she did not have the good sense to be discreet and simply enjoy a quiet affair. Maybe she also wanted to hurt her husband.

George got to know of the lovers' plan and had no intention of allowing himself to be humiliated, even if he did not love his wife. Then mysteriously, on 2 July 1694, Königsmarck disappeared and was never seen again. The rumour spread that he had been killed with George's connivance. Königsmarck's body was thrown into the river Leine, apparently weighed down with stones so that it would not bob back up to the surface. One courtier, Don Nicolò Montalbano, was paid 150,000 thalers (about 100 times the annual salary of the highest-paid minister in Hanover). Later rumours claimed that Königsmarck was not drowned but hacked to pieces and buried beneath the Hanover palace floorboards. George realised that it would damage his chances of inheriting the throne of England should he become known to be a killer and so he denied everything and spread the rumour that robbers had murdered the Count.

A novel written in 1708 dramatised what became one of the scandals of the century. Then an account written in 1754 suggested the real villain was the plump Countess of Platen. This anonymous version of events is not necessarily reliable, according to a thorough thesis by John Veale, written in 2001.

In 1898, Ernest Henderson in the *American Historical Review* examined research on the murder and the attempt to blame the Countess. He made fun of a number of theories, especially a French one which claimed Königsmarck had been thrown alive into a hot oven. More seriously, Henderson alleged much material that would reveal the truth had been destroyed on the orders of the Electors of Hanover who, of course, became the Kings of England – 'They were determined that no written records on this matter should remain'. Some sources even claimed a nice gory touch – that George had used Königsmarck's bones to make a stool on which he liked to rest his feet.

George's marriage to Sophia Dorothea was dissolved in 1694

and she was blamed as the guilty party. With her father's approval, George then had his ex-wife imprisoned in Ahlden House near Celle. Sophia Dorothea's admirer Leibniz wrote that 'they would never have believed her so guilty at Celle if her letters [to her lover Königsmarck] had not been produced'. Her punishment was severe: she was not allowed to see her children or her father, not permitted to remarry and only allowed to walk within the mansion and its courtyard. She could, however, ride in a carriage outside her castle under guard escort.

Sophia Dorothea's son George was eleven years old when his father imprisoned his mother. This is the kind of event the Life Events Scale does not begin to contemplate. She wrote to her husband saying that she repented of what she had done and begged him to let her see him 'and embrace our dear children'. Her ex-husband remained unmoved, however, and never saw her again. Their son resented his father's actions and the fact that his mother had been humiliated. He infuriated his father by keeping a portrait of his mother in his room. Again the family history of the royals offers extreme examples well beyond usual case histories. Few psychologists have been able to study cases where one parent has another imprisoned and kept away from their children for over thirty years. Sophia died in 1726. George was never allowed to see his mother again. He had been the victim of a 'custody battle' and the damage inflicted would affect his own behaviour towards his eldest son.

George the jailer did not blame himself one jot for these catas-trophes. Instead, he blamed his parents for forcing him into a loveless marriage and vowed not to make the same mistake with his son – the boy would have to meet and desire his bride-to-be. It was one of his few endearing decisions. So, in June 1705, using the false name of 'Monsieur de Busch', George visited Caroline of Ansbach. The English envoy to Hanover, Edmund Poley, reported the young man was so impressed by 'the good character he had of her that he would not think of anybody else'. Caroline was clever, even intellectual, and counted Leibniz among her friends. George proposed and was accepted. On 2 September 1705, the couple married.

The bridegroom quickly forgot what his father had done to protect him from a loveless marriage, though, and they were soon at odds. The younger George was keen to fight against France in Flanders, but his father would not allow him to join the army until he had a son and heir. George and Caroline duly obliged when, in early 1707, Caroline gave birth to a son who was christened Frederick, but her husband was still not permitted to join the army.

Caroline then gave birth to three daughters and one other son. The couple were devoted to their children, with one exception. That exception was their oldest son, Frederick, and they were initially at least not to blame because, yet again, George's father behaved in a cruel way: he decided to keep Frederick in Hanover, well away from his parents.

These Continental melodramas did not escape Queen Anne's attention. She refused to see any of the Hanoverians, which suggests that she thought there was some truth in the rumours that George was a murderer. As a staunch Protestant, though, she felt it would be better to have a killer on the throne of England than a Catholic. After all, some murderers like Henry I, Edward IV and Henry VIII had been decent kings. It was now twenty years since Königsmarck had died and the scandal was largely forgotten.

After Anne died in 1714, the Elector of Hanover came to England with his eldest son. George I was crowned at Westminster, though there was no great enthusiasm among his new people. Over a century earlier, James I had been a foreigner but he spoke good English despite his heavy Scottish accent. For the next 200 years, many of the kings and queens of England spoke better German than English – and not one of their wives was born in England. Caroline of Ansbach became Queen, as did Charlotte of Mecklenburg-Strelitz, Caroline of Brunswick, Adelaide of Saxe-Meiningen and Alexandra of Denmark. Victoria, of course, married Albert of Saxe-Coburg-Gotha who, according to some rumours, even had some Jewish blood. They were all immigrants and had come to rule a country that distrusted Johnny Foreigner, even if his headgear happened to be a crown.

As soon as the new King was crowned, his son was made Prince of Wales. Caroline arrived in Britain in October 1714 with their daughters. She and George begged his father to allow them to bring their eldest son Frederick as well, but George I insisted his grandson stay in Hanover. He was making it very clear who had the ultimate authority. The Prince of Wales was upset and set about making it obvious that, while his father was a German who could not understand the ways of the English, he was no Fritz Foreigner. Absurdly, the Prince claimed that he had not a single drop of blood in his veins that was not English. In fact, his veins contained only one trace element of English blood, as he could count the very English Elizabeth of York among his ancestors.

As his English was lamentable, George I insisted on carrying on the affairs of England in French. His Hanoverian advisers all spoke French but a number of his English ministers did not, so all state papers had to be produced in two languages: French and English. The only Hanoverian who spoke good English, French and German was the Prince of Wales so his father had to rely on him and invited him to sit in on meetings of the ruling Council. This gave the Prince more power than his father wanted him to have. Now the battle between the two men, which had festered since the Prince's father had imprisoned his mother, became more bitter.

The new King made a poor impression on his new subjects. The Earl of Chesterfield wrote that George was 'an honest dull German gentleman ... Lazy and inactive even in his pleasures which were, therefore, lowly and sensual'. The most stylish account of the court comes from Lady Mary Wortley Montagu, the only woman in history to get a husband because she could quote Horace in the original Latin. She wrote of George I:

In private life he would have been called an honest blockhead; and Fortune, that made him a king, added nothing to his happiness, only prejudiced his honesty, and shortened his days. No man was ever more free from ambition; he loved money, but loved to keep his

own, without being rapacious of other men's. He would have grown
rich by saving, but was incapable of laying schemes for getting; he
was more properly dull than lazy, and would have been so well
contented to have remained in his little town of Hanover, that if the
ambition of those about him had not been greater than his own, we
should never have seen him in England: and the natural honesty
of his temper, joined with the narrow notions of a low education,
made him look upon his acceptance of the crown as an act of usurp-
ation, which was always uneasy to him. But he was carried by the
stream of the people about him, in that, as in every other action of
his life. He could speak no English, and was past the age of learning it. Our customs and laws were all mysteries to him, which he
neither tried to understand, nor was capable of understanding if
he had endeavoured it. He was passively good-natured, and wished
all mankind enjoyed quiet, if they would let him do so.

George's mistress was even duller and a coward too, Lady Mary
sniped. The woman refused to come to England as she thought
its natives 'were accustomed to use their kings barbarously, might
chop off his head in the first fortnight'. As a result, George I often
travelled back to his native Hanover and saw far more of Caroline
and George's son Frederick than the child's parents did. Initially,
that upset them as they missed their son.

A caring or indeed sensible father would not have provoked
another row but George I did just that. In July 1716, he refused to
make his son Regent as the Prince had every historical precedent
to expect. Instead, he was given limited powers, as 'Guardian and
Lieutenant of the Realm'. The young George was furious, as well
as upset by the fact that his father was going to see his son. He
decided to needle his father in return and courted popularity with
the natives. As part of his campaign, the Prince of Wales dined in
public at Hampton Court, which seemed to impress his subjects.

Two events boosted the Prince's popularity. When Caroline
became pregnant again, she let it be known that the child would be
born in England. There was much public sympathy for her when

the baby was stillborn. The Prince then had what might be cynically called a 'lucky break'. While he was at the Drury Lane Theatre, an assassin tried to kill him. Instead of being delighted his son was safe, the King became jealous because the young man was now popular with the public.

When the Prince's second son, Prince George William, was born a few months after the Drury Lane incident, the King hit on a novel provocation. Though he knew his son disliked the man, George I made the Duke of Newcastle one of the child's sponsors at the christening. There seems to have been a misunderstanding between the Prince and the Duke. The Duke thought the Prince said: 'I shall fight you out.' (What was actually said, no one can precisely report.) The Duke took it as an insult and challenged the Prince to a duel, which gave the King a chance to indulge his penchant for imprisoning members of his own family. George I confined his son and daughter-in-law to their apartments in St James's Palace just as he had confined Sophia Dorothea. The heir to the throne could not risk his life fighting a duel, the King ruled. In Hanover, no one would have objected but someone now reminded the King of a legal nicety that a German would not know, coming from barbarous parts. In 1679, Charles II had agreed to the Habeas Corpus Act, which ruled the state could not detain someone without legal cause. The Prince could therefore sue his father for false imprisonment.

To avoid such embarrassment, the King expelled his son from St James's Palace, but he was so angry he added a nasty twirl of revenge. He got advice from the leading judges as to whether he could keep control of the Prince and Princess of Wales's children and not allow them to leave St James's Palace. In what may have been the first custody case in English law, the judges said the King had the right to keep his grandchildren and deny their parents access. George I did not hesitate to do so.

Meanwhile, George and Caroline were desperate to see their children. They once secretly visited the palace and Caroline fainted and George 'cried like a child'. The King called Caroline 'cette diablesse Madame la Princesse' (the devilish Princess) but she could intimidate him because she was intelligent. When she pleaded to be allowed to see her children, the King allowed both parents to 'enjoy' what social workers today would call a 'supervised access visit' once a week. The Prince wrote abject letters in which he apologised for any offence he had caused His Majesty; his father did not answer. Father and son were now truly at war.

Then comedy turned to tragedy. George William, whose christening had caused the row, fell ill when he was three months old. He was choking and coughing all the time. It would have been sensible to move him to the country, where the air was much fresher but the King did not allow that. Caroline and George were at their son's side when the infant died in February 1718.

After these rows, the Prince started to support the King's political enemies. In siding against him, his son set a pattern for the next century, where the heir would often be conspiring against the monarch who, in return, often dreamed of getting rid of his troublesome son.

The King visited Hanover and his mistress again from May to November 1719. This time, he did not even make his son guardian of the kingdom, but established a regency council. It was yet another humiliating rebuff.

In 1720, the English economy was nearly wrecked by the South Sea Bubble, the crazy speculation in shares in a company which offered the mirage of riches from the Pacific. Sir Robert Walpole, who is generally held to be England's first Prime Minister, realised the country must have stability and encouraged the King and his son to settle their differences. Neither man was exactly keen and the Prince was soon disillusioned. First, his father did not make him Regent when he returned to Hanover to see his mistress yet again. Second, he would still not allow George and Caroline to have their three daughters back.

The King was cruel but his son was not easy himself, as Lady Mary Wortley Montagu dissected:

The fire of his temper appeared in every look and gesture; which, being unhappily under the direction of a small understanding, was

every day throwing him upon some indiscretion. He was naturally
sincere, and his pride told him that he was placed above constraint;
not reflecting that a high rank carries along with it a necessity of a
more decent and regular behaviour than is expected from those who
are not set in so conspicuous a light. He was so far from being of
that opinion, that he looked on all the men and women he saw as
creatures he might kick or kiss for his diversion; and whenever he
met with any opposition in those designs, he thought his opposers
impudent rebels to the will of God, who created them for his use,
and judged of the merit of all people by their ready submission to
his orders.

The 'kick or kiss' Prince succeeded when his father died on 11 June
1727, on his way to Hanover. Caroline and George's three daughters were finally allowed to go home to their parents. While the
girls knew they should be overjoyed, they did not find it easy to
adjust to the mother and father they did not know well.

The new King decided not to attend his father's funeral in
Hanover. His English subjects were pleased because they saw this
as proof that George II loved England more than Hanover. There
was a final twist to the rows between father and son: George II
suppressed his father's will because it attempted to split his 'empire'
so that one grandson would inherit Britain and another would
inherit Hanover. Both British and Hanoverian ministers considered the will unlawful, as George I did not have the legal power to
choose his successors personally. Critics supposed that George II
hid the will to avoid paying out his father's legacies.

The relationship between the new King and his eldest son was
also antagonistic but there was the added complication that George
I had refused to allow Frederick to come to London. The orthodox
view is that children who are left by their parents are angry at them
but this separation had made the parents also angry towards their
son: they left Frederick waiting in Hanover for another year. When
he finally arrived in London in 1728, he was twenty-one years old
and had not seen his parents for fourteen years.

Only weeks after he arrived, Frederick started to plot against his parents. His first gambit was theatrical. He backed the Opera of the Nobility as a rival to Handel's royal opera. More seriously, he imitated his own father's less than filial behaviour and sponsored a court of 'opposition' politicians. George II called his eldest son 'a half-witted coxcomb'. James Parton, who in 1868 wrote one of the first biographies of Victoria, sniped that George II's eldest son was 'stupid even for a Prince'.

The King chooses his son's wife

The great cricket writer C. L. R. James wrote: 'What do they know of cricket who only cricket know?' Frederick, like many immigrants, sensed that one way to understand his new country was to understand its favourite sport. By 1728, that was cricket.

Frederick quickly became genuinely enthusiastic. He bet on games, formed his own team sometimes and even played himself, though he was not much of a batsman or bowler. In August 1732, the *Whitehall Evening Post* reported that Frederick attended 'a great cricket match' at Kew. The next year, he gave a guinea to each player in a Surrey v. Middlesex game. Luckily, the Hanoverians did not persuade their German subjects to take up cricket, which would no doubt have resulted in Germany winning Test after Test.

It sometimes seems the Hanoverians could have written the ultimate text on how to provoke sibling rivalry. George II's favourite son was not his eldest boy but his younger brother so the King now studied whether it might be possible for Frederick to succeed only in Britain, while William would become Elector of Hanover. But George II was wilier than his father and did not think he could just issue a fiat; he was learning English ways.

Soon after he arrived in England, Frederick became friendly with Lord Hervey, a minor aristocrat whom Alexander Pope satirised as 'Sporus'. Hervey was extremely effeminate 'as to even bring his sex into question', according to a friend he later quarrelled with, William Pulteney. Pulteney was being unnecessarily vitriolic – Hervey had eight children by his wife and also shared a mistress, Anne Vane, with

Frederick. Hervey and the Prince even wrote a play together under the pseudonym Captain Bodkin, but it was so dreadful it was only staged once. A few years later, the two men fell out and Hervey wrote bitterly that Frederick was 'false ... never having the least hesitation in telling any lie that served his present purpose'.

In terms of the history of royal parenting, what is remarkable is that Frederick's parents would have agreed. Most of the period from 1730 to 1742 was taken up with new and vicious family battles between George II, his wife and their eldest son.

Naturally, Frederick did not see himself as half-witted or false. He encouraged the poet James Thomson to write a masque, *Alfred*, which hinted at some connection between Frederick, who had never even taken part in a battle, and Alfred the Great, who had defeated the Vikings. Ironically, Frederick also urged Thomson to write a song that has endured: 'Rule Britannia'. Again, this could be seen as a typical attempt on the part of an immigrant to endear himself to his new country.

Inevitably, Frederick and his parents quarrelled about his future wife. The first potential bride was Lady Diana Spencer, an ancestor of the modern Princess Diana and the favourite grandchild of Sarah, Duchess of Marlborough, the woman who had been Queen Anne's domineering friend. The Duchess offered the massive dowry of £100,000. Frederick was deeply in debt and enthusiastic, but the King and Walpole forbade the marriage. The last thing either wanted was for Frederick to become independently wealthy, which would make him less dependent on them. The second would-be bride was Wilhelmine, daughter of Frederick of Prussia, who would also bring a handsome dowry. The King was not keen on this match either but continued talks for diplomatic reasons. Frustrated by the delay, Frederick sent his own envoy to the Prussian court. When the King discovered his son had taken this initiative, he scuppered the marriage plan.

An instance of Oedipal contortions

The most scandalous author on the sexual mores of the eighteenth century was Giacomo Casanova, who did sometimes sleep with both a mother and her daughter, or daughters. Not even Casanova described a family where a mother discussed the sexual prowess of her son, though. As far as I know, Freud did not do so; nor did those pioneers of sexology Havelock Ellis, Krafft-Ebing or Kinsey. Again, the long royal case history provides something unique.

In the 1730s, Frederick's mother became convinced that her son was impotent and discussed the issue with Hervey. He claimed Frederick sometimes referred to himself as Hercules or 'as if he were the late King Poland'. That monarch, Augustus the Strong, was supposed to have fathered 354 children, which accounted for his nickname, but Frederick was clearly uncertain as to his potency. Hervey also told the Queen that her son sometimes suffered 'with a despondency of having children and in so pathetic a tone that he is ready to cry and seems to think it is impossible'. At times, Caroline realised this conversation was hardly one a mother should have and begged Hervey to change the subject, but on many other occasions she insisted on discussing Frederick's sexuality further. Hervey once informed the Queen that Anne Vane, the woman he had shared with Frederick, had confided that the Prince was extremely ignorant 'to a degree inconceivable but not impotent and my firm belief is that he is as capable of having children as any man in England'. At one point, the Queen asked Hervey if he could find out from Lady Dudley (who was supposed to have slept with half the men in London) whether her son 'was like other men or not'.

Finally, in 1736, the half-witted, and perhaps impotent, coxcomb was married to the sixteen-year-old Augusta of Saxe-Gotha. Frederick did not choose her, of course: his father did. But Frederick was so deeply in debt that he had to accept. When she first met her in-laws, Augusta prostrated herself on the floor, a gesture which impressed George II and Queen Caroline. Frederick also seemed pleased by Augusta. During the wedding, he fortified himself with several glasses of jelly (Frederick had perhaps heard that his mother doubted he could make love to a woman).

The young couple did not have an easy time on their wedding night. Caroline insisted on being present while Augusta undressed.

Frederick then arrived. Hervey reported: 'Everyone passed through their bedchamber to see them where there was nothing remarkable but the Prince's nightcap which was some inches higher than any grenadier guard's in the whole army.' The couple were finally allowed some privacy in which to start their marriage.

There is a possible and perverse interpretation of Frederick's mother's behaviour. Caroline had not seen her eldest son from when he was seven years old. Mothers are sometimes attracted to their sons. The interest Caroline showed in her son's sexuality may mean she had some desire, conscious or unconscious, to sleep with him. There is no clear evidence for this speculation but it does make some sense, given her behaviour. (Freud's friend Princess Marie Bonaparte, the aunt of Prince Philip, seriously contemplated sleeping with her son.)

Caroline's obsession with her son's prowess in bed continued after the marriage. Hervey reports that the Queen asked him whether it might be possible for Frederick to arrange for another man to lie with Augusta without his wife realising it.

'Nothing so easy,' Hervey assured the Queen.

'Is it possible?' the Queen mused.

Hervey then suggested an ingenious method. For a month, he said, 'I would advise the Prince to go to bed several hours after his wife.' The Prince should spray himself with a powerful perfume so that he wafted a distinctive scent. He should then get up again, saying he had to urinate and sprinkle a waiting double with the same perfume (the highly scented double needed to be much the same size as the Prince). The double would then get into bed with Augusta and she, Hervey believed, would be fooled because of the scent. The Prince's substitute could then make love to Augusta and, of course, get her pregnant. Hervey was not joking and the Queen did not take it as a joke.

Frederick's marriage also had financial implications. He told Anne Vane that they could not carry on as lovers and gave her a pension of £1,500, with a bonus of £20,000 on the day she married someone else. Having made these promises, Frederick asked his father to ask

Parliament for a better allowance, but the King refused. In the end, a compromise was reached but Frederick felt humiliated and got his revenge when his father fell badly ill with piles and a fever in January 1737. Frederick spread the rumour that the King was dying so George II had to rise from his sick bed and attend a number of society events to prove his death was far from impending.

The family could not stop deceiving and detesting one another, it seems. So, when Frederick told his parents that Augusta was pregnant, the Queen did not believe it for one moment. She went to see her daughter-in-law and was made even more sceptical when Augusta was vague about when she was due to give birth. 'For my part I do not see she is big,' the Queen told Hervey.

The Queen then insisted that the baby be born at Hampton Court, where she and the King were living, so inevitably, their son wanted the child born somewhere else. When Augusta started her labour, her husband sneaked her out of Hampton Court in the middle of the night to make sure his parents could not witness the birth. After the suspicions surrounding the birth of the Old Pretender, royal births were witnessed by members of the family and senior courtiers to guard against 'suppositious' children in warming pans. George II and the Queen were horrified when they learned that their son had whisked Augusta away and made her travel along bumpy roads in a carriage that shook wildly. They dashed to St James's.

The Queen was relieved to discover that Augusta had given birth without witnesses to a 'poor, ugly little she-mouse' rather than to a 'large, fat, healthy boy'. Her attitude and these unpleasant games poisoned the relationship between mother and son still further; Frederick was banished from the King's court.

The row led to a frantic exchange of letters in August 1737, as Frederick tried to mend fences with his parents. He wanted the King to know that his son was his most devoted servant, but George II told him that he thought taking Augusta out of Hampton Court 'to be such a deliberate indignity', which His Majesty 'resents to the highest degree'. For the next three weeks, Frederick grovelled to no avail. On 10 September, the King condemned 'this extravagant and undutiful behaviour' and refused to accept that his son was sorry, given the many instances where Frederick had offended him for years. 'It is my pleasure that you leave St James's,' the King concluded, as soon as that did not cause Augusta any inconvenience. In an attempt to further humiliate his son, he also allowed the correspondence to be published.

Caroline fell fatally ill in November 1737. On her deathbed she uttered one of the least loving assessments a mother ever spoke. She said, 'At least I shall have one comfort in having my eyes eternally closed, I shall never have to see that monster again.' Now the sins of one generation ricocheted on the next.

Frederick got his own inevitable revenge. When Augusta became pregnant again in 1738, he removed his whole family from the Palace. The baby was so weak he was not expected to live. George, however, stubbornly stayed alive. Stubbornness would be one of his characteristics until he died, eighty-one years later. The birth of an heir to Frederick guaranteed the succession of the House of Hanover but George II and his son remained hostile towards each other.

Frederick's innings – the word seems fitting, given his passion for cricket – was finally ended by an abscess on the lung in 1751. The abscess is usually attributed to a blow by a cricket or a real tennis ball, but there is no proof of this macabre, albeit attractive idea. If it were true, Frederick would be yet another heir who died not just before his time but also as a result of violence. In his study of the Georges, the novelist William Makepeace Thackeray quoted an obituary poem, which shows the esteem – or not – in which the Prince was held.

> Here lies Fred
> Who was alive and is dead
> Had it been his father
> I had much rather
> Had it been his brother
> Still better than another
> Had it been his sister

No one would have missed her
Had it been the whole generation
Still better for the nation
But since 'tis only Fred
Who was alive and is dead
There's no more to be said

Poor Fred was not just unkind but unfair, according to Veronica Baker-Smith in her aptly named 2008 study, *Royal Discord*. She argues Fred has been 'undeservedly' consigned to a mere 'footnote in history'. Few parents, she suggests, have so maligned one of their children.

'Mad' King George III and his son

Frederick's twelve-year-old son now became heir to the throne. As usual with the House of Hanover, his father preferred his younger brother. George had been seen as something of a dunce but he became the most diligent and perhaps the craftiest of the Hanoverian Kings when it came to manipulating the ego-driven politicians of his era. As a parent, George III is perhaps best known for performing what might be called the 'reverse Oedipus'. According to Freud, sons want to kill their fathers. George III took the conflict between Hanoverian fathers and their sons to a new extreme as he tried to kill the Prince of Wales. He was thought to be mad at the time but it could be argued that he knew perfectly well what he was doing – his boy had finally driven him to serious violence.

The first two Hanoverian Kings and cricketing-mad Frederick were acutely aware that they were foreigners. George III spoke German to his mother but he was born in England and did not speak English with an accent. When he was ten, he took part in a family production of Joseph Addison's play *Cato* and said in a specially written prologue: 'What, tho' a boy! It may with truth be said, A boy in *England* born, in England bred.' He would use those lines again.

Augusta had very little faith in the education that George II provided for her son once he became his heir. She told Bubb

Dodington, a major landowner who had loaned Frederick substantial sums of money, she did not know what they taught the boy but 'she was afraid it was not much'. Augusta sensed she should let her boy play with other children, but she was afraid because of the 'profligate way' so many aristocratic children were being brought up. Now that he was Prince of Wales, George became even more isolated from boys of his own age. Lord Waldegrave, grandson of the doctor who had delivered the Old Pretender, became George's governor and complained that 'the mother and the nursery always prevailed'.

Waldegrave did not have a flattering view of the boy. He thought George was honest, but he had a dull spirit. He gave a subtle analysis of his charge, noting that: 'His want of application and aversion to business would be far less dangerous, was he eager in the pursuit of pleasure; for the transition from pleasure to business is both shorter and easier than from a state of total inaction.' Astutely, he noted that George would often withdraw to be alone 'not to compose his mind by study or contemplation but merely to indulge the melancholy enjoyment of his own ill humour'. George did not like Waldegrave any more than Waldegrave liked him and later sniped that his governor was a 'depraved worthless man'.

Augusta appealed to the Earl of Bute for help in teaching her son; Bute had been a friend of Frederick's and had married Lady Mary Wortley Montagu's daughter. Her choice caused tension with the King, who disliked Bute for a number of reasons. He was Scottish and George II worried that any Scot truly yearned for the return of the Young Pretender, the grandson of James II. Bute was also unusually well educated and a good botanist. He believed Augusta's son should study science as well as history, which would teach him the duties of a constitutional monarch, which the Hanoverians still had trouble understanding.

Bute became far more than a tutor; he became a substitute father and, as a teenager, George often tried to justify his behaviour to him. For example, he wrote to Bute: 'It is very true that ministers have done everything they can to provoke me, that they have called me a harmless boy…' Then he complained: 'They have also treated my mother in a very cruel manner (which I shall neither forget nor forgive to the day of my death) because she is so good as to come forward and to preserve her son from the many snares that surround him.' George promised Bute that he would 'ever remember the insults done to my mother' and also to defend his tutor.

By his teenage years, George realised that he was lazy and added: 'I will throw off that indolence which if I don't soon get the better of will be my ruin.' An angry young man, he was mainly angry at himself. He should be given some credit for being self-critical, though. On 25 March 1757, he admitted to Bute, 'I am conscious of my own indolence', which was 'my greatest enemy' and only a good friend like Bute would have tolerated it. Again, the Prince promised to fight this flaw in himself and 'you will instantly find a change'. A few weeks later, George begged Bute to have patience and promised that he would 'apply with the greatest assiduity if that is possible to regain the many years I have fruitlessly spent'.

In 1759, George fell in love with Lady Sarah Lennox, but Bute advised against the match and George meekly accepted his veto. 'I am born for the happiness or misery of a great nation,' he wrote, 'and consequently must often act contrary to my passions.'

George II died two weeks before his seventy-seventh birthday and his 22-year-old grandson became King in 1760. Though naturally nervous, George III was politically more astute than might have been expected. The boy who had recited the lines about being born and bred in England now made much of that in his accession speech. He offered a variation on the words he had spoken in Addison's play, trumpeting: 'Born and educated in this country, I glory in the name of Britain.' Hanover was a pesky principality on the unattractive mainland of Europe, which was packed with foreigners. It was 'a horrid electorate which has always lived on the vitals of this country'. Up yours, Fritz, in effect! Insulting the Germans was far more effective in winning public confidence than his father's toying with cricket.

Finding the young King a wife now became a priority and an obsession for his mother. For all his diatribes against foreigners, George let his foreign mother choose a foreign wife for him. Augusta of

Saxe-Gotha settled on Princess Charlotte of Mecklenburg-Strelitz, who was seventeen years old, only a year older than Augusta had been when she married Frederick. Charlotte was hardly one of the most desirable Princesses of Europe. Virtually no one had heard of Mecklenburg-Strelitz, which was easily confused with the larger but equally unmemorable principality of Mecklenburg-Schwerin. Mecklenburg-Strelitz had been established after a dispute with yet another puny principality, the duchy of Mecklenburg-Güstrow. To make matters even more ridiculously Ruritanian, there were two Dukes of Mecklenburg who did not recognise each other. Sadly, they do not seem to have challenged each other to a duel but, had they done so, they would probably have used make-believe swords.

The Strelitz duchy was one of the most backward regions of the Hapsburg Empire. Charlotte's family was so poor that she could bring no dowry. She was a devout Lutheran, however, and, though no striking beauty, at least she had white and even teeth. Charlotte was also reasonably intelligent and lively. She had one tremendously useful attribute, too: she came from a family that bred prodigiously. She was the eighth of ten children and her great-grandfather had nineteen children by two wives – and twelve of them survived. Her family genes were top class.

At the end of August 1761, Charlotte set out for England. The King sent Admiral Anson to bring his bride over from Rostock. Anson had sailed the Pacific so he should have been able to cope with bringing a ship across the North Sea but he seems to have lost his bearings. What should have been a three-day cruise turned into a nine-day nightmare. Anson was supposed to make for Greenwich, where a grand reception was waiting for the future Queen, but, instead, he docked at Harwich. The next morning, Charlotte had to travel to London on the rickety Essex roads, but she was resilient. When she finally got to St James's Palace, she behaved with considerable grace, though she did not prostrate herself as Augusta had done when she met the royal family for the first time. The next day, the total strangers, Charlotte and George, were married.

Against the odds, the marriage was happy and the couple coyly called each other 'Mr and Mrs King'. George III was not interested in the usual Hanoverian vices – women, gambling and fashion. He pottered about his palace grounds often dressed like a farmer and never visited Germany after he became King; in fact, he never went beyond the south of England. Weymouth was his favourite holiday resort.

Mr and Mrs King had fifteen children: nine sons and six daughters. Their first child, a boy, was born a year after the wedding and in a splendid bed which cost £3,780, an unusual luxury as George was stingy. He had managed to live on his income as Prince of Wales, something that would influence his attitude to his sons. Other than for the Prince of Wales, he did not make any provision for his children until 1778, by which time two of them were in their teens.

The arrangements Charlotte made for the birth of her first child suggest she had very definite ideas on giving birth. She insisted on moving to St James's Palace because the ventilation was better in the palace there. The labour lasted just five hours. Her son was given a spoonful of purging mixture as soon as he was born and 'was quiet and looked extremely well'.

The country celebrated: guns were fired at the Tower, bonfires lit and large quantities of liquor distributed free. Mother and baby thrived, though the baby had some sort of fainting fit on 22 August. After being given a little peppermint water, however, Prince George recovered at once.

Charlotte seems to have been a child-bearing diva. Her second son, Frederick, was born so quickly that there was no time for the doctor to arrive, which annoyed the physician. Frederick soon became his father's favourite, which sowed the seeds of the poor relationship between the King and his oldest boy. Charlotte's third son, William, was born on 21 August 1765. His mother returned from a dinner in Richmond feeling a little unwell and popped him out without any fuss a few hours later. When she was thirty-three weeks pregnant with her fourth child, the Queen danced merrily with the King of Denmark. She danced even longer – till 4.45 a.m.

on the King's birthday on 4 June 1771 – just before she gave birth to their eighth child. The splendid genes were working.

Charlotte also had a clear sense of her duties as a mother. She carped that she could never quite trust the attendants because 'it is impossible for servants however true they may be in their affections to have the feelings of a parent'. Like most aristocrats of the era, she did, however, use wet nurses. She was so successful at producing healthy children that, when her eighth son, Octavius, died at the age of four, it was said that she finally became a true mother. It was almost as if seeing a child die young was a rite of passage. She lost her next son when he was a small boy, too.

Wet nurses and flogging

In his *Royal Confinements*, Dewhurst argues wet nurses often endangered children, which makes it all the more remarkable that thirteen of Charlotte's children survived. Many wet nurses did not wash properly and if they did not feel like feeding the child, or were not producing milk, gave babies cow's milk without boiling to sterilise it – the idea of sterilisation would not be accepted for another seventy-five years. Wet nurses also often fed babies 'pap', a form of gruel made by soaking meal or bread in water, or cereal cooked in broth. The nurse chewed the pap first, which could spread infections. A number of doctors tried to persuade aristocratic women not to use wet nurses, but with relatively little success. W. M. Craig, who wrote a fawning biography of Charlotte, reminded his 'fair and amiable countrywomen of the sacred obligation that they are under to sustain and strengthen the children they bring into the world with the all sufficient nutriment of their own bosoms'. Vanity was the problem, he argued. 'Is there anyone so enchanted by the public admiration of her own beauty as to prefer it to the thankful smiles of a lovely infant that clings close to her breast?'

Craig excused the Queen from any such vanity. Charlotte had 'caught the tenderness of maternal feelings on her landing in this country' and 'grieved she could not be to her son all that a mother should be' but she had so many royal duties. So she 'submitted and endeavoured to make amends by a most scrupulous attention to other points in watching over the young Prince'. That 'most scrupulous attention' would turn out to be not good enough to prevent her young Prince from being one of the most absurd monarchs to place his backside on the throne.

When Prince George was born, there was no parade of potential wet nurses as there had been in 1689 when Mrs Pack was chosen. Margaret Scott, a descendant of the Buccleuch family, was chosen and she was still in milk as she had recently given birth to her twelfth child. Mrs Scott was very proud of her Buccleuch ancestry and took it upon herself to interfere in the nursery until the Prince was weaned. The King liked her, but Charlotte did not and she learned the lesson: all her other wet nurses were not so well connected as Mrs Scott.

Charlotte adored her eldest son and was charmed by his precocity. When he was four and was asked what he was doing, George replied, a philosopher in embryo, 'I make reflections.' His mother decided to teach him the rudiments of German, English and counting herself with the help of a governess, Lady Charlotte Finch. George was a good pupil and, by the time he was eight, he could speak French, German and Italian as well as English. The clever boy basked in his mother's love. But queens were not supposed to teach their children. The King interfered and insisted his son be handed over to more conventional teachers. Prince George was obviously spoilt, but he had been willing to learn from his mother; the separation changed him and he became a difficult pupil.

The King was extremely upset when one of the new teachers, a M. de Salzas, would not explain why he refused to carry on teaching the Prince; the reality was that the boy had become impossible. More discipline was the answer, the King assumed. He handed his son over to two clergymen, Dr Markham and Cyril Jackson. They were given 'the injunction to treat him as they would any other private gentleman and to flog him whenever he deserved it'. They did so with little pity. The Prince blamed his father and it could be argued that he never quite recovered from being so brutally treated.

When George was fourteen, the King again changed the Prince's tutors but his son was by then hot-headed and quite unwilling to accept discipline. His new teachers, Bishop Hurd and Reverend Arnold, tried to flog him and his brother William but the Princes would not let them. In fact, George grabbed the cane and tried to give their teachers six of the best. Arnold, who seems to have been stronger than the Bishop, 'tore the weapon from his hand and roughly administered to him the punishment with which they had been threatened'. Years later, George's sister Sophia told a friend that she had seen her two oldest brothers 'held by their arms to be flogged like dogs with a long whip'. The children were flogged not just when they were lazy or disobedient; William was even flogged for having asthma. Perhaps it is not surprising that the King's fourth son, Edward, became infamous for his brutality towards the men under his command.

There is no evidence that George III was sadistic but he seems to have believed thrashing would teach his sons not to be arrogant or lazy, and he may have believed he would have been less lazy in his teens, had Bute thrashed him. The last King who had been thrashed so often and with such conviction had been James I, who grew up to be an exceptionally intelligent and hard-working man. Hardly any of George and Charlotte's children might be said to have possessed those qualities.

I have suggested that intelligent children are more likely not to be traumatised should they be abused. One benefit of studying the long history of the royals is that it highlights the inadequacies of psychological theory. Research by the National Children's Home shows that one-third of men who sexually abuse children were sexually abused themselves but this prompts the question: why do two-thirds of abused boys not repeat the pattern? Intelligence is part of the answer, I have suggested, but it does not explain why George and William or, later, George V and his brother Eddy turned out to have such different personalities.

T. H. White condemned George as a 'poltroon', but the novelist J. B. Priestley was kinder and said in *The Prince of Pleasure* that George was not the 'cold-hearted libertine which he was so often reputed to be but he was really a soft-hearted overgrown boy. So far as he was a man, he was not a bad one but a foolish one.' Neither author got near the truth, it seems. Like Henry VIII, George was a narcissist but, unlike the Tudor, he would become a frustrated narcissist.

From his loving mother, George also picked up one destructive interest. Charlotte was very concerned about her children's health and believed in the then fashionable remedies of bleeding and cupping. Her son became addicted to these. Sadly, they were not his only addictions. By the time he was seventeen, the Prince set about exploring London's low life. He made two unfortunate friends: Jack Payne and the Duke of Cumberland, who is described in a memoir by Lloyd as 'a good natured but feeble minded man', whose whole life was devoted to 'weakness and dissipation.' Dissipation became the Prince's greatest hobby.

In 1781, George was given a separate establishment – in other words, a grand house with servants of his own. He flung himself with zest into debauch, getting drunk, chasing women and gambling. At the end of the eighteenth century, two new crazes which had not been available previously – opium and nitrous oxide (or laughing gas) – became fashionable. After the young chemist Humphry Davy tested the effects of nitrous oxide on himself, many aristocrats gave laughing-gas parties. The effects of both opium and laudanum on writers and artists between 1770 and 1820 have been studied in works such as Hayter's *Opium and the Romantic Imagination* but no one seems to have examined use by the aristocracy in any detail. The Prince used laudanum constantly and it affected his behaviour. Until De Quincey published his classic *Confessions of an English Opium-Eater* in 1821, few people even thought opium harmful. The artist Thomas Phillips (who produced some classic illustrations of George IV and whose work is on display in the National Portrait Gallery) gave a good contemporary account of the Prince, and could be describing someone whose wayward behaviour was influenced by drug use:

The Prince is influenced by caprice and has no steadiness. He has the power of giving a proper answer to whoever addresses him on any subject but nothing fixes him. The person who last spoke to him makes an apparent impression but it is gone when the next person or subject comes before him.

Phillips said of the Prince that 'his tailor or bootmaker will occupy his mind' quite as much as an important politician.

By now, the Prince owed fabulous amounts to money lenders. He often sent his chef to handle some of the more delicate negotiations with his creditors. Mr and Mrs King, a decent Lutheran mother and a somewhat bourgeois-minded father, despaired of their eldest.

When the Prince turned twenty-one, he received a grant of £60,000 from Parliament and an annual income of £50,000 from his father, but these huge sums were not enough for his extravagances. His stables alone cost £31,000 a year. Mr and Mrs King lectured, reasoned and nagged, but George would not cut his spending or reduce his use of laudanum. One memoir in 1783 criticised the King for treating his son with 'ill-judged parsimony', which was bound to lead to trouble. Just as earlier heirs had done, the Prince soon sided with the opposition, now headed up by the formidable Charles Fox, one of the greatest orators ever to grace the House of Commons. Fox was also a hopeless gambler, so he and the Prince had much in common. Meanwhile, the King became furious at what he saw as his son's betrayal.

George and Charlotte also despaired of their son's romantic adventures. Instead of settling down with a nice German wife, the Prince first fell in love with one of the Queen's ladies-in-waiting, Miss Hamilton, who discouraged him. Then he fell for Mary Robinson, an actress who had played Perdita. He signed many notes to her as 'Florizel', a nickname that stuck. Referring to actresses, Miss Hamilton warned that 'a female in that line has too much trick' and might well be dangerous to him. The King just thought his son had been 'a thoughtless boy' in dealing with Mary and looked on her and other young women as temptresses.

He could not sustain that illusion for long as his son then became infatuated with Maria Fitzherbert, who was even more unsuitable. Six years older than the Prince, Mrs Fitzherbert was also a Roman Catholic. It seems the Prince was doing everything he could to upset his parents. He was not content to enjoy Mrs Fitzherbert as his mistress; he wanted to marry her. That would cause problems.

The Royal Marriages Act of 1772 obliged any heir to obtain the monarch's consent to any marriage. Knowing his father would never give that, the Prince decided to marry Mrs Fitzherbert in secret at her house in Mayfair. If news of this marriage leaked out, there would be uproar and the Prince would never receive another sou, either from the King or Parliament.

The daughters of Mr and Mrs King

Fortunately, the experience of the King and Queen with their daughters was much happier. The girls were more restrained than the boys and the diarist Fanny Burney has left many charming details of their behaviour. She wrote most about the Princess Royal, who was born in 1766 and their youngest Princess Amelia, who was born in 1783. The King 'dotes on her', Fanny noted, and the Queen allowed her to carry Amelia in her arms to her sentimental father.

In February 1786, Fanny was playing a game which involved putting Amelia in a phaeton and driving about boisterously. The young Princess was in no mood to understand or accommodate when Fanny was tired.

'Do come and play with me,' Princess Amelia insisted and kept on pulling at Fanny's gown.

'We shall disturb the King, Ma'am,' Fanny said, hoping to quieten the little girl.

But Papa did not intimidate his little daughter. Princess Amelia dashed over to him while he was talking earnestly to a Mr Smelt and called, 'Papa, go!'

'What?' cried the King.

'Go, Papa, go you must,' the Princess insisted. So Papa the King took his little daughter in his arms and began playing with her and kissing her. When a few days later Amelia burned one of her fingers playing with wax, the King 'watched the advancement of her pain with great solicitude'. But he could also rib his daughter in the nicely teasing way of good parents, for he jested that Princess Amelia 'would not be denied. Miss Burney is now the first in favour with her.'

Having fun with his daughters did not solve the King's problems with his oldest son, though. In 1787, Charles Fox proposed to obtain a huge parliamentary grant to deal with George's never-ending debts but London society was fizzing with rumours that the Prince had secretly married. Fox denounced these rumours as lies which, of course, did not please Mrs Fitzherbert. The Prince was trapped between his furious wife, his furious parents and an equally furious Parliament. Meanwhile, the King and Queen had heard the rumours and were beside themselves with their son, who accused them of not understanding him.

Eventually, Parliament granted the Prince £161,000 to settle his debts and £60,000 for improvements to Carlton House. Despite these fabulous sums, the Prince still felt aggrieved because his father refused to give him any place in the running of the country.

George III's crisis

In 1788, the personal crisis for which George's reign is best remembered took place when he suffered a breakdown of sorts. The arguments as to whether the King was mad, suffering from porphyria or had been poisoned by arsenic in the cosmetics he used have never been finally resolved. Arsenic is the current favourite as samples of the King's hair were examined in 2005 and revealed high levels of the poison. The King certainly behaved in ways he had never done before. For example, he made his first and only attempt to seduce a woman other than his wife. Charlotte accepted that her usually loving husband was literally not in his right mind. What she – and the country – saw as a tragedy, their eldest son regarded as an opportunity, though.

By November, the King could not fulfil his duties. Descriptions of his behaviour suggest he was manic as he sometimes spoke for hours without stopping. Far odder, it was claimed that he shook hands with a tree, thinking the oak was the King of Prussia. That may have been exaggerated as it is more usual for schizophrenics in a florid state to say they are Christ or Napoleon. The nearest well-documented example is perhaps in the case histories of Oliver Sacks, who is a neurologist, not a psychiatrist. In *The Man Who Mistook His Wife for a Hat*, Sacks describes a patient who did just that, but the man's problem was organic and he never recovered.

R. D. Laing and many other psychiatrists have claimed there are some rational reasons for even the oddest symptoms and this seems a useful view as to what happened next. On 5 November 1788, the King attacked his son and tried to smash his head against a wall. One observer claimed foam was coming from the King's mouth and his eyes were so bloodshot that they looked like currant jelly. The assault was put down to madness rather than fury at the way his son had behaved for the past ten years. Perhaps it was no accident that the King chose Guy Fawkes Day to attack his son: Guy Fawkes had, after all, wanted to get rid of an earlier King.

There were bitter battles between doctors as to who should have the honour of dealing with the 'royal malady'. Eventually, a fierce 'mad doctor', Francis Willis, was chosen. Willis had the Queen's confidence at first and put George in a straitjacket. A special chair was constructed to hold the King down. Sometimes, Willis applied poultices which were supposed to draw out 'evil humours'. Willis became harsher and sometimes even had the King beaten to force the evil humours out. The Prince, who had been flogged so much as a boy, appears to have enjoyed the fact that his father was being punished.

As the King could not fulfil his duties, Parliament had to appoint a Regent. The leaders of the main parties, Charles Fox and the younger Pitt, wrangled over the terms. Fox suggested the Prince's powers should include the power to appoint the Prime Minister. Pitt refused to agree because he was afraid that the Regent would remove him from office for the Prince was far closer to Fox.

Then a miracle happened. Or a tragedy, at least as far as the Prince was concerned: the King recovered for no apparent reason, which made his son unhappy, although he had to pretend otherwise. The Queen even stopped the Prince seeing his father twice because she thought a visit from his son would be upsetting and might trigger a new bout of the 'royal malady'. The Prince did write polite letters which rejoiced in his father's recovery but he and some cronies, including Jack Payne, went to the fashionable club, Brooks, on 17 February 1790. Payne imitated the King's behaviour and 'howled like a monkey'. The King was as mad as ever, they all grinned.

The miracle was that, despite Willis's treatment, George recovered – and quite suddenly. When the King became well enough to resume his duties, his eldest son was disappointed. The extent to which the Queen's relationship with her once-adored son had changed is clear in one further detail. When she arranged a concert to celebrate the King's recovery, she did not wish her son to attend. She reminded him that the concert was to thank those who had stayed loyal to the King during his illness: the Prince simply did not fit the bill.

A naval father

From the early 1780s, George III and Queen Charlotte were concerned that the Prince would corrupt the younger children and did their best, in particular, to keep his brothers away from him. George's third son was quite close to his brother when they were young, but William then became the first royal Prince sent to join the Navy to gain experience of the world. No previous Prince had even been in actual command of a canoe.

When he joined the HMS *Prince George*, William was just thirteen years old. He learned how to navigate, keep the men in order and even how to cook. He was treated like all the other young would-be officers but he was the only one to be accompanied by a tutor. The tutor could not prevent William from being arrested with shipmates after a drunken brawl in Gibraltar, but, as soon as the authorities realised they had jailed a Prince of the royal blood, they released him with profuse apologies.

Twenty-two of the King's letters to Prince William were discovered in 2008 and, while they hardly compare with James I's *Basilikon Doron*, they offer an affectionate mix of good advice and typical royal anxieties. The King told Prince William:

> You are now launching into a scene of life where you either prove an Honour, or a Disgrace to your Family; it would be very unwelcoming of the love I have for my children, if I did not at this serious moment give you advice [on] how to conduct yourself.

George III advised his son to behave humbly.

> Though when at home a Prince, on board of the *Prince George* you are only a Boy learning the Naval profession; but the Prince so far accompanies you that what other Boys do, you must not. It must never be out of your thoughts that more Obedience is necessary from You to Your superiors in the Navy, more politeness to your Equals, and more good nature to your Inferiors than from those who have not been told that these are essential for a Gentleman.

William did well in the Navy and was promoted to lieutenant. He served during the American War of Independence and George Washington entertained the idea of seizing him while the Prince was visiting New York. The British got wind of the scheme, however, and assigned guards to escort William and so the plot was foiled.

William eventually became one of Nelson's captains, which delighted the King. Nelson himself had a good opinion of the Prince: 'In his professional line, he is superior to two-thirds, I am sure, of the [Naval] list; and in attention to orders, and respect to his superior officer, I hardly know his equal.' William was finally made a rear admiral but then his sea career did not progress any further, which he found very frustrating.

Though William and George III enjoyed a better relationship

than most Hanoverian sons had with their fathers, the frustrated rear admiral now put pressure on his father and he did so in a way that no other royal ever seems to have done. William threatened to run for the House of Commons for the constituency of Totnes in Devon. This might have been marvellous political theatre and precedent – imagine if Prince Charles or Princess Anne offered themselves for election – but George III was appalled by the prospect. William was much easier to buy off than his elder brother, though. The rear admiral settled for being made Duke of Clarence and St Andrews and Earl of Munster. His father apparently grumbled, 'I well know it is another vote added to the Opposition.'

In 1791, William started to live with an Irish actress, Dorothea Bland, who called herself 'Mrs Jordan'. For the next twenty years, they produced children as enthusiastically as Mr and Mrs King did. All their ten (who were, of course, illegitimate) were given the surname 'FitzClarence' after their father's Duchy. Rather like his own father, William seems to have enjoyed a quiet home life. He told a friend: 'Mrs Jordan is a very good creature, very domestic and careful of her children. To be sure she is absurd sometimes and has her humours but there are such things more or less in all families.' The phrase is telling as it makes it very clear that William did not see Dorothea as a mistress but to all purposes as his wife. He seems especially to have looked forward to family get-togethers, as Mrs Jordan wrote: 'We shall have a full and merry house this Christmas, 'tis what the dear Duke delights in.' The King accepted the fact that his son was living in sin but thought, typically, that this particular state justified halving Mrs Jordan's allowance.

It is not surprising George III was constantly worried about the debts that his sons ran up. By the mid-1790s, the Prince of Wales owed moneylenders something like £630,000 – almost £50 million in today's money. His father refused to bail him out, so the only solution was for the Prince of Wales to marry a rich wife, which provoked more conflict between the Prince and his long-suffering parents.

The tragicomedy of the wife George III chose for his son

The Prince of Wales was given the choice of two possible brides; both were German and George's first cousins. Princess Louise of Mecklenburg-Strelitz was the daughter of Queen Charlotte's brother, while Caroline of Brunswick was his father's sister's daughter. Caroline did not have a good reputation; the Queen had heard rumours that she had become the lover of an Irish officer in her father's army. Ironically, this made her an excellent choice as far as the Prince's latest mistress, Lady Jersey, was concerned. She believed Caroline would be less of a rival than Louise and persuaded the Prince that she was the best woman for him.

Prince George sent one of his courtiers to Brunswick to inspect Caroline. James Harris found the would-be bride dressed in a slovenly way and thought she had not washed for days. Her coarse language also disturbed him, but, instead of coming back to London to warn George that he might be making a terrible mistake, Harris devoted himself to improving Caroline. After four months, he thought she was presentable and brought her to England. George was not impressed, however, as, the moment he saw Caroline, he said, 'Harris, I am not well, pray get me a glass of brandy.' For her part, Caroline was equally unimpressed and complained George's portrait had obviously been painted years earlier and that he did not look so dashing now. 'I think he is very fat and nothing like as handsome,' she declared. The night before the wedding, George sent his brother, William, to tell Mrs Fitzherbert that she was the only woman he would ever love. He then proceeded to get roaring drunk – it was apparently the only way he could face the wedding.

Some time later, George said that he and Caroline only had sex three times, but that was sufficient for her to congratulate her husband on how large his penis was. She could only know that, he concluded, if she had slept with other men; his parents had made him marry a harlot. The royal couple separated within weeks, though they remained under the same roof. Three times was enough, however, as Caroline became pregnant. Nine months after the wedding, she gave birth to a daughter. Expert Queen Charlotte was involved in the preparations for the birth and told the Chamberlain not to order the cradle he intended to buy. Communication went through a palace official, it seems, as Charlotte instructed him to tell her eldest son: 'I, as an experienced woman in such matters, say it should be without rockers to it.'

Prince George became very anxious during the last stage of his wife's labour because producing an heir would bolster his own position. He invited many grandees to attend the birth, including the Archbishop of Canterbury, the Chancellor, the Lord President, four dukes and Lord Jersey, the husband of his mistress. Jersey carried a letter to the King and Queen, saying Caroline had given birth to 'an immense girl'.

George III was delighted and the girl was called Charlotte after the Queen. Ignoring the friction between his son and daughter-in-law, the King added: 'You are both young and I trust will have many children.' It was a forlorn hope. Three days after Charlotte was born, George made a will in which he left his fortune to Mrs Fitzherbert, 'who is my wife in the eyes of God and who is, and ever will be such in mine.' The Prince added: 'To her who is called Princess of Wales I leave one shilling.' The will was not just hostile to Caroline but, implicitly, to his parents who had arranged the marriage. It was not the final insult, though: the Prince's will also stated that Caroline should play no part in bringing up their child. When she complained, George banned her from seeing their daughter unless a nurse and governess were present.

As the immense baby Charlotte grew up, both her parents tried to use her as a pawn in their ongoing battle. In August 1797, her mother left Carlton House and rented a house in Blackheath in south London. She claimed to be a devoted mother, but Charlotte saw very little of her; George was even less interested. When Charlotte was eight, he moved her out of his own home into Montague House, which was next door. There, Charlotte grew up with little contact with either parent and was looked after by strangers. She had one of the bleakest of all royal childhoods.

George III's life is threatened; his son's reactions

I have argued that, by comparison with most people, royals endure rather more life events, and few are more upsetting than assassination attempts. George III was attacked twice. The first attempt was in 1786. The would-be assassin was Margaret Nicholson, who he treated rather kindly, insisting she needed a mad doctor as she had tried to kill him with a kitchen knife that was hopelessly blunt. Relations between the King and the Prince were already so bad that Charlotte did not tell her son either that his father had been attacked, or that he had survived. Then, in May 1800, George III was shot at in the Drury Lane Theatre – just as his grandfather had been in 1716. The assassin missed but the attack, perhaps to the Prince of Wales's chagrin, did not trigger a new bout of the royal malady; that only happened ten years later.

When the King broke down again, it was generally assumed that he suffered a recurrence of his earlier madness, but he was now seventy-two years old and seems more likely to have been suffering from senile dementia. He still had moments of lucidity, though: he believed that he became depressed when his youngest and favourite daughter, Princess Amelia, fell ill with consumption. Amelia was, in fact, far from being an obedient daughter as she passionately pursued the Earl of Euston and wrote astonishingly intimate letters to him (in one, she hoped he would not be disappointed by her sexual parts). But the King almost certainly did not know of these erotic letters. When she was dying, he visited his daughter every day and gave her 'every consolation that could be drawn from religion though his own heart suffered dreadfully in witnessing the pains he could not alleviate'. After she died, he insisted on keeping a lock of her hair. Amelia's nurse noted: 'The scenes of distress and crying every day were melancholy beyond description.'

The Prince of Wales finally got the power he wanted and became Regent in 1811. By now, he was using remarkable amounts of laudanum. After spraining his ankle, he took 250 drops at one sitting and then continued on a steady dose of 100 drops every three hours. Sir Henry Halford, the Prince's physician, feared his patient's use of

the drug would drive him mad and it certainly affected the way he
treated his daughter. England was now a place with a senile King
and an addict for Regent. It is ironic that, while both these men
were still 'ruling', the country managed to defeat Napoleon. The
Battle of Waterloo may have been won on the playing fields of
Eton, but the victory owed nothing to the royals.

Once he was Regent, the Prince of Wales was determined to
triumph over the wife his parents had forced on him. Caroline was
accused of having had a child by another man. She had managed to
conceal her pregnancy, she claimed, because she was so fat that no
one could tell whether or not she was with child. Gleefully, George
set up what became known as 'the Delicate Investigation', whose aim
was simple: he wanted evidence that would allow him to divorce the
wife he hated. Their daughter Charlotte was now ten years old and
became the victim of their battle. Her father told her that she could
not see her mother while the Delicate Investigation was proceeding.

The most graphic evidence was appropriately indelicate. A footman, Joseph Roberts, observed that Caroline 'was very fond of
fucking', but could one really believe the word of a servant against
that of a Princess, especially when she remained very popular with
the public? There was no clear proof of Caroline's guilt, so George
reluctantly allowed Charlotte to see her mother again. He imposed
one condition: his daughter could not play with William Austin,
whom, the Prince believed, was Caroline's illegitimate son that she
had managed to bring into the world without anyone knowing.

George was inconsistent in his attitude towards his daughter
Charlotte, sometimes sentimental, sometimes unpleasant, sometimes mean. He gave her a stingy allowance for clothes and imposed
one bizarre rule: she liked the opera, but her father ordered that she
had to sit in the rear of the box and leave before the end of any
performance.

By 1811, George's brother, Prince William, was so deeply in
debt himself that he had to give up Mrs Jordan. The jilted actress
commented: 'Money, money, my good friend, has, I am convinced,
made HIM at this moment the most wretched of men,' before

adding: 'With all his excellent qualities, his domestic *virtues*, his love for his *lovely* children, what must he not at this moment suffer?' She was given a generous allowance of £4,400 per year and custody of their daughters, as long as she went away and never set foot on the stage again. When she did take up her acting career again, to repay the debts her son-in-law had incurred – William took custody of their daughters. Soon afterwards, Mrs Jordan fled to France to escape her creditors and died, impoverished, near Paris in 1816. William was now a single man, with eleven children to look after but he took his responsibilities more seriously than one might expect.

Charlotte's Quadrille
– the Princess, the Orange, the Russian and Leopold

When Charlotte was seventeen, she and her father started to fight over whom she should marry. As she was likely to become Queen in her own right, Charlotte could have her pick of European Princes. Her father favoured William of Orange but he disgraced himself by getting drunk the first time he met her. Charlotte, who had not shown any political instincts until that moment, informed her father that a future Queen of England should not marry a foreigner like 'the detested Dutchman', as she called William. The Prince of Wales suspected she was as devious as he had been with Mrs Fitzherbert and that Charlotte really wanted to marry another William, the Duke of Gloucester. He confronted the pair and thundered he would never allow the match.

'He spoke as if he had the most improper ideas of my inclinations,' Charlotte wrote, 'I see that he is compleatly poisoned against me, and that he will never come round.' The newsletters had much fun with stories about whether Charlotte would marry 'the Orange or the Cheese' – Gloucester was 'the Cheese' as the county's cheese was tasty.

In June 1814, Charlotte gave in to her father and signed a marriage contract with the Orange, but she had her mother's roving eye and fell in love with a Prussian cavalry officer. The Prussian galloped

away, however, having seen that preparations for the wedding were
in full swing. Then Charlotte met what she had been looking for
perhaps all the time: a young man with a triple-barrelled German
name, Prince Leopold of Saxe-Coburg-Saalfeld. She invited him to
call on her and they spent nearly an hour alone without a chaperone.
As soon as he left Charlotte, Leopold wrote to her father apologising
for any indiscretion. The real trouble with him, however, was that
he was too poor and the Prince of Wales, as usual, needed money.

If George was all for the marriage to the Orange, Caroline was
bound to be against it. She and her daughter now found an original way of annoying the Prince: if Charlotte married the Orange,
she would have to live in the Netherlands, a sacrifice she could
only contemplate if her mother lived with her. Fat and fond of sex,
Caroline would shock the bourgeois burghers of Amsterdam, so the
Orange would not agree and Charlotte broke off their engagement.
Her father responded by doing what a number of Hanoverians
had done before – putting his child under house arrest. He told
Charlotte that he was going to send her to Windsor the next day,
where her grandmother, the Queen, would talk some sense into
her. Charlotte, a perfect teenager, ran screaming out into the street
– her laudanum-addled father had not taken the precaution of
having the house surrounded by guards. She had no idea how to
hail a cab, however, but a gallant passer-by found her a hackney. As
she clambered inside, Charlotte instructed the cabbie to take her to
her mother's house in Blackheath.

Within hours, members of the royal family arrived in Blackheath,
including Frederick, Duke of York, George III's second son. He did
not come as a sympathetic uncle, eager to help in a crisis, but with
some sort of legal document which forced Charlotte to return to
her own home. After much bickering, she was allowed to spend
the night at her mother's on the strict understanding that she went
straight to her father's house the next day.

The runaway Princess became the talk of the town. Father and
daughter had a tearful reconciliation, but George still sent Charlotte
to Windsor, where again she was under house arrest. The servants

were instructed never to let her out of their sight. Her grandmother now had to juggle a senile husband, a clutch of troublesome sons and a furious, headstrong teenager. Giving birth was simple by comparison.

Charlotte managed to smuggle a note out to her favourite uncle – Augustus, the Duke of Sussex – who seized the chance to annoy the Prince of Wales. A few days later in the House of Lords, the Duke asked the Prime Minister (Robert Jenkinson, Earl of Liverpool) whether Charlotte was free to come and go. George was furious and blamed Sussex for making a bad situation worse – and public. The two brothers never spoke again.

Following this incident, Charlotte was abandoned once more: at the end of July 1814, George told her that her mother was about to leave England for a very long time. Charlotte was upset, but her relationship with her mother was by now so damaged that she did not feel anything she might say would make a difference. Even worse, her mother was casual about leaving. Charlotte simply said: 'For God knows how long, or what events may occur before we meet again.' In fact, Charlotte would never see her mother again.

Throughout these dramas, Charlotte still hoped that her Prussian cavalry officer would whisk her off, but, in mid-December, she 'had a very sudden and great shock' when she learned that he had married someone else. She wrote that she would 'take the next best thing, which was a good tempered man with good sence' (her spelling left much to be desired), before adding: 'that man is the P of S-C', by which she meant Leopold, the Prince of Saxe-Coburg. Her father, however, refused to give up hope of the lucrative marriage to the Orange, even though Charlotte was adamant. 'No arguments, no threats, shall ever bend me to marry this detested Dutchman,' she wrote.

The 'next best thing' to the 'detested Dutchman' was flattered by Charlotte's attentions, but Leopold was fighting against Napoleon and could not come to visit her. That did not stop Charlotte formally requesting her father's permission to marry him. The chaotic political situation on the Continent, George said, made it impossible for him to even consider such a folly; he did not add there was an even greater problem, Leopold's poverty. But his daughter persisted and, in January 1816, she wrote to her father: 'I no longer hesitate in declaring my partiality in favour of the Prince of Coburg – assuring you that no one will be more steady or consistent in this their present & last engagement than myself.' Whether he was genuinely touched by Charlotte's pleas or too tired to keep on fighting is not clear, but George finally summoned Leopold. The father, who had bungled his own love life, interviewed his daughter's suitor to see if the young man was suitable. Their talk went well and Charlotte then had dinner with Leopold and her father. She wrote of Leopold:

> I find him charming, and go to bed happier than I have ever done yet in my life ... I am certainly a very fortunate creature, & have to bless God. A Princess never, I believe, set out in life (or married) with such prospects of happiness, real domestic ones like other people.

George now told Charlotte that Leopold 'had every qualification to make a woman happy' but, almost at once, the Prince behaved eccentrically. He did not allow her to spend much time with her suitor because he had managed to convince himself that, if she saw too much of him, she would become bored. George was projecting what Phillips had described as his 'lack of steadiness' onto his daughter.

Charlotte's mother did not bother to return for the wedding. She was in Italy, where she was enjoying herself with an Italian maître d'. The honeymoon was spoilt by the fact that the couple spent it at Oatlands Palace, which stank and was overrun by dogs. Bride and groom were also not feeling altogether well, but Charlotte wrote that Leopold was 'the perfection of a lover'. Marriage made her more relaxed, perhaps for the simple reason that Leopold loved her as her parents had never really done with any consistency. Christian Stockmar, Leopold's adviser, noticed that Charlotte was much calmer and more in control of herself than before. Leopold wrote: 'Except when I went out to shoot, we were together always, and we could be together, we did not tire.' When Charlotte became too excited, Leopold would say only, 'Doucement, chérie' ('Gently, my love'). Charlotte seems to have liked that, and began calling her husband 'Doucement'.

At the end of April 1817, Leopold told his father-in-law that Charlotte was pregnant. The public placed bets on whether it would be a boy or a girl. Speculation thrived. Economists calculated the birth of a Princess would raise the stock market by 2.5 per cent, but the birth of a Prince would increase it by 6 per cent.

Though Stockmar had a degree in medicine, Charlotte was entrusted to Sir Richard Croft, who was not a doctor but an *accoucheur* (male midwife). Croft suspected his patient had been stuffing herself while pregnant and insisted that she eat very little. Insufficient calories probably slowed down the progress of her pregnancy.

A few weeks before she was due, Charlotte wrote a somewhat disturbed letter to her mother, who was still disgracing herself abroad. 'Oh my mother,' she said, 'when I look to the dark probabilities, even shadows shake my courage and I feel myself the victim of terrors which reason would almost demonstrate absurd.' She felt surrounded by strangers, 'with a single exception' – Leopold. If she survived, she would do her best to restore her mother to her proper place, but 'a pang of terror shoots across my bewildered brain'. It sounds like a plea from an anxious daughter to a mother who showed no enthusiasm to return to be by her side.

Charlotte was due to deliver on 19 October, but nothing had happened by the end of the month. On the evening of 3 November, her contractions began, but she was weak because of Croft's starvation regime. In the morning, he summoned a doctor and an obstetrician; they all began to fear Charlotte might be unable to deliver the baby.

A traumatic labour
Again, 5 November proved to be a fateful date in royal history. At 9 p.m., the baby was delivered, but the child was stillborn. George and the rest of the royal family were assured that the mother, at

least, was doing well. Utterly exhausted, Charlotte reacted calmly. It was the will of God, she told her midwife, that the baby should have been born dead. She was finally allowed to eat a little. Leopold, who had remained with his wife throughout the labour, obviously thought she was in no danger. He took some opium and collapsed into bed.

Three hours after she had given birth, Charlotte began vomiting violently and complained of pains in her stomach. Croft was alarmed to find his patient was very cold, could not breathe easily and was bleeding. He put hot compresses on her, then the accepted treatment for postpartum bleeding, but it did not help. Croft called in Stockmar and urged him to wake the Prince to come and see his wife. Stockmar ran to Leopold's bedroom but could not rouse him from his opium-induced slumbers and so he ran back to the Princess.

Charlotte seized his hand and said: 'They have made me tipsy.' Stockmar was so shocked by her condition that he decided to try to wake Leopold again. He was leaving the room when he was startled to hear Charlotte say, 'Stocky! Stocky!' He turned round, walked over to the bed and realised those were her last words: she was dead. The post-mortem examination concluded that she had died as a result of a haemorrhage, although there was perhaps less blood than might be expected.

Charlotte's father was sick with grief, but, as he so often did, could not behave decently. He was too distraught to attend her funeral. When she heard that Charlotte had died, her absent mother fainted in shock and, as soon as she had revived, waxed tragically: 'England, that great country, has lost everything in losing my ever-beloved daughter.' She too did not attend her 'ever-beloved daughter's' funeral.

Leopold did attend the funeral and took the death of his wife very badly. He wrote to Sir Thomas Lawrence:

Two generations gone. Gone in a moment! I have felt for myself, but I have also felt for the Prince Regent. My Charlotte is gone from the country – it has lost her. She was a good, she was an admirable woman. None could know my Charlotte as I did know her! It was my study, my duty, to know her character, but it was my delight!

Stockmar later wrote that Leopold 'has never recovered the feeling of happiness which had blessed his short married life'. But Charlotte's tragic death was far from the end of Leopold's involvement with the British royal family, their marriages and their children.

William – the new heir

The tragedy meant that one day Prince William was very likely to become King. William was not merely the heir, but might well produce heirs. He was only in his early fifties, but he had a good breeding record as he had fathered ten children with Mrs Jordan and at least one with another mistress. Since the country would now have to pay them, William's debts became less of an issue, unlike his children. He insisted any wife had to be prepared to act as a mother to his team of eleven illegitimate children. The prospect did not appeal to a number of eligible European Princesses but, finally, the inevitably German, Princess Adelaide of Saxe-Meiningen, agreed to have him and his brood. She was twenty-five years old and quite strong willed. Adelaide soon took her husband, his children and his finances in hand: she insisted he take proper exercise, cut down on his over-eating and made him drink less wine and more barley water. Invigorated by a young wife and barley water, William had no difficulty in fulfilling his conjugal duties. Adelaide became pregnant at least five times, but she had three miscarriages and her two surviving daughters died young.

Remarkably tolerant, Adelaide even made no fuss when her husband commissioned a statue of his dead mistress, Mrs Jordan, and two of their children. William wanted the memorial placed in Westminster Abbey but the Dean refused to allow this memento of immorality to be set on sacred ground. The delinquent triptych was shipped down the Thames to Mapledurham, where a more tolerant clergyman housed it in his church (the vicar happened to be one of William's many illegitimate sons). There, the statue remained until a distant descendant of William's, the fifth Earl of Munster, presented it as a gift to Elizabeth II. It now stands in Buckingham Palace. Given the recent marital history of the royals, one cannot think of a better place for it.

In 1820, George III died. His son was again too indisposed to attend a family funeral – George IV's doctors put it down to anxiety, laudanum and too much whisky. Any psychoanalyst would also suggest other reasons; George would have to behave well when what he really wanted was to dance with joy now that his father had finally expired. For Freud, the death of his father was his making, freeing him to develop psychoanalysis; for George, it was his final unmaking.

Once he assumed the throne, for which he had been itching for decades, George's first problem was his wayward wife. He promised Caroline a fortune if she stayed in Italy and only crossed the Channel in her coffin. Caroline, however, had every intention of placing her ample bottom on the throne. She was the first, though hardly the last, embittered Princess of Wales to enjoy public support against an unfeeling husband. Cheering crowds welcomed her back to London. George should have realised that it was unwise to act against her, but common sense was never his forte. He was, as T. H. White noted, 'a poltroon', and so he asked Parliament to impeach Caroline for 'licentious, disgraceful, and adulterous intercourse'.

Proceedings began in the House of Lords in August 1820. The King only received a slim majority, but angry demonstrations in Caroline's favour made it impossible to put her on trial. In the end, the opium addict survived the slut – she died three weeks after her husband's Coronation. Technically she was the Queen, but when she tried to attend the Coronation ceremony, she found armed men preventing her from entering Westminster Abbey.

As he grew older, George IV often suffered delusions about what he would have liked to have been and to have done; in his opium-disintegrating mind, he even managed to convince himself he had commanded a division at the Battle of Waterloo. It was pure fantasy, of course.

When George lay dying at the end of May 1830, William went to see his brother. Together, they wept, as they had managed to stay fond of each other. George wittered pieties to his brother: 'God's will be done. I have injured no man. It will all rest on you then.'

Perhaps because of his time in the Navy, perhaps because of his long and, for a long time, happy relationship with Mrs Jordan, and perhaps too because of his sensible wife, Adelaide, William was more realistic than his brother had been. He knew that he was unlikely to reign long as he was over sixty years old and his successor would probably be a child. William liked children and meant to do his best, but it would prove very difficult. His eleven-year-old niece was already the victim of what we now call 'emotional abuse'. Today, any conscientious social worker would have taken Victoria into care and, working with other agencies, placed her mother and her mother's lover on trial for child abuse.

6

VICTORIA, ALBERT AND THE DANGERS OF GREAT EXPECTATIONS (1821–63)

George III's fourth son, Edward, the Duke of Kent and Strathearn, played just a small part in the dramas of his father's reign. The Duke went into the military but he could not even manage half a battalion decently; he infuriated his superiors because he was too violent. He was obsessive about discipline and so brutal to his men that, after a disastrous spell in Gibraltar, he was never given another significant command.

In 1818, the Duke married Marie Luise Victoria of Saxe-Coburg-Staalfeld, the sister of Leopold, Charlotte's widower. It was Victoria's second marriage. Her first husband, Charles, Prince of Leiningen, married her after losing his first wife, who happened to be Marie Luise Victoria's aunt. Today, this would lead to intense psycho punditry on what the consequences of marrying your uncle might be. Again, the history of the royals and the Freuds run in strange parallel. The young Freud faced a similar dilemma when an uncle from Odessa wanted to marry his niece. Freud's mother saw no difficulty but Sigmund pointed out that, when a man of fifty-nine wants to marry a girl of sixteen, he has only one motive. Freud's will prevailed, as it usually did in his family. Niece–uncle incest seems to have been more common than might be imagined among nineteenth-century Jews and royals, though.

The Duke was determined that his child should be born in England. He too was deeply in debt and had to borrow £5,000 to transport his wife, their servants and much bed linen from

Germany to England. A month before the Duchess was due to give birth, they reached London, where the Duke had to meet his creditors. He had the good sense to be polite to them so they did not insist on seizing everything he owned.

At 4.15 a.m. on 24 May 1819, the Duchess gave birth at Kensington Palace to their first and only child. Victoria has been the subject of many fine biographies, including those by Elizabeth Longford, Cecil Woodham Smith and Christopher Hibbert. The Queen also kept a diary, writing up to 2,500 words a day from the age of thirteen. She allowed a biography, *Eminent Women of the Age*, to be co-written by James Parton and Horace Greeley in 1868. Although often unctuous, James Parton did not just have access to private papers, but also discussed her childhood with the Queen personally. Victoria was also the subject of a chatty contemporary book by Grace Greenwood, the first woman to be hired as a journalist by the *New York Times*.

At a critical moment in her reign, Victoria also wrote a book herself, followed by a sequel, in a moment when the Queen wanted to let her subjects feel she was not remote. Today, we tend to think of Victoria as a buttoned-up matriarch, who was, as the cliché goes, 'not amused'. She had a keen sense of image, however, and was the first British monarch to write in a confessional mode and to allow some of those writings to be published. As a result, we sometimes have a surprisingly honest account of some of her ambitions and anxieties, both as a child and as a parent. Victoria's troubled family history may help to explain why she tried so hard to make the royal family seem respectable and, perhaps even more remarkably, ordinary. Twenty years into her reign, she wrote a letter to her eldest daughter in which she stressed Princes and Princesses should not delude themselves they were made of superior flesh and blood somehow different to that of the poor, the peasants and the working classes.

Victoria's 132 dolls
Victoria was born into a complex stepfamily. Her mother, Princess

Victoria, already had two children, Carl and Feodora, by her first marriage. When Victoria was born, her grandmother wrote to her daughter:

> I cannot express how happy I am to know you are, dearest, dearest Vicky, safe in your bed with a little one, and that all went off so happily. May God's best blessings rest on the little stranger and the beloved mother! Again a Charlotte – destined, perhaps, to play a great part one day, if a brother is not born to take it out of her hands. The English like queens, and the niece of the ever-lamented, beloved Charlotte will be most dear to them. I need not tell you how delighted everybody is here in hearing of your safe confinement.

The constant reminders of Charlotte turned out to be darkly apt, for the infant Victoria soon found herself in a house of mourning. In January 1820, eight months after she was born, her father suddenly died of pneumonia. The Duchess was devastated, as her marriage to Edward had been unexpectedly happy.

Six days after her father died, Victoria's grandfather, George III, also passed away. The widowed Duchess of Kent had every reason to return to her palace in Coburg, where she could live cheaply on the legacy of her deceased first husband, but she believed her daughter might become Queen of England. George IV wanted the Duchess to leave England, but, when she insisted on staying, he felt obliged to let her live in Kensington Palace. The place was run down and had become a refuge for a number of impoverished nobles who were often visited by bailiffs. Parton put it tactfully: 'Queen Victoria can doubtless well remember the time when her mother was pestered with duns [bailiffs] and when her own allowance of playthings was limited by her mother's poverty.' He also made much of the fact that the Duchess found it hard to live on £6,000 a year. She was fortunate that her brother, Leopold, had become rich after Charlotte died as he had found himself in the improbable situation of being asked to become King both of

Belgium and of Greece. Leopold turned down Greece and became King of Belgium. He was relatively generous to his sister.

After Parton's book was published, Victoria penned some of her own childhood memories. She remembered crawling on a yellow carpet and being told that, if she cried and was naughty, her uncle Sussex (who lived next door) would hear and come to punish her. Victoria was also scared of bishops, who wore frightening wigs and aprons. She liked visiting her uncle Leopold when he was at Claremont because she was allowed to listen to the music in the Great Hall when there were dinner parties. The family servants, including Baroness Spath, who had served her mother for years, 'all worshipped the poor fatherless child' that she was. Spath had a habit of kneeling in front of her, but Princess Feodora, Victoria's half-sister, recalled the toddler was taught to apologise to the servants if she had been rude to them.

Victoria was brought up in a household where German was spoken. She did not start to use English much until she was three years old. In the 1820s, even likely queens did not receive the sophisticated education they had done three centuries earlier. Victoria was not expected to read Aristotle in the original Greek or to write poems as Elizabeth I had done. Her somewhat traditional grandmother was, in fact, worried the child would come under too much pressure and wrote to her daughter: 'Do not tease your little puss with learning. She is so young still.'

After the death of her husband, Victoria's mother appointed John Conroy as head of her household. Conroy became a key figure in Victoria's childhood, but his whole career depended on one fortunate introduction. Until he was forty, he was just an ordinary officer in the Royal Artillery. Conroy did, however, marry well and his father-in-law introduced him to the Duke of Kent, who appointed him as one of his equerries.

Conroy was a good organiser and became a favourite of the royal couple. When the Duke died, he offered his services to his widow. The Duchess and Conroy became very close and the Duke of Wellington believed they were lovers, as did many others at court. Throughout Victoria's childhood, the Duchess and Conroy felt vulnerable because the court did not like or approve of them.

After her father died, Victoria became third in line to the throne and so it seemed prudent to ensure that she received good care. In 1824 her nursemaid, Mrs Brock, was dismissed and a German woman – Louise Lehzen, who had looked after Victoria's half-sister, Feodora – took charge. Feodora was now too old to need a nanny. Lehzen was 'a handsome woman, despite her pointed noise and chin, clever, emotional, humourless', according to the historian Christopher Hibbert. Victoria's mother was confident, as was Conroy, Lehzen would bring the child up according to their wishes; the woman was, after all, only a foreign servant.

When she was four years old, Victoria contracted dysentery. Even the poltroon King was for once concerned, but, after a while, the Duchess reassured him that their little daughter had recovered. A year later, George IV invited her to Windsor – 'When we arrived at the Royal Lodge the King took me by the hand saying, "Give me your little paw."' She recalled: 'His Majesty was large and gouty and that he wore a periwig.' He gave his niece a miniature of himself set in diamonds, which his last mistress – Lady Conyngham – pinned on the girl. Victoria remembered feeling very proud. The next day, she and Lehzen met the King as he was driving in his Phaeton. 'Pop her in,' said the King and he took her for a drive.

When the Duchess's son by her first marriage – Prince Charles of Leiningen – came to England, he found Conroy charming and a pleasant companion. Conroy assured him that he had 'unlimited affection', both for the Duchess and for her small daughter, adding that, when he was dying, the Duke of Kent had entrusted the care of his wife and child to him. He had even pledged part of his property to guarantee the Duchess's debts, he boasted. Charles did nothing to discourage his mother from trusting Conroy.

Conroy also told Charles that he hoped to give Victoria 'an upbringing which would enable her in the future to be equal to her high position'. Charles may have been impressed, but the court regarded Conroy as an ambitious upstart, whose father had been a mere barrister. As we have seen, George I kidnapped his son's children. George IV had far better reasons for insisting Victoria live with him, but the man who had not exactly been a devoted father to his own daughter was hardly likely to exert himself for his niece.

The Duchess and Conroy both knew their future depended on the young Victoria, but, instead of giving her love and security, their own insecurities led them to try to control the girl. Conroy devised what came to be known as 'The Kensington System'. The System is too grandiose a name but Conroy obtained some support from Charles Leiningen, who, much later in 1841, dictated a long memorandum justifying it – *A Complete History of the Policy Followed at Kensington, Under Sir John Conroy's Guidance.*

The Kensington System

In 1972, the Chinese Foreign Minister and Mao's friend, Chou en Lai, was asked what the results of the French Revolution of 1789 had been. He replied apparently it was still too early to see. As the story moves from the past to a more recent era, I am reminded of this splendid quip but the results of royal parenting are easier to discern than those of the French Revolution. The way that Albert and Victoria brought up their children – especially their first-born, Victoria, their eldest son, Bertie, and their third child, Alice – had long-lasting effects on the royal family. Queen Elizabeth II is the great-granddaughter of Bertie; Prince Philip is the great-grandson of Princess Alice and this long family case history makes it clear that a pattern of reaction and counter-reaction persists. We can still, nearly 175 years on, see the effects of Victoria and Albert's attempt to make sure their children were a credit to them.

The details of the Kensington System were obsessive and flouted the finest educational thinking of the period. Rousseau, Froebel and Pestalozzi believed children needed freedom – freedom to play, freedom to think and freedom to grow. Froebel and Pestalozzi were theorists of education, who influenced Maria Montessori in setting up the kindergarten system. The social philosopher Rousseau is most famous for his treatise *The Social Contract* (1762).

There is no evidence that Conroy studied any writer on childcare and he dreamed up the Kensington system whose main aim was denying Victoria freedom so that he and the Duchess could control every aspect of her life. Victoria was never allowed to be apart from either her mother or her governess. Lehzen could not let the girl out of her sight until the Duchess took over at night-time, when Victoria had to sleep in her mother's room.

She could never see anyone unless either her mother or Lehzen was present. One detail shows the petty nature of the dependency that the system tried to foster: Victoria was never allowed to walk downstairs without holding either her mother's hand or Lehzen's.

Conroy wanted to keep Victoria isolated from other children and her mother complied with this. Somewhat grotesquely, while Victoria did not see much of other children, she was given a collection of dolls. Eventually there were 132 of them, many of which represented characters from books, plays and operas. They lived in boxes. Most historians have suggested that playing with these dolls must have damaged Victoria because they could hardly replace real child companions, but the point is debatable.

Stephen MacKeith, who was at one time chief psychiatrist to the British army, studied children who create imaginary worlds, often using dolls to people them. These 'paracosms' were sometimes obsessive and often complicated. The Brontë children had one called 'Gondal' and one of MacKeith's subjects had developed a railway system spanning the globe, with stations even in the middle of the oceans. These 'paracosms' allowed emotionally vulnerable children to create a world they could control and, MacKeith argued, Victoria did not stop playing with these dolls until she was fourteen or even fifteen. It may be that they helped her to cope with the problems caused by the Kensington System. Her only companion of her own age was Victoire, Conroy's daughter, and she did not like her.

While keeping her under constant surveillance, Conroy and the Duchess wanted the public to be aware of Victoria and to realise that the likely heir was thriving, so the little girl was quite often taken for walks in the gardens of Kensington Palace. Anyone who wanted to could observe the spectacle of the happy child from afar.

A system that required a nanny to be present day and night created dependency but not the dependency the Duchess and Conroy wanted to achieve. Soon 'dear, good Lehzen' became more important to Victoria than any other adult, including her own mother. Moreover, far from being a malleable underling, Lehzen encouraged Victoria to distrust Conroy, her mother and her mother's friends. Unlike most of the others who surrounded Victoria, Lehzen had no ambitions of her own other than to do the best for her charge.

Victoria took to calling Lehzen 'Mother' and 'dearest Daisy' in private. Later, the Queen wrote: 'She knew me from six months old and from my fifth to eighteenth year devoted all her care and energies to me with the most wonderful abnegation of self, not even taking one day's holiday. I adored though I was greatly in awe of her.' Indeed, as Victoria's diary entry notes: Lehzen was 'the most affectionate, devoted, attached, and disinterested friend I have.' She was strict, but used no corporal punishment according to the accounts of the royal household. Girls were not flogged, but they were often smacked; Lehzen was exceedingly liberal. Tensions in Kensington Palace grew as Conroy and the Duchess realised the Princess loved Lehzen deeply.

In 1827, Victoria became second in line to the throne. Conroy now complained not very subtly that the Princess should not be surrounded by commoners and so the King agreed to make him a knight commander of the Hanoverian Order. For once, 'Dear good' Lehzen became annoyed and even the self-obsessed George IV could see this could be damaging and so, to placate her, he decided to honour Lehzen, too. He was canny enough to make her a Baroness of Hanover, rather than give her an English title. She is the only royal nanny ever to have been ennobled.

Curiously, while Conroy and the Duchess controlled every detail of Victoria's life, they accepted the King's right to appoint a tutor. Despite his own frivolities, George IV chose a very traditional

PARVVLE PATRISSA, PATRIÆ VIRTVTIS ET HÆRES
ESTO, NIHIL MAIVS MAXIMVS ORBIS HABET.
GNATVM VIX POSSVNT COELVM ET NATVRA DEDISSE,
HVIVS QVEM PATRIS, VICTVS HONORET HONOS.
ÆQVATO TANTVM, TANTI TV FACTA PARENTIS,
VOTA HOMINVM, VIX QVO PROGREDIANTVR, HABENT
VINCITO, VICISTI, QVOT REGES PRISCVS ADORAT
ORBIS, NEC TE QVI VINCERE POSSIT, ERIT. *Ricard Morysini Car.*

A portrait of a young Edward VI, decorated in full royal garb. The formality of the picture does not hint at the vulnerability of the young royal, who was plagued by ill-health throughout his short life. © Getty Images Ltd

James I, his wife Anne of Denmark and their children. © Getty Images Ltd

Appearing older than their years, the children of Charles I. © Getty Images Ltd

George III with his wife, Queen Charlotte, and a mere six of their fifteen children. No other British King and Queen have succeeded in having a larger number of legitimate offspring.
© Getty Images Ltd

Queen Victoria and Prince Albert had breakfast with their family nearly every day and were always involved in planning their activities. © Getty Images Ltd

Each royal child had his or her own cradle. © Lawrence Gresswell

ABOVE AND BELOW The fort at Osborne House on the Isle of Wight where Victoria's children and grandchildren played. © Lawrence Gresswell

LEFT David and George, the eldest sons of George V. © Getty Images Ltd

RIGHT If George V's sons didn't have their kilts shipshape, their father was apt to reprimand them. © Getty Images Ltd

The former King Edward VIII pictured with his love Wallis Simpson in 1952.

ABOVE A relaxed shot of the young Princess Elizabeth and her sister Princess Margaret, accompanied by the customary canine comrade. © Press Association

BELOW No psychologist could fault the loving eye contact the women of the royal family made with Princess Elizabeth's two oldest children. © Press Association

Princess Diana plays with son William; both appear radiant and content. © Getty Images Ltd

character. George Davys had been a student at Oxford and was the vicar of a small parish in Lincolnshire. He taught the Princess French, German (which she hardly needed to be taught since she spoke it every day with Lehzen), some Latin, English, geography, mathematics, politics, art and music. She liked history, especially. Meanwhile, Lehzen taught her dancing and deportment.

Kensington Palace was a hive of power games. In 1828, Lehzen's best friend, Baroness Spath, was dismissed on Conroy's orders. It was rumoured that she had seen 'familiarities' between him and the Duchess. As she had known the Duchess for years, she dared warn her of the risks of being too close to Conroy; almost at once, Spath was taken in by Victoria's half-sister Feodora, now married to a German prince. It is likely that Victoria was upset by these changes.

In January 1830, William's wife, Adelaide, decided the family had had enough of Conroy and wrote to the Duchess, saying that it 'was the general wish' that she should not allow Conroy 'too much influence over you but keep him in his place'. Adelaide did not refer to any incident Spath might have witnessed but felt it was enough to point out that Conroy had never lived 'in court circles' and so could not be expected to behave properly. Adelaide was relatively tactful and added that, 'In the family it is noticed that you are cutting yourself off more and more from them with your child.' She blamed Conroy and said the royal family 'believe he tried to remove anything which may obstruct his influence so that he may exercise his power alone and alone too one day reap the fruits of his influence'. The Irish upstart hardly had the rank to prevent the royal family from communicating with Victoria. Incensed, the Duchess showed the letter to Conroy. The result was violent hostility between the two of them and William and Adelaide; Victoria was caught in the crossfire.

Feeling under pressure, the Duchess and Conroy invited the Bishops of London and Lincoln to meet Victoria and examine how well she was being educated. With what seems like mock humility, the Duchess wished to know if 'the course hitherto pursued in her education has been the best, if not where has it been erroneous'. She reminded the Bishops that, as Victoria was just shy of six months old when her father died, 'her sole care and charge devolved to me'. The Duchess had been a stranger among the English and had denied herself the comforts of returning to Germany, 'rejecting all those feelings of home and kindred that divided my heart'. She presented herself as very much the martyr. Victoria passed the examination triumphantly and her fine performance strengthened her mother and Conroy's position against the court.

Around this time, Lehzen slipped a copy of the genealogy of the House of Hanover into one of Victoria's lesson books. It was the first time that Victoria realised she would probably be the next monarch. After a pause, she is reported to have said, 'I will be good' before adding that she now understood why Lehzen had 'urged me to learn so much, even Latin. My cousins, Augustus and Mary, never did, but you told me that Latin is the foundation of the English grammar and of all the elegant expressions.' The revelation that she might become Queen also prompted Victoria to write in the margin of the book: 'I cried much on learning it and ever deplored this contingency.'

Lehzen reminded her that she would not succeed if Adelaide had children. Victoria was not disappointed and said, according to Lehzen: 'For I know the love Aunt Adelaide bears me and how fond she is of the children.'

Victoria was controlled, but not always confined to Kensington Palace. Her mother sometimes took her on outings, including one to Ramsgate, where a writer admired the Princess, who was 'in all the redolence of youth and health'. Victoria was wearing 'a plain straw bonnet, with a white ribbon round the crown; a coloured muslin frock, looking gay and cheerful, and as pretty a pair of shoes on as pretty a pair of feet as I ever remember to have seen from China to Kamschatka'. The Princess was playing on the beach with her mother and William Wilberforce. For once, Conroy does not seem to have been around.

Victoria's mother had ignored Adelaide's criticisms of Conroy. When William was crowned in 1831, he wanted to punish the

Duchess and announced that, although Victoria was his heir, she was not going to walk immediately behind him in the procession, as tradition required. Furious, the Duchess refused to attend the Coronation. Victoria was deeply disappointed.

Almost as soon as William was crowned, the family quarrelled again. The King was now sixty-five years old and might die, while Victoria was under eighteen and still a minor. Her mother wanted to be named Regent, but William resisted because he feared Conroy would have too much influence. The Duchess and Conroy retaliated by putting intense pressure on Victoria to appoint Conroy as her private secretary and treasurer. Victoria was just ten years old at the time, but she did not sign the paper they put in front of her.

Victoria's grandmother learned of these quarrels and wrote to the Duchess when the child celebrated her eleventh birthday: 'It is only by the blessing of God that all the fine qualities He has put into that young soul can be kept pure and untarnished. How well I can sympathise with the feelings of anxiety that must possess you when that time comes!'

I was struck by Victoria's use of the word 'anxiety' in a very modern sense when she spoke of Bertie; here, even earlier, we find a similar use. Freud did not invent neurotic anxiety.

The Duchess had told her mother that she was afraid her daughter would take some revenge when she took up the throne. When she later allowed Parton to publish this exchange, Victoria did not mind the public being reminded of the problems her mother caused her.

By July 1834, hostilities between the King, Queen Adelaide and Kensington Palace became so raw that the Duchess wrote to Stockmar for help. She suggested he mediate between the warring members of the family. Stockmar's memoirs show that he thought he could do nothing – 'How can my words help when nobody wishes to change and nobody wishes to give in?' The difficulty lay largely in the personality of Conroy: he might be devoted to the Duchess, Stockmar tactfully noted, but he was also 'vain, ambitious, most sensitive and most hot-tempered'. Stockmar refused to blame Lehzen as the Duchess wanted him to and insisted the problem lay 'in the innate personality of the Princess, in the inner circumstances at Kensington and in the behaviour of Sir John to the Princess'. He blamed Conroy for making himself 'the sole regulator of the whole machine'. It was clear that 'every day the Princess grew up, she became resentful of what must have looked to her as an exercise of undue control over herself'.

Parliament seems to have been unaware of the family rows. We have seen the intrigues surrounding the appointment of Regents who would take over should the monarch be either a minor or inca- pacitated. In 1831 Parliament had named the Duchess as Regent, if the King should die before Victoria was eighteen. William was not pleased, especially as the Duchess did not let him see his niece as often as he wished. Now that Parliament had approved her as would-be Regent, the Duchess offended the King by moving into the rooms in Kensington Palace that he had reserved for himself. She also snubbed his illegitimate children and sniped that William was 'an oversexed oaf'.

When Victoria was old enough to need a lady-in-waiting, Stockmar suggested the Duchess discuss possible candidates with her daughter. The Duchess was in no mood for compromise, however, and appointed Lady Flora Hastings. Stockmar foresaw trouble, and he was right.

In 1835, the Duchess again wrote her daughter a stern letter, demanding she have a less intimate relationship with Lehzen. Victoria's half-sister Feodora was appalled and wrote to Queen Adelaide, asking her and the King to do whatever they could to protect the governess. Though the Duchess and Conroy had day- to-day control of Victoria, the heir was now sixteen years old and, like Elizabeth I three centuries earlier, very determined. Lehzen clung on at the Palace and, when Victoria became seriously ill, it was she and not her mother who nursed her devotedly for five weeks.

Family tensions boiled over at a formal dinner in 1836 when William IV said he intended to live until Victoria was of age, as her mother and her entourage were not to be trusted. The Duchess was predictably outraged. After the dinner, she scolded Victoria bitterly in the tapestry room at Windsor because the King had drunk his niece's health, an incident to which we shall return later.

Leopold could have been a calming influence, but he was now King of Belgium and sided with his sister against the other King in London. William IV and Queen Adelaide had decided it was time to dangle Victoria in front of possible husbands. They invited the Prince of Orange and his sons to visit as the Oranges were always ready to tie the knot with a future British monarch. Leopold and the Duchess at once suggested to Prince Albert of Saxe-Coburg that he should visit, too. William IV knew Leopold was keen on Albert marrying Victoria and told the Duchess that he would not receive the young man at court and the Saxe-Coburgs should not stay at Kensington Palace.

At this, Leopold had an epistolary hissy fit and wrote to the Duchess:

> The relations of the King and Queen therefore are to come in shoals and rule the land when your relations are forbidden. Really and truly I never heard anything like it and I hope that it will a little rouse your spirit now that slavery is abolished in the British Colonies. I do not comprehend why your lot alone should be so kept a white little slavey in England for the pleasure of a Court who never bought you, as I am not aware of their having gone to any expense on that head or the King even having spent a sixpence for your existence.

He ranted on that he expected that he would not be allowed to visit England and he was sure that the King would be 'excessively rude to your relations'.

Victoria was now in the midst of conflict between her mother and Conroy, William and Adelaide, and her beloved uncle Leopold. No wonder she clung to Lehzen. After she attended a ball on 13 May 1836, Victoria gave Leopold a bitchy account of the Oranges. Both the boys were 'very plain and look heavy, dull, and frightened and are not at all prepossessing. So much for the Oranges, dear Uncle.'

Victoria's letters at the age of fifteen show her to be very competent and a credit to Lehzen and her other teachers. In the 1880s, Stockmar's son edited his father's memoirs and included a section where Stockmar accused the Duchess and Conroy of spreading rumours that Victoria was 'mentally undeveloped'. These stories were absurd to anyone who met Victoria or had even received a letter from her, but Lord Melbourne, the Prime Minister, was worried she might not be fit for the throne – he had not been able to judge her capabilities for himself. Stockmar's memoirs claimed the Duchess and Conroy tried to 'shut up' Victoria until she signed the long-drafted document guaranteeing Conroy the job of private secretary when she became Queen. Conroy told the Duchess to 'keep her under duress until she had extorted this engagement from her'. The Duchess, Stockmar claims, was too timid to protest and Victoria too spirited to agree. But the plot was high treason, he added.

Thirty years later, Charles Fulke Greville, who had been a Clerk of the Council between 1821 and 1852, published an account of this period. Queen Victoria 'attacked him most savagely', according to Stockmar's son. In a letter to Theodore Martin of October 1874, the Queen accused Greville of 'dreadful indiscretions and disgracefully bad taste'. Stockmar's son points out, however, that Victoria never claimed Greville lied, only that he was guilty of 'many derelictions'. The Queen did not behave impeccably herself as she threatened to reveal damaging details about Greville's own history and character.

Victoria also added notes to the manuscript of the Kensington System, in which she scribbled 'Untrue', for example, at the point where it claimed Conroy had mortgaged his own properties to guarantee her mother's debts. Though emotionally abusive, her childhood did not cripple Victoria; she seems to have been among those intelligent children who could make some sense of why they were badly treated and so she coped better. In addition, she had two further advantages: Lehzen was a stable presence and the dolls had allowed Victoria to 'act out' some of her anxieties.

The intellectual Prince

Victoria's future husband also had a childhood riddled with tensions. Prince Albert was a minor Prince of a minor German duchy. In 1824, when he was just five, his mother was exiled from court. Louise of Saxe-Gotha-Altenburg had finally had enough of her husband's endless affairs and decided that she herself would be unfaithful. She then secretly married her lover, Alexander von Hanstein, the Count of Pölzig and Beiersdorf. When their marriage was discovered, she never saw her children again and died of cancer at the age of thirty.

Hoping to give the boy stability as well as a good education, Albert's father, the Ernst, Duke of Saxe-Coburg-Gotha, appointed Christoph Florschütz his son's Prince-instructor. When Albert was ten, Florschütz introduced him to philosophy – it made great demands of him but he coped. At seventeen, Albert and his brother Ernest visited Brussels. Their uncle Leopold had arranged for them to be taught by a remarkable man: Alphonse Quetelet. He had started as an astronomer, but, after a few years, turned his attention from the stars to statistics. Quetelet had the original idea of using probability theory in social science and dreamed of a 'social physics' that discovered possible relationships between crime and climate, crime and poverty, education and excessive drinking.

We still use one of Quetelet's ideas today, as he devised a simple measure for classifying people's weight relative to the ideal weight for their height. Many contemporary texts on health refer to the Body Mass Index, or Quetelet Index. Quetelet transformed young Albert into a would-be polymath, who could discuss philosophy, history, architecture and science with the best in those fields. The minor Prince went on to the University of Bonn, where two of his teachers were major intellectuals: the philosopher Fichte and the poet Schlegel. Fichte had what now seems a far-fetched ambition: he wanted to find a philosophical basis for the personality of God. He impressed Albert, however, who remained interested in metaphysics all his life.

What Albert did not realise was that he himself was being studied. Leopold wanted to know whether the young man would make a good husband for his niece and so he asked his trusted adviser Stockmar to assess Albert. When the plan was first mooted in 1836, Stockmar told Leopold that he needed more time to make a fair judgement.

When Albert and Victoria were seventeen years old, the Prince came to England with his father and brother. Both teenagers knew that some members of their family wanted them to marry. Albert was a little shocked by the manners of the English court and its tendency to 'party', as we would put it now, as frivolity did not come naturally to him. He also tended to fall asleep around nine-thirty in the evening, so when he had to attend a great dinner and 'then a concert which lasted till one o'clock. You can well imagine I had many hard battles to fight against sleepiness during these late entertainments.'

Victoria does not seem to have noticed Albert's habit of dozing off. She recorded her own impressions: 'The Prince was at that time much shorter than his brother, already very handsome, but very stout. He was most amiable, natural, unaffected, and merry; full of interest in everything; playing on the piano; drawing; in short, constantly occupied. He always paid the greatest attention to all he saw.'

Her cousin seemed very serious, Victoria wrote, remembering 'how intently' Albert listened 'to the sermon preached in St Paul's on the occasion of the service attended by the children of the different charity schools. It is indeed rare to see a Prince, not yet seventeen years of age, bestowing such earnest attention on a sermon.' By the stern standards of Fichte, however, the sermon was candy floss. Albert returned to Germany unsure as to the impression he had made on Victoria, however, and was afraid he would spend his life as a minor German Prince.

There are many instances of individuals somehow managing to live until a birthday or an anniversary that matters to them. William IV wanted to avoid the Duchess becoming Regent and clung onto life until Victoria turned eighteen. Less than a month later, on 20 June 1837, the King died in the middle of the night. At 6 a.m., as the Archbishop of Canterbury saluted the new monarch, Victoria 'maintained her self-possession; but on hearing these tremendous words, the realisation of so many hopes and fond imaginings, she threw her arms about her mother's neck and sobbed,' Parton wrote. But, in a few moments, the Queen recovered herself and remained composed when her uncle, the Duke of Sussex (who had once terrified her), knelt in front of her: 'Do not kneel, Uncle,' she said, 'for I am still Victoria, your niece.'

Victoria got down to business at once. She held a Privy Council, interviewed a number of ministers and officials, wrote four long letters and, after dinner, appointed Dr James Clark as the first of her physicians. Throughout her life, she had over 200 physicians, though many hardly got to see the Queen, let alone treat her.

Victoria may have thrown her arms around her mother but she was not about to allow the Duchess, let alone the Kensington System, to rule her life any longer. One of the Queen's first commands was to have her bed removed from her mother's room and insist she should be allowed an hour a day by herself. Conroy was banned from her apartments. Victoria's relations with her mother remained cold and distant for the next twenty-three years. The new Queen knew how to offer reward and obtain revenge. Lehzen now became more powerful; tradesmen needed her signature before their bills could be paid. Conroy was furious.

As soon as she was Queen, Albert wrote to 'his dearest cousin' on 26 June 1837:

> I hope that your reign may be long, happy, and glorious, and that your efforts may be rewarded by the thankfulness and love of your subjects. May I pray you to think likewise sometimes to your cousins in Bonn, and to continue to them that kindness you favored them with till now. Be assured that our minds are always with you.

Conscious he was just a minor Prince, Albert added humbly: 'I will not be indiscreet and abuse your time.' Victoria does not seem to have answered this letter, which worried Albert a good deal. Parton claimed: 'The only excuse the Queen can make for herself is in the fact that the change from the secluded life at Kensington to the independence of her position as Queen Regnant put all ideas of marriage out of her mind.'

But Leopold had not abandoned his plans for Victoria's marriage and now demanded an up-to-date report on Albert. Stockmar had to accompany the Prince on a walking tour of Switzerland and northern Italy and reported that Albert had 'great powers of observation, was prudent and showed self-control'. The nineteen-year-old was fit to marry Victoria, but, before anything could be done, there was another drama which further soured relations between the Queen and her mother.

Early in 1839, the companion who had been foisted on Victoria – Lady Flora Hastings – complained of pain in her lower abdomen. Sir James Clark, the Queen's physician, said he could not diagnose what was wrong without examining her. When Flora refused to allow him to do so, he assumed she was pregnant. Lehzen, who was now so influential that she discussed Flora with the Prime Minister, Lord Melbourne, told him that Flora was 'with child'. On 2 February, the Queen wrote that she suspected Conroy to be the father. When Flora finally let the royal doctors examine her, they discovered she had cancer of the liver. Conroy and Flora's brother attacked the Queen and her 'fellow conspirator' Lehzen for besmirching Flora's good name. Meanwhile, Leopold saw the crisis as an opportunity: he instructed Albert to go to England without waiting to be invited.

Three years had passed since the cousins had first seen one another. Parton described a classic example of love at not quite first sight; when Albert arrived at Windsor on 10 October 1839, Victoria met him. She was dressed 'in evening attire, and invested with the dignity which the very title of Queen seems to carry with it. Nor was the change in him less striking in a maiden's eyes. The Prince had grown tall, symmetrical, and handsome.' 'Symmetrical' meant that Albert had become less stout; he had also grown a becoming moustache.

Albert had 'a gentleness of expression, and a smile of peculiar sweetness, with a look of thought and intelligence in his clear blue eye, and fair, broad forehead, which conciliated everyone who looked upon him'. Parton finished with a flourish: 'He was the very Prince of romance – just the hero wanted for the dazzling fiction of which Victoria was the gentle heroine.'

Though still angry with her mother, Victoria took Albert to visit her the night he arrived, but there was a comic hitch. Albert did not have the proper clothes to attend a formal dinner and etiquette 'could not be dispensed with', Parton added. We do not know where Albert ate that night.

Four days later, Victoria told Lord Melbourne that she had made up her mind to marry Albert. 'You will be much more comfortable,' he said somewhat patronisingly, 'for a woman cannot stand alone for any time in whatever position she may be.' Melbourne seems to have forgotten that Elizabeth I managed perfectly well without a man by her side or in her bed.

Albert was very much the social inferior and was not told of Victoria's decision until the next day, when he got back from hunting. He gave his grandmother, who was, of course, also Victoria's grandmother, a romantic description:

The Queen sent for me alone to her room and declared to me in a genuine outburst of love and affection that I had gained her whole heart, and would make her intensely happy if I would make her the sacrifice of sharing her life with her, for she said she looked on it as a sacrifice. The only thing which troubled her was that she did not think that she was worthy of me. The joyous openness of manner in which she told me this quite enchanted me, and I was quite carried away by it. She is really most good and amiable, and I am quite sure Heaven has not given me into evil hands, and that we shall be happy together. Since that moment Victoria does whatever she fancies I should wish or like, and we talk together a great deal about our future life, which she promises me to make as happy as possible.

As soon as Albert left, Victoria recorded her feelings in her diary: 'How I will strive to make him feel as little as possible the great sacrifice he has made! I told him it was a great sacrifice on his part, but he would not allow it.'

That afternoon, she wrote to her uncle Leopold, who had engineered the match after all:

> My mind is quite made up. The warm affection he showed me on learning this gave me great pleasure. He seems perfection, and I think that I have the prospect of very great happiness before me. I love him more than I can say, and shall do everything in my power to render this sacrifice (for such in my opinion it is) as small as I can. He seems to have great tact – a very necessary thing in his position. These last few days have passed like a dream to me, and I am so much bewildered by it all that I know hardly how to write; but I do feel very happy.

Had she not had a country to reign over, Victoria might have made a successful romantic novelist. Naturally, Uncle Leopold was delighted.

On 10 February 1840, the couple married at the Chapel Royal in St James's. Victoria wore a white satin dress trimmed with orange blossoms, very large diamond earrings and a diamond necklace. Albert was in the uniform of a British field-marshal – promotion was rapid if you married the Queen – and wore the collar and star of the Order of the Garter. They went to Windsor Castle for their honeymoon.

The marriage worked well, both emotionally and sexually, though Victoria would often complain that women were not to be regarded as 'breeding rabbits'. When she was four months pregnant, an eighteen-year-old barman, Edward Oxford, fired two pistols at her carriage while she was driving with Albert. On 11 June 1840, *The Times* reported:

> The Prince who, it would seem, had heard the whistling of the ball, turned his head in the direction from which the report came, and

Her Majesty at the same instant rose up in the carriage, but Prince Albert as suddenly pulled her down by his side. The man then drew from behind his back a second pistol, which he discharged after the carriage.

Oxford was charged with High Treason. His attempt was the first of seven on Victoria's life. She was sturdy, however, and nine months and eleven days after her wedding, she gave birth to her first child, a girl who was called Victoria and nicknamed 'Princessy'. Two days later, Albert wrote to his father that his wife 'is as well as if nothing had happened. She sleeps well, has a good appetite, and is extremely quiet and cheerful.'

Victoria was enchanted by her husband's tender loving care, which she compared somewhat remarkably to that of a good mother – the mother she felt she had not had. There could not have been 'a kinder, wiser, or more judicious nurse', she added. When Princessy was born, Albert persuaded his wife to make peace with her own mother, though the relationship always remained strained. In 1842, he also persuaded her to send Lehzen away with a generous pension. His real opinion of the governess was vitriolic; he called her a 'crazy, stupid intriguer with a lust for power'. Once she was out of the way, Albert had no rival for Victoria's attention.

His education had made Albert a formidable reader. He studied what the best minds in Europe had said about how to bring up children. Jean-Jacques Rousseau, Froebel and Pestalozzi all emphasised the need for children to have freedom. Victoria ought to have been in favour of this after her own experiences, but it turned out to be not quite so simple.

Rousseau and mother's milk

In *Emile* (1762), Rousseau provided ideas on every aspect of childcare. He argued against swaddling and that mothers should not farm their own children out to wet nurses. No one has ever made greater claims for the magic of a mother's milk. According to Rousseau, if mothers fed their own children, 'morals will reform themselves, nature's sentiments will be awakened in every heart, the state will be re-peopled.' Victoria, however, had wet nurses for her family.

Rousseau praised Locke's ideas of toughening children 'against the intemperance of season, climates, elements; against hunger, thirst, fatigue'. They needed to learn from experience. Rousseau gave an example of a father who took his son out to fly kites and immediately turned what should have been fun into a test. The father asked his boy to work out where the kite was by looking only at its shadow.

'We have made an active and thinking being,' Rousseau said, before adding: 'It remains for us, in order to complete the man, only to make a loving and feeling being – that is to say, to perfect reason by sentiment.' Without any evidence, he then argued that children could not understand complex human emotions or abstract concepts until they reached their teenage years. The leading child psychologist of the mid-twentieth century, Jean Piaget, who headed up an institute in Geneva named after Rousseau, made the same claims but with some evidence at least. Rousseau's theories could be published in Calvinist Geneva, but not in Catholic France because Rome made children recite the Catechism. Rousseau argued this was mere parroting since the child had no idea what abstract concepts such as God meant.

Albert also read the radical Swiss Pestalozzi, whose most famous work was *How Gertrude Teaches Her Children*, and Froebel, who developed the first kindergarten. Both stressed the need for children to feel free and freedom meant not being constantly badgered by their over-anxious parents. Victoria felt she had been controlled by a mother who had not really loved her, and also by Conroy. She did not react by letting her children run wild and free, however, but by providing them with, as she saw it, love as well as control. Victoria had never been convinced that her mother truly loved her and wanted the best for her, but she and Albert did love and want the best for their children. That changed everything.

Princessy was unlikely to inherit the throne and so she was put under less pressure than her eldest brother, Bertie. The Queen was often amused by her. On 6 October 1841, Sarah Lyttelton noted, 'The Princess hid her head under her nurse's arm yesterday and that the Queen peeped round to see why she did it' – 'HRH was detected in that safe corner sucking her necklace which is forbidden. Then the Queen said "Oh fie naughty! Naughty!" Upon which the child looked slyly at her and held up her mouth to be kissed. It is lucky another is coming.' Lady Sarah then added the immortal phrase quoted at the beginning of this book: 'The Queen is like all young mothers, *exigeante*.'

Princessy could have perfect toddler tantrums. She kept on shouting, 'Wipe my eyes!' all the time when she was 'roaring', which presumably means when she was crying. The baby also showed 'morbid love of one nursery maid'. Lady Sarah told her daughter-in-law that Madame de Maintenon said that mothers who complained about the slow progress of their daughters 'should always be sweet to the children and pray for them. God would see the rest.'

Princessy was clever, though rarely placid. On 7 May 1842, when her daughter was just over seventeen months old, the Queen came into Lady Sarah's bedroom just in her dressing gown because she wanted the governess to look at 'the most lovely of rainbows'. Lady Sarah was delighted but the small Princess howled and seemed to have 'unconquerable horror'.

A few months later, Lady Sarah noted:

My little Princess is all gracefulness and prettiness, very fat and active, running about and talking a great deal. She is oversensitive and affectionate and rather irritable in temper at present. But it looks like a pretty mind only very unfit for roughing it through a hard life which hers may be.

When Lady Sarah's daughter-in-law wrote to ask how to cope with her own baby's crying fits, Lady Sarah was sympathetic:

I can't wonder you're uneasy about them – *j'ai passé par là*. But there is no occasion, believe me, to suppose they mean bad temper at her age. As to checking them I fancy taking very little notice of them is not a bad thing. I own I am somewhat against punishments; they wear out so soon and one is never sure they are understood by the child as belonging to the naughtiness.

It is a pity Lady Sarah never dared say that to the Queen and Prince Albert.

Naughtiness was always a danger in the nursery. On 10 October 1842, Lady Sarah told her daughter-in-law: 'The Queen said to Princessy, "Two little girls are coming to see baby tomorrow."' The 'two little girls' were the daughters of Lady Dunmore. When Princessy heard that:

> She got upon tiptoe put her head down on one side and with the most extreme slyness of manner answered, 'Naughty.'
> 'No, no,' said the Queen, 'they are very good little girls.'
> 'Kying,' persisted Princessy.
> 'No, no, they never cry,' the Queen said.

Lady Sarah was struck by the 'drollery' of Princessy's questions, 'so meant to be joking and malicious'. She felt the two-year-old Princess was more like a four-year-old child. Later that week, when the six-year-old Charley Edgecumbe came to see her, Princessy was all 'coquetterie, hiding behind the curtain for him to find her – holding out her frock and dancing up and down before him'.

Albert's way with the children enchanted his wife. Lady Sarah wrote that it was not every 'Papa who would have such patience and kindness' and that patience often got 'a flashing look of gratitude from the Queen'.

The couple's next child was born on 9 November 1841. Bertie would test their patience, but neither his father nor his mother could ever see that they made unreasonable demands of him because they never doubted either that they loved him or that they wanted the best for him. Albert drew up complex rotas specifying the duties of every servant who came near the children.

On 10 February 1843, when Bertie was only fifteen months old, Lady Sarah noted that he 'talks much more English than he did though he is not articulate like his sister. He understands a little French and says a few words but is altogether backward in language.' She thought him very intelligent, though there were a 'few passions and stampings occasionally'. But Bertie soon learned his manners at least, as he 'bows and offers his hand beautifully besides saluting à la militaire'. He was supposed to be fluent in at least three languages – German, English and French – by the time he was four, but, while 'Princessy gets on very well', Lady Sarah noted, Bertie was still not perfectly trilingual.

Prince Albert hated the way he had been treated and treated his own sons very differently. This, in turn, would affect the way George V treated his own children, which contributed to Edward VIII's decision to abdicate.

Albert and Victoria's third child, Alice, was born in April 1843. Her birth made up the royal couple's mind to buy a larger palace as they felt Buckingham Palace did not have enough room for nurseries. In 1845, they bought Osborne House on the Isle of Wight, which Albert inevitably improved. There, the children could have sufficient space, though their bedrooms were furnished very sparsely and had little heating. They were taught unprincely skills, such as cooking, gardening and carpentry.

As she grew up, the outside world fascinated Alice. She visited tenants on the Balmoral estate and once escaped from her governess at the chapel at Windsor to sit in a public pew (she later explained that she wanted to understand ordinary people). In 1854, her mother took her on a tour of London hospitals, where soldiers who had been wounded in the Crimean War were being treated. Alice became fascinated by Florence Nightingale's work and this would have effects a century later.

Bertie and his bumps

Victoria and Albert had six more children, all but one of whom
married kings, princes and princesses, so that they were linked with
every European royal family. The Queen and Albert spent time
with their family – they had breakfast with them nearly every day
and were always involved in planning their activities. When one
governess wanted to resign because her mother was seriously ill,
Grace Greenwood wrote:

> The Queen, who had been much pleased with her, would not hear
> of her making this sacrifice, but said, in a tone of the most gentle
> sympathy, 'Go at once to your mother, child; stay with her as long
> as she needs you, and then come back to us. I will keep your place
> for you. Prince Albert and I will hear the children's lessons; so in any
> event let your mind be at rest in regard to your pupils.'

Victoria loved her eldest daughter but that did not mean she
let her get away with much as Princessy grew older. Greenwood
explained that when Princessy was 'a wilful girl of about thirteen,
sitting on the front seat, [she] seemed disposed to be rather familiar
and coquettish with some young officers of the escort'. Victoria
gave her daughter disapproving looks but Princessy deliberately
dropped her handkerchief over the side of the carriage. When 'two
or three young heroes sprang from their saddles to return it to her
fair hand, the awful voice of royalty stayed them. "Stop, gentlemen!"
exclaimed the Queen, "leave it just where it lies. Now, my daughter,
get down from the carriage and pick up your handkerchief."' The
Queen was not about to allow her daughter to become too grand or
too wilful – 'It was hard, but it was wholesome.' Greenwood then
added a cultural quip. 'How many American mothers would be
equal to such a piece of Spartan discipline?' Despite this, Princessy
had a far easier time than her brother.

Spartan discipline did not improve Bertie, and Albert made
the mistake of seeking advice from Stockmar, who wrote pomp-
ous memos in which he recommended the boy 'should be the

repository of all the moral and intellectual qualities by which the [state] is held together and under the guidance of which it advances in the great path of civilisation'. For a year, Albert and Victoria searched anxiously for the paragon who would turn their son into this splendid repository. When Bertie was eight, they finally chose Henry Birch, who had been captain of the school at Eton and won four university prizes at Cambridge.

Birch was aptly named because he was a disciplinarian and insisted Bertie even had to study on Saturdays. He taught mathematics, geography and English, and appointed suitable experts to give the young Prince lessons in religion, German, French, music, drawing and writing. No child in the land was driven harder than poor Bertie.

It is a sign of the obsessive pressure that Albert placed on his son and tutor that Birch had to send him a report every day. Birch complained that Bertie was 'extremely disobedient, impertinent to his masters and unwilling to submit to discipline'. The child could not concentrate on playing or 'attempt anything new or difficult without losing his temper'. The anxious Birch was trying to please anxious parents and tried both 'severe punishment' – beating Bertie – and also laughing at him. Neither approach worked. At Eton, Birch said, boys 'were formed as much by contact with others as by the precepts of their tutors' but Bertie spent far too much time with adults and found himself 'the centre round which everything seems to move'. He hardly knew any children his own age, apart from Alice and Princessy. His relationship with Alice was especially close.

In January 1852, Birch left Windsor because his mother had grown insane and he needed to look after her; he was replaced by Frederick Gibbs, who was offered the then very generous salary of £1,000 a year. Bertie came to detest Gibbs even more than he did Birch. His new tutor made him work six to seven hours a day, starting at eight every morning. After he had slaved at his books all day, Bertie had to ride, drill and do gymnastics. At the end of each day, the Queen saw that her son hung his head 'and looks at his feet and invariably within a day or two has one of his fits of nervous and unmanageable temper'. Victoria, who had hated being controlled as a girl, was now allowing her own son to be controlled but she never doubted that she loved Bertie and that it was all for his own – and eventually the country's – good. Albert had studied all the philosophers who preached the need for children to be free, but he was too consumed by anxiety – anxiety to do good, anxiety to impress his wife, anxiety to make sure England got a king who would be a credit to the family – to be sensible and moderate.

Three of Gibbs's assistants dared to protest Bertie was being driven too hard, but their arguments made no impression. The librarian at Windsor – Dr Becker, who taught Bertie German – found the courage to warn Albert that Bertie's angry outbursts were the result of frantic attempts to stuff his mind with facts, facts and more facts. Becker recommended a less intense approach and that everyone should respond to Bertie's outbursts of temper with kindness. He said: 'Encouragement of every kind is what the child wants to a high degree. The expression of too high expectations which he finds himself unable to meet discourages him instantly and makes him unhappy.' He also urged Albert and Victoria not to mock their son when he failed. Becker failed in his task and a little sibling rivalry did not help. Princessy was 'a child far above her age' but she 'puts him down by a word or a look', the Queen said. She worried this was damaging 'their mutual affection'.

Victoria and Albert ignored Becker's recommendations and instead turned to Sir George Combe, then Britain's leading phrenologist. The absurd 'science' of phrenology argued that, by studying the bumps on the skull, one could understand the brain within. Poor Bertie had his head shaved so that the specialist could feel every inch of his skull. Combe became pessimistic and told Bertie's parents their boy needed special care to counteract his less-than-satisfactory bumps.

Unfortunately, Prince Albert also felt he had to produce perfect children and devised endless schedules and programmes of improvement for them. He was the first royal to have been very well educated since James I, but good education did not give him good judgement when it came to his family. His behaviour towards them was obsessive and neurotic. It might be argued that it resembled that of many immigrant parents, who are often eager to ensure their children do well in a society they do not quite understand.

In 1860, Queen Victoria wrote in her journal:

> Bertie continues [to be] such an anxiety. I tremble at the thought
> of only three years and a half being before us when he will be of age
> and we can't hold him except by moral power. I try to shut my eyes
> to that terrible moment. He is improving very decidedly – but oh it
> is the improvement of such a poor or still more idle intellect.

The use of the word 'anxiety' by the Queen is again oddly modern.

Predictably, sometimes the most acute conflicts between royal parents and their offspring came when the children were teenagers and Bertie is a notable example. After being battered by this over-intense education, he was sent to Cambridge University, where he exasperated his tutors. The only lectures that he attended regularly were those given by Charles Kingsley, author of *Westward Ho!*

The irony was that Bertie was not without talent. Benjamin Disraeli, Victoria's favourite Prime Minister, described him as informed, intelligent and of sweet manner. Bertie displayed not just charm but competence too in 1860 when he was in his late teens and his parents allowed him to visit North America. No Prince of Wales had set foot there since America had won its independence. Bertie went first to Canada. In Montreal, he opened the Victoria Bridge and laid the cornerstone of Parliament Hill, Ottawa. He then travelled to Washington and stayed for three days with the President, James Buchanan, at the White House. He met Henry Wadsworth Longfellow, Ralph Waldo Emerson and Oliver Wendell Holmes.

Bertie handled a delicate mission well, but his parents did not praise him lavishly when he returned home. To put his achievement into context, by the time he was seventeen, George IV had only run up debts. At a similar age, the rather more virtuous Princess Elizabeth had been allowed to make one radio broadcast for the children of Britain, while her son had never carried out one public engagement.

Princessy as a mother

By the time Bertie came back from America, Princessy had married Fritz, the Crown Prince of Prussia. Some of the most touching examples of Victoria's love for her daughter are to be found in the letters they exchanged. Princessy wrote that she had never imagined she could be as happy as she was with her husband. When their first son was born, Fritz would bring him to his wife every morning in his basket. He telegraphed England that 'my baby is lovely and improved every hour'. Four days after Wilhelm was born, the proud parents sent Queen Victoria a lock of his hair. Princessy told her mother that she thought the baby took after her brothers, Bertie and Leopold. 'You need not be afraid I shall be injudiciously fond of him,' Princessy wrote, 'although I do worship him as I do Fritz, Papa and you, though of course all and each in a different way then I feel he is my own and he owes me so much and has cost me so much.'

When Princessy came back to visit England in 1859, she wrote to Fritz: 'I have left my homeland to find paradise with you.' But there was a blot on their paradise: their son, Wilhelm, had a withered arm and would soon become a troubled boy.

It may be useful to compare Wilhelm's childhood with that of a minor, but far more disabled Anglo-Irish aristocrat, Arthur Kavanagh. He was born in 1831 with severely underdeveloped arms and legs. His umbilical cord had somehow become wrapped around his limbs and cut them off, so Arthur was just a 'torso', as he would put it later. His mother Harriet was lucky in that her doctor, Boxwell, was not just familiar with the theories of Pestalozzi but, unlike Prince Albert, he also heeded them. If children were encouraged, they could conquer their handicaps.

Princessy behaved much as one imagines her father would have done had one of his children been handicapped: intensely. She and her husband commissioned the building of a machine which was supposed to straighten Wilhelm's back and improve his bad arm. By the time he was two, the servants were finding it difficult to bring him up properly and the child developed tantrums as bad as Bertie's. Princessy told her mother that she was concerned because her son screamed for hours, making everyone around him tense and distressed.

In England, Princessy and her mother also discussed the more pleasant matter of whom Alice should marry. Victoria said she wanted her children to marry for love, but in practice that meant they had to find a spouse from among the small pool of European royalty who were also Protestants. The Queen asked Princessy to produce a list of eligible princes. Inevitably, this included an Orange but he was obsessed with a Catholic arch-duchess. Princessy also suggested Albert of Russia, but Fritz said his cousin would not do for 'one who deserves the very best', as Alice did.

As a last resort, Princessy suggested Prince Louis of Hesse. He had no money but seemed to be a promising young man. Victoria sent Princessy to inspect the 'goods', as she put it, and to decide whether Louis or his brother Henry was more suit-able. The brothers were invited to Windsor in 1860, ostensibly so they could watch the Ascot Races with the royal family; while they were watching the races, the Queen could be watching them. Both Princes cantered well enough, but Victoria saw how well Louis and Alice got along. They became engaged in April 1861. The Queen persuaded the Prime Minister, Lord Palmerston, to vote Alice a dowry of £30,000. Prince Albert worried about the lack of a decent palace in Hesse and wanted a new one built to his specifica-tions, but the ungrateful Hessians did not wish to pay for this. Alice was unpopular even before she arrived in her new country.

Princessy was not very popular in nearby Prussia either. The Germans saw her as an Englishwoman who did not understand their country, just as the English viewed Albert as a German who did not understand them. Princessy did not endear herself by becoming furious when she found that a Prussian nanny had covered her children with German eiderdowns instead of softer English blankets. The Kaiser got to hear of this and was not pleased.

These cultural clashes came to a head over the question of breastfeeding. The Kaiser ordered Princessy not to breastfeed Wilhelm and her first two children. When finally she was allowed to breastfeed some of her younger children, she loved the experience. 'To have a baby at the breast is the greatest joy of womanhood,' she wrote to her mother. 'I am always overjoyed when she stretches out her little arms to me and shows me in every way how content she feels at my breast.' The Kaiser was opposed to breastfeeding, and once decreed Princessy could only go on holiday if she left her three children behind, 'and turn the baby over to a wet nurse immediately'. Royal children sometimes did not 'belong' to their parents, but to the head of the family.

A year of deaths

With the death of Queen Anne's only son, 1700 had been a year of calamities for the royal family and 1861 would be just as tragic. The Queen Mother had never made up with her daughter but had been allowed to live at Frogmore, a royal residence rarely visited by Victoria. When Victoria's mother fell ill early in 1861, it was young Alice who went to look after her. She played the piano and nursed her grandmother through the final illness. When her mother died, she and Victoria had not really reconciled and the Queen broke down with grief. She relied heavily on Alice, to whom Albert said: 'Go and comfort Mama.' The Queen wrote to Leopold that 'dear good Alice was full of intense tenderness, affection and distress for me'. It is tempting to suggest that Victoria, who had ruled since 1837, felt guilty because she had more or less abandoned her mother who, as far as she was concerned, had failed her in letting Conroy impose the Kensington System.

After his successful trip to America, Bertie wanted to join the army but his parents denied him this, even though the Crimean War had ended and England was at peace. Visiting America had made Bertie more confident. He travelled to Ireland with his parents' permission, but took part in army exercises without telling them that he was doing so. Bertie did not just learn about military manoeuvres, though. While there, some officers smuggled a very willing actress into his tent. Nellie Clifden became the first of Bertie's many lovers.

Unfortunately, a rather stuffy colonel reported the affair to Victoria and Albert. Albert was ill when the news of Bertie's disgraceful behaviour reached Windsor. Nevertheless, he felt that he must rush up to confront his son, who was by then in Cambridge, because it was such a serious crisis: the Prince of Wales could not jolly in bed with trollops. Albert told his son that he was not only breaking his mother's heart but also endangering the monarchy. Already there had been three attempts to assassinate Victoria, Marx and Engels had published *The Communist Manifesto*, and there were agitations in France and Germany. The French royal family had fled to England for safety; England had seen the Chartist riots. Bertie managed to keep his temper, apologised to his father and promised to have nothing more to do with actresses and to reform.

By the time Albert got home to Windsor Castle, he was seriously ill. Over the next three weeks, his condition grew critical and he became so weak that he could hardly talk. On 10 December, Victoria wrote to Princessy, 'Papa had an excellent night' but 'it was very trying to watch and witness' his illness. She was being optimistic. A day later, Albert took a turn for the worse. During her father's illness, Alice remained by his bedside. She sent for Bertie by telegram, without their mother's knowledge, for Victoria had refused to tell her son anything as she blamed him for Albert's illness.

On the morning of 14 December, the Queen asked if Albert was strong enough to give her a kiss. He did so and then fell into a sleep. She left the room 'and sat down on the floor in utter despair'. When she went back, Albert was comatose – 'I took his dear left hand which was already cold though the breathing was quite gentle and I knelt down by him.' Albert took two or three more breaths, 'the hand clasping mine and all, all was over'. The Queen stood up, kissed his forehead and 'called out in a bitter and agonising cry, "Oh my dear Darling!"'

Victoria and Albert each had troubled childhoods and had created a close, cocoon-like marriage to give each other emotional security. Albert's death robbed Victoria of that essential stability and it would have taken a formidable maturity for her to face the pain of his loss calmly, especially perhaps as he had died only a few months after her mother. Now, true sorrow followed on from the guilt when her mother died, shattering her.

In the family, Victoria could still function and dominate, however. Seven months after Albert died, the marriage Princessy had arranged for her sister Alice took place. It was a sombre, very private occasion, in the shadow of their father's death. Alice married Louis of Hesse in the dining room at Osborne House. She was allowed to wear white during the wedding, but, before and after the ceremony, she had to wear mourning black. Ushered in by her four sons, the Queen was screened from the other guests by them. Victoria struggled to hold back the tears, Bertie remained composed, but Arthur and Leopold cried throughout. The Queen wrote to Princessy that the ceremony was 'more of a funeral than a wedding' and told the poet laureate Tennyson that it was 'the saddest day I can remember'.

The honeymoon at Ryde on the Isle of Wight could hardly be jolly in the circumstances and matters grew worse when Victoria decided to visit the couple. In order not to upset her mother, Alice tried not to seem 'too happy'. In this, she failed and her obvious happiness made the Queen jealous of her daughter.

The normal healing process of time did not help Victoria: she could not accept Albert's death and blamed the son she saw as inadequate for it. In her mind, if Bertie's debaucheries had not forced Albert to rush to see him, he would not have died and her life would not have been ruined. She wrote to Princessy that she could never forgive Bertie and 'I never can, or shall, look at him without a shudder'. Naturally, the personal and political consequences of all this were profound. The monarch was never as unpopular as Victoria became in the 1860s when she simply refused to perform what the public saw as her duties.

It is also worth looking at this period in Bertie's life in terms of the life-events theory. He had great success in America; he then lost his virginity and had to cope yet again with his father's recriminations. His grandmother had died shortly before; his father soon followed, and then his mother blamed him for his father's death. Victoria kept a diary in which she wrote up to 2,500 words a day and kept up a correspondence with Princessy. It was a safety valve in which she would have recorded her feelings in great depth. In 1893, however, she told her youngest daughter, Beatrice, to burn many of her letters and diaries. In fact, Beatrice copied all the diaries and edited them while doing so, 'deleting all the bits she knew Grandmama would not have wished preserved. Beatrice then burned the originals. This work occupied her for thirty-nine years,' Alice's daughter, Princess Victoria, wrote in her unpublished recollections.

Beatrice really proved herself a dutiful daughter. It is plausible to imagine the sections Grandmama did not wish to be preserved were full of bitterness, much of it directed towards the unfortunate Bertie. When he finally ascended to the throne in 1901, he recovered the letters his mother had written to Disraeli. Edward VII then had these destroyed also.

There is again a curious parallel with Sigmund Freud, who burned his diaries and letters at least twice in his lifetime and made sure many surviving letters and documents would never be read. The Library of Congress in Washington DC houses nineteen boxes of Freud's papers, which are closed in perpetuity. At least we know how many of his boxes are sealed, however. When it comes to the Royal Archives, we do not even know what documents cannot be read. It is reasonable to suppose some are less-than-loving letters from kings and queens, scolding their children.

Soon after Albert died, Queen Victoria appointed William Gull as one of her physicians. Gull is best known for having identified the condition of anorexia nervosa, but he had previously been in charge of the psychiatric wards at Guy's Hospital. Though he knew about depression, he failed to help the Queen to cope with her own, which lasted for over ten years. Both Disraeli and Gladstone urged her to come out of what could almost be called hibernation and to resume her duties, but she refused. The Queen was lucky, however, as the Victorian press was somewhat willing to respect her privacy.

Eventually, Victoria was persuaded to give her people some trifle to show that she still cared for them. The trifle was that she permitted the publication of her *Highland Journals* in 1868. The diary, Greenwood noted naïvely, 'exhibits to us the picture of a happy family, always delighted to escape from the trammelling etiquette and absurd splendors of their rank, and capable of being pleased with those natural pleasures which are accessible to most of mankind'. The Queen's relationship with Bertie was anything but happy, of course.

Bertie's exile

Bertie was not the first dissolute Victorian aristocrat whose mother could not bear to have him near her after a traumatic episode. In 1849, Arthur Kavanagh was caught making love to one of the servant girls on the family estate. His mother was apoplectic: the idea that a cripple with no arms and no legs should have sex appalled her, so Lady Harriet sent him off with his brother and a sour young clergyman to tour Sweden and Russia. Arthur got into a fight in Moscow and had to flee the city, taking a boat down the Volga. He landed in Baku, on the Caspian Sea, where he outraged his clerical tutor by spending Christmas in a harem. The local sheik thought a man with no arms and no legs was hardly likely to appeal to his concubines, but he was deluded.

Arthur then crossed the mountains of Persia on a pony and took a boat to Bombay. Meanwhile, his outraged mother cut off his letters of credit. Circumstances forced Kavanagh and his mother to reconcile a year later after his fully limbed brothers had died – one

of consumption, another in a fire. Kavanagh inherited huge estates
and was elected to the House of Commons in 1866. He is the
most disabled person ever to sit in Parliament and one of the least
recognised heroes of British history.

Queen Victoria used the same tactic as Lady Harriet had but, for
decades, there was no reconciliation between herself and her eldest
son. The Queen arranged for Bertie to tour the Middle East and he
visited Egypt, Jerusalem, Damascus, Beirut and Constantinople.
She was still just as angry with him when he returned and
punished him by refusing to allow him the slightest role in running
the country. Instead, she decided to find him a wife. In March
1863, Bertie married Alexandra, daughter of the future King of
Denmark. He was twenty-one; she was eighteen. She was a beautiful young woman and Tennyson wrote some routinely rhapsodic
lines for her:

> Sea king's daughter from over the sea,
> Alexandra
> Saxon and Norman and Dane are we
> But all of us Danes in our welcome of thee,
> Alexandra

The birth of Bertie and Alexandra's first child ten months after
they married did not lift Victoria's depression, but, as ever, she
summoned up enough energy to meddle in the couple's affairs. She
wrote: 'Bertie should understand what a strong right I have to interfere in the management of the child or children.' Victoria wanted
the boy to be called Albert in memory of her own beloved Albert.
Bertie and Alexandra did not wish to do so, but they complied with
this request, although they themselves always called him 'Eddy'.
Alexandra did not have the strength of character to stand up to
Victoria. Ironically, Bertie's first son turned out to need far more
control than his father had done, and that was precisely what Bertie
refused to provide as a result of his own unhappy experiences.

Seventeen months after Prince Albert Victor (or 'Eddy') was

born, Victoria received a telegram in the early morning to say Bertie had a second son. Again, the Queen wanted to call him Albert, but this time the family used the name George.

In dealing with his children, Bertie had no problems in controlling his temper. He rarely became angry because of anything that they did. Alexandra made a profound impression on her second son: George later recalled that he grew up around two extremely beautiful women and one was his mother. Alexandra worked at it; she had an educated sense of style and summoned drapers and dressmakers to create splendidly fashionable clothes. 'I know better than all the milliners and antiquaries,' she wrote. 'I shall wear exactly what I like and so shall my ladies. Basta.' This early fashionista had to survive in a court still dominated by her formidable mother-in-law, who continued to oppress the family with her depression. For consolation, Alexandra turned to her children, and especially to her sons.

Alexandra spent far more time with her children than most upper-class women of her time. She tended to baby them, partly to compensate for Bertie's eternal absences. After two or three years, the marriage became formal and decently mannered but distant. If Bertie wasn't at the races, he was at the casino and, wherever he was, he was likely to be with other women. He often came back home at 3 a.m. Alexandra complained of his taste for 'female Paris notorieties' and 'various Russian beauties'.

Alexandra's children were her only source of fun and joy: she liked to play hide-and-seek with them, or to toboggan down the palace stairs on silver trays. She told her friend, Annie de Rothschild, that the Princes were 'dreadfully wild, but I was just as bad'.

Shortly before Bertie and Alexandra had Eddy, his sister Alice had had her first daughter: Princess Victoria of Hesse, who became Prince Philip's grandmother. The young Princess would soon find herself on the move, however, because of a war that pitted sister against sister. When the Prussians invaded Hesse in 1866, soldiers loyal to Princessy and her husband fought with those who owed loyalty to Alice and her husband. Princessy did not have to worry about her children but Alice's daughters, Victoria and Ella, were sent to England to live with their grandmother until the war ended.

In February 1873, the family had another shock. Alice's two-year-old son Friedrich was diagnosed with haemophilia. He cut his ear and it bled for three days – bandages could not stop the flow of blood. In late May, Friedrich and his brother Ernst were playing in their mother's bedroom. Friedrich was too young to know he had to be eternally careful. He climbed onto a chair by an open window. The chair tipped over and Friedrich fell. He survived the fall and would almost certainly have lived if he had not been a haemophiliac. A few hours later, he died of a brain haemorrhage. It was twenty years since the Queen had given birth to her haemophiliac son, Leopold, and the new victim showed the bleeding disorder in the royal family was hereditary.

In terms of life events, Victoria enjoyed and endured a real panoply. She certainly had a full life and one that affected the royal family for generations. The childhood of Bertie's first son would be deeply influenced by the excessive expectations Victoria and Albert had had for their children. For his part, Bertie was determined not to make the same mistakes that his parents had made with him. He was indulgent with his children – and far too indulgent with his eldest son.

7

THE DANGERS OF TOO LITTLE DISCIPLINE: EDWARD VII AND HIS ELDEST SON (1864–1910)

Victoria was not impressed by the way her grandchildren were being brought up. She nagged Princessy about Wilhelm, and Bertie about Eddy and George. Victoria had noted that Wilhelm was arrogant and this worried her. She also warned Princessy of the danger of being too close to her son because 'I often think too great care, too much constant watching leads to the very dangers hereafter which one wishes to avoid.' Princes, she added, were at risk because they were flattered and no one had 'the courage to tell them the truth or to accustom them to those rubs and knocks which are so necessary to boys and young men'.

The Queen was especially concerned about Bertie's children. When Eddy was six, and George was five, she complained: 'They are such ill-bred, ill-trained children I can't fancy them at all.' Bertie might well have replied that he knew far too much about the rubs and knocks that the Queen recommended for boys. He became more and more frustrated as she still excluded him from any role in government and consoled himself with mistresses and gambling. He seduced, and was seduced, by Lady Randolph Churchill, Alice Keppel (the great-grandmother of the Duchess of Cornwall) and the actress Lillie Langtry. He was even forced to appear as a witness in the 1870 divorce case brought by Sir Charles Mordaunt against his wife, who had a succession of lovers. Bertie had spent hours alone with Mrs Mordaunt and few believed their encounters to be innocent.

The Mordaunt case was the first of three scandals that threatened the reputation of the royal family between 1870 and 1890. To have her son give evidence in a divorce case appalled Victoria and confirmed her view that Bertie was hopelessly debauched and unfit for any responsibility. Time after time, he begged her to change her mind but to no avail. Yet again the relationship of a monarch to a Prince of Wales was unhappy and destructive.

Even if Bertie had been a saint, Victoria would probably have insisted on choosing the tutors for his children. John Neale Dalton, a curate in the church at Osborne on the Isle of Wight, had impressed her and she sent for him. But Dalton turned out to be far more complicated than the Queen knew: his closest friend from Cambridge was Edward Carpenter, who became a pioneer of the rights of gay men. Whether the two men were lovers is uncertain but they were certainly close. Carpenter dabbled in the Victorian homosexual underworld, a world where, in discreet houses, rich men could meet what we would now call 'rent boys'. Dalton knew Carpenter visited such houses.

In 1873, Queen Victoria gave Eddy's brother, George, a watch for his birthday and, as so often, it became an occasion for stressing what was expected of him, though he was only eight years old. She hoped: 'that it will serve to remind you to be very punctual in everything and very exact in all your duties. I hope you will be a good, obedient, truthful boy.' I have been unable to find out if she gave Eddy a watch too but he certainly did not grow up to be good or obedient.

In January 1874, Bertie and Alexandra visited St Petersburg for the wedding of his brother, the Duke of Edinburgh, and the Grand Duchess Maria of Russia. Dalton stayed behind with the Princes at Osborne. He spent as much time riding ponies with them as giving them any proper lessons. Dalton had a reckless streak as he allowed the Princes to shoot at him while he pretended to be a deer. Whether anyone could have made Eddy learn much is doubtful, though: he was lazy, astonishingly so. Dalton complained that the Prince's mind was 'abnormally dormant'. Alexandra worried about her eldest boy and nagged George not to be bad-tempered with his tutor. In a leather-bound volume recording the Princes' progress, Dalton noted that George suffered from 'fretfulness of temper' and 'self-approbation'. That did not stop his tutor writing, 'I thought much of my darling little Georgie' and signing his letters to 'dearest boy with much love'. He also wrote very affectionately to Eddy.

When Eddy was nine, Bertie thought it might make sense to split the brothers up, but Dalton argued against this, as Eddy required 'the stimulus of Prince George's company to induce him to work at all'. Dalton's memo was sent in the first instance, of course, not to Eddy's parents, but to Queen Victoria. The tutor added, 'the mutual influence of their characters' which were totally different 'in many ways is very beneficial'. It would be even harder to educate Eddy if he were away from his brother. Dalton also believed Eddy was of some use to George 'as a check against that tendency to self-conceit which is apt at times to show itself in him'. Clergymen of the time were perhaps inclined to watch for pride but, from a psychological point of view, Dalton's assessment is intriguing. George brimmed with 'self-conceit' at times. The obvious explanation for Freud at least would have been that George's mother adored him, as Alexandra manifestly did. Her adoration made her second son at times arrogant.

By the time the Princes neared their teens, Dalton thought they should be sent off to sea together. Queen Victoria had some doubts: 'I have a great fear of young and carefully brought up boys mixing with older boys and indeed with boys in general and the things they may hear and learn from them cannot be over-rated.' Despite these anxieties, she finally allowed her grandsons to join the Navy. In 1877, when Eddy was thirteen and George was twelve, they were sent to the Royal Navy's training ship, HMS *Britannia*. For some years, the boys would be separated from their parents. Dalton accompanied them as chaplain and eventually published the sermons he preached on the high seas.

When George was an old man, he told his librarian, Sir Owen Morshead, that HMS *Britannia* 'was a pretty tough place and, so

far from making any allowances for us for our disadvantages the
other boys made a point of taking it out on us on the grounds that
they'd never be able to do it later on'. Clearly, neither of the Princes
dared turn to Dalton for protection because the other midshipmen
would have thought this pathetic. There was a lot of fighting between
the cadets, as well as an unofficial hierarchy. George complained:
'They used to make me go up and challenge the bigger boys – I was
awfully small at the time – and got a hiding, time and again.' The
persecution stopped, however, when one of the big boys landed a
formidable blow on the princely nose and the ship's doctor forbade
any more fighting.

After the ban on fighting the cadets found another way to bully
George. They were not allowed to bring any food on board and
'the big boys used to fag me to bring back a whole lot of stuff'.
Perhaps due to a lack of cunning, George could never conceal his
contraband so he would get into trouble, but, worst of all, 'it was
always my money and they never paid me back'. He told Morshead
that he supposed his fellow cadets thought 'there was plenty more
where that came from', although in fact he only received a shilling
pocket money a week. Strangely, his indulgent father who frittered
thousands away kept his son short.

After their spell on the *Britannia*, the boys were sent to sail on
the HMS *Bacchante* on a three-year world tour. Many writers and a
few psychiatrists have mused on the effects of an English boarding-
school education, which promoted separation anxiety. During the
days of Empire, it was quite common for Anglo-Indian families
especially to send their boys to England and sometimes the parents
did not see them for years.

Churchill described the Navy that the Princes entered as an
institution that ran on rum, sodomy and the lash. There were a
few cases of captains punishing their men for 'uncleanness', such
as the gay sailor James Jones in the early nineteenth century, but,
in general, homosexuality was not openly admitted though even
Princes may have been at some risk of becoming involved in homosexual activities. An anonymous naval officer wrote of the secrecy

surrounding what the Irish writer and poet Oscar Wilde would describe as 'the love that dare not speak its name'.

What we know is less sensational. The Princes got into trouble because they got themselves tattooed on their noses. 'How could you have had your impudent snout tattooed,' their mother wrote and went on to mock fondly, 'What an object you must look and won't everybody stare at the ridiculous boy with an anchor on his nose.' Sensibly, she asked why her sons could not have chosen to be tattooed on less visible parts of their bodies. Dalton was drawn into the debate and promised the parents that 'the Princes' noses are without any fleck, mark or scratch or spot of any kind'. The Princes may have been unmarked when Dalton wrote but they then got themselves tattooed in Tokyo, Kyoto and even Jerusalem, where they attended a Passover service. Eddy, for once, must have been impressed for he listened attentively to the Jewish prayers.

In his biography of George V, Philip Ziegler argues that, after being taught by Dalton for years, the Princes were less well educated than the average public schoolboy of the time. George often made spelling mistakes, while Victoria complained to Bertie that at least he 'spoke German and French when you were five or six' but his own children were not even much good at English. Alexandra seems to have discouraged George from learning German, as she described the language as 'that old Sauerkraut'.

For six years, Eddy, who had not been disciplined with any consistency by his father, was in the Navy. We know surprisingly little about this period but he does not seem to have learned the kind of self-control most young aristocratic sailors did. He was eighteen when the *Bacchante* returned to the UK. What one can learn of his subsequent history suggests that he was weak and, to be charitable, easily tempted.

George had enjoyed his time on the *Bacchante* and decided to make the sea his career. Since he was not the heir to the throne, there was no reason why he should not go into the Navy. He attended the Royal Naval College at Greenwich, where his best subject was practical navigation; he also achieved first-class honours in gunnery. At the age of twenty-one, George was sent to serve on HMS *Thunderer*. His father wrote to the captain: 'I feel that in entrusting him to your care I cannot place him in safer hands, only don't spoil him please.'

Bertie had picked up some of Dalton's concerns about George's self-conceit. He begged Captain Henry Stephenson to treat the Prince just like any other officer and added: 'I hope he will become one of your smartest and most efficient officers.' The Prince would only fail if he were allowed to be lazy. In a rather sweet way, Bertie told his son not to eat too much meat and not to smoke too much. Then, in a fine show of hypocrisy, he also warned him against spending too much time in the disreputable coffee houses of Malta. By contrast, George's sentimental mother ignored the fact that her son was now a lieutenant and wrote to him as if he were still a small boy, and gave him 'a great big kiss for your lovely face'.

In 1889, Bertie was proud when his son got his first command: Torpedo Boat no. 79. Queen Victoria was worried because, as far as she was concerned, torpedo boats were dangerous. George, however, distinguished himself by rescuing a ship whose engines had failed. Meanwhile, as he became older, Bertie kept in touch with his favourite sister Alice and often complained to her that their mother still excluded him from any serious political role.

Alice had never forgotten her visit to the wounded soldiers tended by Florence Nightingale. When Hesse became involved in the Austro-Prussian War, she was heavily pregnant, but that did not stop her from running field hospitals. Like her father Albert, she was intellectual and enjoyed metaphysical speculation. She became friends with the theologian David Friedrich Strauss, who criticised the traditional sentimentality of Victorian religion.

In 1878, Alice travelled to England to spend a holiday in Eastbourne accompanied by her daughters, Victoria and Ella. The girls were treated to a tour of the House of Lords and charmed their grandmother. Princess Alice was a healthy woman of thirty-four and could not have imagined this would be the last time she saw

her mother. At the end of the year, the Hesse court was hit by diph-
theria. Alice nursed her family for a month before falling ill herself.
She died on the seventeenth anniversary of her father's death,
14 December 1878, in Darmstadt. Her eldest daughter Victoria
wrote: 'My mother's death was an irreparable loss. My childhood
ended with her death, for I became the eldest and most responsible.' Alice's death had one unexpected effect, though. Her daughter
Victoria wrote: 'My mother's death broke through many of the
outward barriers' and the Queen offered Alice's children 'consistent
signs of affectionate pity and interest'.

The girls felt at ease with their grandmother. Victoria offers the
nice details that in private the Queen now took off her widow's
cap and that she sprayed herself with a delicate orange-blossom
perfume. The Queen, her granddaughter noted, never perspired
and her hands 'used to be like hot bricks'. When she was grown
up, Victoria tried to find this perfume which she knew came from
Grasse in southern France but she never managed to procure it.
Queen Victoria came over to Hesse when her granddaughters were
confirmed at various times in the Lutheran faith.

Princess Alice's death led to trouble. The Queen expected the
bereaved husband to grieve properly, but instead Louis of Hesse
became entangled with the disreputable Countess Chapsky,
as Princess Victoria called her. In her recollections, Alice's daughter,
Princess Victoria, provides some details that show on this occasion the
Queen and her son Bertie could behave in a united, and terrifying,
fashion. Both thought the Countess quite unsuitable. They rounded
on Louis and forced 'my father to have his marriage annulled as the
lady's past and reputation made it impossible for my unmarried
sisters to grow up with her', Victoria wrote. Indeed, the Countess
was given lavish compensation to go away. 'The whole episode was a
nine-day scandal in Europe and a painful one to my father and us,'
Victoria noted. It was, however, one of the first signs that the Queen
and her son were mending their relationship, at least partially.

Bertie's eldest son, however, continued to be trouble. After he left
the HMS *Bacchante*, Eddy was sent to Cambridge. He showed no

interest in his studies but Bertie was more tolerant than Albert had been and did not insist on his son passing examinations. Dalton ceased to be his tutor and James Kenneth Stephen was appointed in his place. It was a dubious choice for Stephen was as involved in the same secretive homosexual underworld as Dalton's friend Carpenter. Stephen seems to have fallen in love with his Prince, which would only have confused Eddy's sexuality further.

In August 1884, Eddy spent some time at the University of Heidelberg studying German with no success whatever. In 1885, he was commissioned as an officer in the 10th Hussars, which provoked a warning that suggests already there were rumours about Eddy's sexuality. The Duke of Cambridge told Bertie it might be best if his eldest son did not stay too long in the regiment. 'The Head Quarters of the Regiment will soon move to Hounslow,' the Duke wrote, adding, 'I do not think that this will be a desirable station for so young and inexperienced a man who would be surrounded by temptations of every sort.'

I have been unable to find out why Hounslow was synonymous with debauch, as far as the Duke was concerned. His advice was not followed and the Duke continued to have the lowest possible opinion of Eddy, who was, he wrote, 'an inveterate and incurable dawdler'. Neither the army nor the university would fail the Prince of Wales's son, however, and, in March 1887, Eddy was promoted to captain. At the age of twenty-three, he was allowed to open Hammersmith Bridge – this seems to have been one of his main achievements in life.

The historian Theo Aronson suggested that Eddy's 'unspecified "dissipations" were predominantly homosexual'. Aronson claimed the Prince had a typical homosexual childhood as psychoanalysts would see it and adored 'his elegant and possessive mother' Alexandra. He also cited Eddy's 'want of manliness', his 'shrinking from horseplay' and his 'sweet, gentle, quiet and charming' nature, and topped this with the incisive analysis that there is 'a certain amount of homosexuality in all men'.

The year 1887 also marked Queen Victoria's Golden Jubilee. Soon after the celebrations, a scandal and a tragedy hit the headlines and caused even greater controversy more than a century later.

Queen Victoria and the Ripper

In late 1888, five prostitutes were murdered in the East End of London. The brutality of these killings led to them being called 'The Ripper Murders'. Although she was now in her late sixties, the Queen took considerable interest in them. A memo of 13 November 1888 records that she feared Scotland Yard's new detective department might not be up to the task of finding the murderer: she wanted more policemen to patrol the streets of Whitechapel. The forensic Queen asked whether the cattle boats had been searched. Had the detectives investigated the number of single men living alone in single rooms for they seemed to be the obvious suspects? She even reminded the Commissioner of the Metropolitan Police that the Ripper's clothes 'must be saturated with blood' and asked why a proper search had not been made to see if such clothes had been abandoned in the East End. The Queen can hardly have guessed that, according to some historians, the Ripper might be someone she knew well.

A second scandal broke eight months later. It involved descendants of some aristocrats who had at times been lovers of the royals for over five centuries. The potential consequences were much more serious than they were six years later, when Oscar Wilde sued for libel after being accused of being a sodomite.

In July 1889, Police Constable Luke Hanks investigated a theft from the London Central Telegraph Office. He questioned a fifteen-year-old telegraph boy, Charles Swinscow, and found he had the considerable sum of fourteen shillings on him. Swinscow confessed he earned the money working as a male prostitute for Charles Hammond. Another Post Office clerk had introduced them. This clerk has a name which one suspects was made up to make a point – Henry *Newlove*. The love that dare not speak its name was, of course, as old as the Greeks but the Victorians sometimes pretended it was new.

Within hours, Detective Inspector Frederick Abberline descended on 19 Cleveland Street with a warrant to arrest Hammond (Cleveland Street runs down into Soho and today has a slightly dilapidated feel). Abberline found the house was locked but he tracked Newlove to his mother's home, a mile north in Camden. Hammond was not there. Abberline suspected that Newlove had got word to Hammond and the owner of the brothel disappeared.

Newlove gave Abberline the names of a number of clients who used the brothel; the most glittering being Lord Arthur Somerset and Henry FitzRoy, the Earl of Euston – a descendant of one of Charles II's bastards. The enthusiastically heterosexual Bertie found it hard to believe and suggested one might as well dream that the Archbishop of Canterbury fancied young men. He did not choose his example well. Edward Benson, the then Archbishop, had been a favourite of the bursar of his college at Cambridge who, according to one of Benson's sons, was in love with his father. Furthermore, after the Archbishop's death, his widow set up home with Lucy Tait, who happened to be the daughter of the previous Archbishop. Oscar's 'love that dare not speak its name' seems to have been singing hymns. All the Benson children, boys and girls, appear to have been homosexual.

Unaware of this background, Bertie told his Comptroller to investigate the allegations. Within a day, meetings were set up with Somerset and his lawyer, as well as with the Commissioner of the Metropolitan Police. They were all left in no doubt that Bertie was 'in a great state', though he did not 'believe a word of it' as far as his son was concerned.

Somerset had considerable contact with Eddy as he ran his stables. Abberline was an intrepid detective, but one did not arrest a friend of the Queen's grandson lightly. He interviewed Somerset, but did not detain him. Abberline was not content to leave it like that, however, and, a few days later, intercepted letters which led him to question Algernon Allies. Allies admitted Somerset had paid him for sex and also that he had worked as a rent boy on Cleveland Street for Hammond. On 22 August, Abberline interviewed Somerset a second time but again he did not, or was not allowed, to hold him.

As soon as Abberline had released him, Somerset left for Germany, where Eddy was taking his summer holiday. The Prince received Somerset and sent him on to Hanover to look at some horses he might buy for his stables. Meanwhile, the press got wind of Abberline's investigation and started to refer to 'noble lords' implicated in some sordid affair. Abberline charged the only suspects he could – Newlove and another rent boy called Veck. Both pleaded guilty to indecency on 18 September but received surprisingly light sentences. It has been suggested they were treated leniently to make sure they did not talk. Hammond, who had run the brothel, was still at large. Then came the news that he had been seen in America. The Prime Minister, Lord Salisbury, ordered there should be no attempt to extradite Hammond back to England and the case against him was quietly dropped, which of course suited the royal family.

Somerset felt safe enough to return to Britain to attend horse sales at Newmarket but left for Dieppe on 26 September, eight days after Newlove and Veck had been sentenced. It seems likely he had been told that he was in danger of being arrested, but not in that much danger as he came back to England four days later. His grandmother, the Dowager Duchess of Beaufort (who could trace her ancestry back to Henry VII's intellectual mother, Margaret Beaufort), had died and he wanted to attend her funeral.

After the funeral, Somerset fled back to France. The Prime Minister, Lord Salisbury, was later accused of warning him that a warrant for his arrest was imminent. Salisbury denied this. Eddy, however, wrote to him a few days later and used a curious set of expressions. He thanked Salisbury and expressed 'satisfaction' that Somerset had been allowed to leave the country. Eddy asked that, if Somerset should 'ever dare to show his face in England again', the authorities would not bother him.

As in the abdication scandal nearly fifty years later, the foreign press wrote far more about the story than the British press. The *New York Times* reported that Eddy had left Britain 'to escape the smoke of the Cleveland Street Scandal in which he was mixed up.

He is something of a wreck.' The paper added that he was not half the man that his brother George was. Eddy's father had his vices, the paper said, but he made up for these with some real virtues, while no one had been able to detect one good quality in Eddy. His dissipations were endangering the monarchy, the paper concluded.

Ernest Parke, editor of *The North London Press*, then managed to persuade some of Hammond's rent boys to talk. Parke wondered why the male prostitutes had been given such light sentences instead of the usual penalty for 'gross indecency', which was at least two years. He also commented on how easily Hammond had managed to escape to America. The rent boys, Parke discovered, had given Scotland Yard the names of some of their aristocratic clients, but no one had been charged. On 16 November, Parke named Henry FitzRoy, Earl of Euston, as having been caught up in 'an indescribably loathsome scandal in Cleveland Street' and added that he too had eluded the law by sailing to Peru.

Parke kept the matter in the public eye and, on 16 December 1889, Newlove and Arthur Newton, Somerset's solicitor, were charged with obstruction of justice. The crown claimed he offered Hammond and the boys money to go abroad so they could not give evidence; a deal was obviously done. Newton pleaded guilty to just one of the six charges against him. He admitted that he had helped Hammond flee but he had committed no crime as there was no arrest warrant out for the man – he had merely tried to protect his client from blackmail. The Attorney General presented no evidence on the other five charges. Newton was sentenced to six weeks in prison, a very light sentence but one which his fellow lawyers considered something of an outrage. In response, 250 London law firms sent a petition to the Home Secretary protesting.

During Newton's trial, the radical MP Henry Labouchère tabled a motion in Parliament that alleged a cover-up to protect the royal family. Labouchère was fiercely hostile to homosexuality and no flatterer of the royals. He was convinced the conspiracy to cover up the scandal went to the top of the government and accused Salisbury of conspiring to pervert the course of justice in hampering the investigation and allowing Somerset and Hammond to escape. During an angry debate, Labouchère declared: 'I do not believe Lord Salisbury.' Members of Parliament can accuse each other of almost anything in the House but not of lying. Labouchère refused to withdraw his remark and was temporarily expelled from the House. His motion was defeated by 206 to 66 – a large majority against, but there were clearly sixty-five MPs who agreed with him.

Even the usually tolerant Bertie was worried by the impact his son's behaviour could have on the monarchy. In letters to his friend Lord Esher, Somerset wrote:

> I can quite understand the Prince of Wales being much annoyed at his son's name being coupled with the thing but that was the case before I left it ... we were both accused of going to this place but not together ... they will end by having out in open court exactly what they are all trying to keep quiet.

Somerset promised he had never mentioned Eddy's name to anyone other than three trustworthy associates. He added, 'Had they been wise, hearing what I knew and therefore what others knew, they ought to have hushed the matter up.' Somerset's sister, Lady Waterford, in a very modern phrase, said of Eddy: 'I am sure the boy is as straight as a line. Arthur does not the least know how or where the boy spends his time, he believes the boy to be perfectly innocent.'

It turned out that Parke had made one claim too many: the Earl of Euston had never set foot in far-off Peru. So Parke was tried for libel and sentenced to a year in prison. The rumours have persisted, however. Sixty years later, George V's official biographer, Harold Nicolson, was told by Lord Goddard (a twelve-year-old schoolboy at the time of the scandal) that Eddy 'had been involved in a male brothel scene, and that a solicitor had to commit perjury to clear him. The solicitor was struck off the rolls for his offence, but was thereafter reinstated.'

Bertie realised he must do something about his son. One possibility was to send Eddy away, either to the colonies or to tour

Europe. He wrote to Sir Francis Knollys, later the Prime Minister's private secretary, that he did not 'dare tell the Queen his real reason for sending Prince Eddy away which is intended as a punishment and as a means for keeping out of harm's way'. It seemed unlikely to him that either of these objects 'would be attained by simply travelling about Europe'.

In October 1889, Eddy did go to India but there was no place on earth where he could not get into trouble with either sex. At sea, he met Mrs Margery Haddon, the wife of a civil engineer. She later claimed Eddy was the father of her son, Clarence Haddon. Eddy's lawyers admitted that there had been 'some relations' between him and Mrs Haddon, but denied he had fathered her child.

Queen Victoria, we shall see, suspected more than Bertie imagined and decided the only answer was to marry Eddy off as soon as possible to a strong woman who would keep him in check. The first potential bride, Princess Alix of Hesse, did not like Eddy and made the poor choice of marrying Tsar Nicholas II instead. She was shot with her husband and children after the Russian Revolution, in 1918.

The second potential bride, Princess Hélène of Orléans, the daughter of Prince Philippe, Count of Paris, adored Eddy, but she was a Roman Catholic. Queen Victoria, who was staunchly Protestant, opposed the match but, when the couple confided their love to her, she relented. Hélène offered to convert, and Eddy offered to give up his right to the throne. Hélène's father had probably learned enough about Eddy not to want him as a son-in-law, though. His daughter was so keen on Eddy that she travelled to Rome to persuade Pope Leo XIII to permit the marriage, but he would not go against her father's wishes.

Eddy now developed an illness that is only referred to as 'fever' or 'gout'. Many biographers argue he was suffering from 'a mild form of venereal disease'. During the course of the illness, he was seen by a young doctor, Alfred Fripp, whose godfather was Canon Dalton. Eddy and Fripp spent much time together and travelled to Scotland and also in England. Theo Aronson claims the two men were lovers.

We know little of the private discussions that took place on the subject of Eddy's marriage. The Royal Archives have conveniently lost their files relating to the subject as a number of historians have found, rather to their surprise. But suddenly, after failing with Hélène, in December 1891, Eddy – to her 'great surprise' – proposed to Mary of Teck.

Mary was the daughter of Princess Mary, one of the granddaughters of George III; she married late and was so fat Queen Victoria despaired of her. Still, her daughter was a minor English Princess. Mary's father was Francis of Teck and of less distinguished stock. He was a minor Viennese aristocrat, who never managed to live within his modest means and did not impress his English relations, although he had served with some distinction at the Battle of Solferino in 1859. Even after he had married into the royal family, the only post he was ever given was Honorary Colonel of the City of London Police Volunteers. Perhaps the most interesting thing about Teck was that it was rumoured one of his relatives had committed incest with a sister and then proceeded to murder his valet when the man found out.

In fact, the Tecks were professional poor relations. The Queen helped by giving them a grace-and-favour lodging in Richmond, but only provided a small allowance. To save money, they travelled throughout Europe, visiting relations who would put them up. On one of these trips, Mary stayed for months in Florence and enjoyed visiting the art galleries, churches and museums. At the age of twenty-four, she was cultured and well educated, but must have despaired of ever finding a husband, let alone one who would one day be King. She did not dream of refusing Eddy, whatever his reputation might be.

The wedding was due to take place on 27 February 1892, but Eddy caught influenza in the pandemic that had raged through Europe from 1889. For Queen Victoria, the fact that he suddenly became critically ill brought back traumatic memories of the death of her own beloved Albert. Eddy's parents, his brother and other members of his family were at his bedside as he lapsed into a coma. Bertie, who had been blamed for his father's death, was distraught as he watched his son die. He wrote to his mother: 'Gladly would I have given my life for his.' Mary of Teck told the Queen that Eddy's mother Alexandra had a 'despairing look on her face [which] was the most heart-rending thing I have ever seen'.

After Eddy died, Queen Victoria wrote to one of her grand-daughters of 'the terrible calamity which has befallen us all as well as the country. The feeling of grief and sympathy is universal and great.' Victoria believed the doctors, who said his death had involved 'blood poisoning'. She sympathised with Mary of Teck, who 'came to see him die – it is one of the most fearful tragedies one can imagine'. The Queen then added a touch of literary criticism, saying, 'It would seem unnatural and overdrawn if it was put into a novel.' Eddy's younger brother George wrote: 'how deeply I did love him; & I remember with pain nearly every hard word & little quarrel I ever had with him & I long to ask his forgiveness, but, alas, it is too late now!'

The British press had not implicated Eddy directly in the Cleveland Street scandal and the obituaries were respectful. Gladstone, who was soon to be Prime Minister yet again though he was now in his eighties, wrote in his diary 'a great loss to our party'. Hermann Adler, the Chief Rabbi of the British Empire, preached a sermon which reminded Jews that Eddy had been 'reverential' when attending Passover in Jerusalem and that 'we all admired the modest, the amiable, the unassuming fashion in which he discharged his public duties'. (Adler was far too worried about the Jewish community trying to cope with thousands of refugees, who had fled from the pogroms in Russia, to be critical of the son of the Prince of Wales.)

Alexandra never fully recovered from her son's death and kept the room in which Eddy died as a shrine. At the funeral, Mary of Teck laid her bridal wreath of orange blossom on the coffin. She must have thought this was the end of her hope for a glittering match.

Queen Victoria was less starry-eyed in private, writing to Princessy about Eddy's 'dissipated life'. Historians have been vitriolic in their assessment. James Pope-Hennessy and Harold Nicolson both portrayed Eddy as lazy, ill-educated and physically feeble.

The Cleveland Street accusations pale into insignificance, however, when compared to the thesis proposed by Stephen Knight, who claimed Eddy committed, or at least had been involved in, the Jack the Ripper killings. Knight claims Eddy fathered a child with a woman in Whitechapel. The monarchy did not need another scandal so either Eddy or several high-ranking men committed the murders – both William Gull, Queen Victoria's doctor, and James Stephen, Eddy's tutor, have been suggested as the killers – to protect the crown. Historians have dismissed these claims as fantasies and pointed out that, on 30 September 1888, when Elizabeth Stride and Catherine Eddowes were murdered, Eddy was at Balmoral, dining with the Queen and some relatives from Germany.

The accusations may have been far-fetched, but two years after Knight published his claims, Gladstone's biographer, Philip Magnus, called Eddy's death a 'merciful act of providence'. After Bertie, the heir to the throne would now be the solid, stolid and sober George, whose grandmother had given him a watch when he was eight years old and told him to be an obedient boy. With Wilhelm a trial and Eddy a disgrace, no one had paid much attention to the boy Dalton had warned suffered from self-conceit.

8

THE ROYAL BULLY

'I am damn well going to see to it that my children are frightened of me!'

George V

George V made this much-quoted remark to Lord Derby, who told it to Randolph Churchill, who in turn told Harold Nicolson: 'Derby was distressed by the way King George bullied his children and he ventured one day at Knowsley when they were walking up and down a terrace to raise the subject.' Derby added that his own children had become delightful companions and begged the King to realise that 'he was missing a great deal by frightening them and continuing to treat them as if they were naughty children'.

According to Nicolson, George was silent for four minutes and then replied: 'My father was frightened of his mother, I was frightened of my father and I am damn well going to see to it that my children are frightened of me!' Some historians question whether the King really did say this, let alone whether he paused for four minutes before doing so.

George's sometimes cruel behaviour to his children was partly a matter of reaction; in this case, a reaction against the way his parents had treated his older brother Eddy. Both his mother and father had indulged Eddy, as Bertie did not want to damage his son in the way the Queen and Prince Albert's demands had damaged him, as he saw it. Bertie had not taken into account the fact that Eddy was both less intelligent and weaker than he himself had been, as well as somewhat muddled as to his sexuality. George, who never mentioned his brother's sexuality, drew a simple lesson: children needed strict discipline and royal children needed that even more than they needed love. He was not about to mollycoddle his own.

But, before becoming a father, George had to find a wife and he was not allowed to choose for himself. Queen Victoria had been impressed by Mary of Teck as a sensible and intelligent young woman. There was no point in wasting a good wife, so, after Eddy died, she decided the girl should marry George. There are two versions of what happened next. One is that George was simply ordered to marry her; the second is that he and Mary, who had both loved Eddy, started to love one another as they mourned. There is probably some truth in both theories.

George and Mary of Teck married on 6 July 1893. One of her bridesmaids was Princess Alice, one of Queen Victoria's many great-granddaughters. Alice had already showed herself to be a feisty girl. When she was four years old, her mother wrote that she had annoyed Queen Victoria by refusing to kiss her hand. The Queen snapped, 'Naughty child!' and slapped her. Alice slapped the Queen back and said, 'Naughty Grandmama!' 'I had to remove the offender,' Princess Victoria noted in her recollections. Grandmama did not tolerate dissent.

Four years later, the outburst had been forgiven and, at the wedding, the Queen thought Alice looked 'very sweet in white satin with a little pink and red rose on the shoulder'. Even in her seventies, she was sharp enough to realise something was wrong with the girl and sent her to an ear specialist (Bertie's wife was also deaf and had responded by withdrawing into herself and her children). Princess Alice, on the other hand, became one of the most flamboyant, eccentric – and heroic – members of the British royal family. Her brothers, Louis and George, were also at the wedding; all three helped make the royal family what it is today.

The wedding was also attended by Wilhelm, Princessy's son. Princessy complained that her son was under the influence of Count Otto von Bismarck, the driving force in German politics as Disraeli and Gladstone had been in British politics. Bismarck made Wilhelm 'have no respect or regard for his parents'. Princessy remained devoted to her second son, Henry, but was realistic about him: 'Though Henry often provokes me, he had a good heart and, alas, Wilhelm has no heart at all.' Yet another relationship between a royal child and his parents had foundered. It is interesting to speculate what the effect on world history would have been had Wilhelm not rejected his British mother.

The Queen took Alice to Osborne on the Isle of Wight for Christmas 1893, where there was a dormitory for all the royal grandchildren. They drove through Cowes and the Queen wrote: 'I love these darling children so, almost as much as their own parents.' Victoria was not the only formidable royal relative Alice had, however. Her aunt, Ella, the Grand Duchess Elizabeth Fyodorovna of Russia, was the first member of the royal family to be canonised for nearly ten centuries.

After the wedding, George and Mary settled down to a quiet domestic life. Their relationship had many silences, it seems. George adored his sentimental mother, who never had the least difficulty in expressing her feelings for anyone. He adored his father, who also rarely had trouble in expressing himself; Queen Victoria was similarly emotionally articulate. George, however, found it hard to express his feelings in person. He and Mary often exchanged loving letters and notes of endearment. It may have been that this reticence suited his wife because she too seems to have been inhibited. Early on in their engagement, she wrote to him, saying she wished she could tell him what she felt more easily. He told her that he understood that reticence all too well.

There is, unfortunately, no contemporary biography of Mary of Teck, which would shed some light on her relationship with her own parents, who were something of a trial to Queen Victoria. The most intimate account we have of Mary describes her as an old woman, when she was a wise and helpful grandmother. Marion Crawford taught the current Queen and Princess Margaret, and knew Queen Mary in the 1930s, when she seems to have been less diffident than in her youth.

Marriage did not make George attractive as far as his official biographer, Harold Nicolson, was concerned. He despaired of his subject when George was in his twenties and carped: 'He may be all right as a young midshipman and a wise old king, but when he was Duke of York, he did nothing at all but kill [i.e. shoot] animals and stick in stamps.' In fact, George played a key part in making the Royal Philatelic Collection one of the best in the world.

In between the shooting and adding to his stamp albums, George did manage his first essential duty – providing an heir. He was still young, only twenty-nine years old, when he became a father. When his first son was born on 23 June 1894, he was in the library reading *Pilgrim's Progress*. 'My darling May was not conscious during those last terrible two-and-a-half hours,' he wrote to Queen Victoria. The baby weighed 8lb and was 'most beautiful, healthy and strong'. The baby David was the future Edward VIII.

David's christening on 16 July 1894 in the White Lodge at Richmond Park was a splendid occasion. The Prince had twelve godparents, and the Prime Minister, Lord Rosebery, was also present. George wrote to his old tutor, Canon Dalton, that he used two bottles of Jordan water, which he had saved from his trip on the *Bacchante*, to bless his son. The only sour note came from Keir Hardie, the first Labour MP, who warned Parliament that the child would be surrounded by sycophants and at the end of the day, 'the country will be called on to pay the bill'.

Historians of the royal family have been puzzled by George and Mary of Teck's behaviour as parents. After David, they had four more sons and one daughter. David's memoirs and other evidence suggest the couple were distant and cold to their children. George was more than able to be warm on paper, however. In August 1894, for example, he told his wife that he had a picture of her and 'darling Baby on my table before me now'. In person, he would find it hard to be so affectionate.

It would be wrong to suggest that the future George V was never a kind father. In some of his letters to his sons, he could be quite playful when the 'chicks', as he called them, were young. When the children had chickenpox, he wrote to David that he hoped neither of them sprouted wings as then 'we should have to go up in a balloon to catch you'.

George and Mary's second son was born on the same day, 14 December, that Queen Victoria's beloved Prince Albert and her daughter Alice had died. She again insisted the boy should be named after her dead husband. Names matter and can cause psychological confusion. His parents did not want to call the boy Albert and always used 'George' or 'Bertie'. It was the beginning of a number of troubles. He was a sickly child and was described as 'easily frightened and somewhat prone to tears'. Albert or George was not allowed to use the hand he wanted to use when he learned to write. He was naturally left-handed, but it was considered bad – indeed sinister – to be left-handed so he was forced to use his right hand. His father always complained that his son's handwriting was poor. George was bullied not just by his father, but also by his first nurse and, to some extent, by his older brother when they were young. Forcing a naturally left-handed child to write with his right hand is now recognised as a classic cause of stammering and George did indeed develop a stammer. He also suffered from chronic stomach problems, as well as knock knees, for which he was forced to wear painful corrective splints. He was, as we shall see, eventually obliged to seek not just speech therapy, but also psychiatric help.

Mary of Teck was no gushing mother, as Alexandra had been. She was not besotted by her babies and found them 'plain'. While she admitted they were 'very nice', the business of having them seemed really unpleasant; it suggests she did not enjoy the sexual side of marriage much and, after she had three children, she negotiated a pause in child bearing with her husband, it seems. Their next child was born two-and-a-half years later after they had gone on one of the many cruises the royals made to show the flag round the Empire.

George's difficulties as a father began when his children stopped being babies. He expected them to behave maturely, or with 'spurious maturity' to use the psychoanalyst D. W. Winnicott's phrase.

(Winnicott was a good friend of Marie Bonaparte and invented the idea of the transitional object.) They had to dress as sailors and were often made to drill and parade. It is tempting to compare him with that other Navy man Captain von Trapp in *The Sound of Music*, but Mary of Teck was no Sister Maria, at least as Julie Andrews played her in the film. Even when she was just their governess, Maria reminded Captain von Trapp that his children were children and stopped him barking commands as if they were on an imaginary battleship. George, however, yelled if his children wore the wrong colour kilts, or their uniforms were not up to scratch, or they did not march in step. Philip Ziegler argues Mary held her husband in awe and was frightened of contradicting him, whatever his behaviour as a father. 'I always have to remember that their father is also their King,' she wrote. She had been brought up all too aware of her parents' inferior position and their poverty.

The little Princes could at least put on a good show for their grandmother. In May 1898, they visited Queen Victoria, who noted: 'David is a delightful child, so intelligent. The baby is a sweet little thing.' The Queen said nothing about George, now the middle child.

In the day-to-day business of bringing up the children, the royal parents relied heavily on a nanny, Lalla Bill, and a nursery footman, whose father had served with the Duke of Wellington. The footman was no respecter of Princes and sometimes spanked David for being rude to Lalla Bill. The third person in charge of the children was a nurse, who turned out to be a very poor choice.

The identity of this nurse has never been revealed. She had worked for the Duke and Duchess of Newcastle, who had given her a good reference, but the woman either changed when she came to Sandringham, or the Newcastles had been blind to her failings. She preferred David to George, but that did not make her treat David kindly; she would twist and pinch his arm before she took him in to see his parents. David seems never to have told his parents what she was doing but he did scream sometimes, which his mother disliked as it was 'jumpy'. The nurse also seems to have deprived

George of food, snatching bowls and plates away from him. Lalla Bill finally told the housekeeper what was going on, but the nurse was not sacked until an investigation was carried out. It emerged she had not had a day off for three years, that she had a difficult husband and she was bitter as she herself had been unable to have children.

When George was five years old, his father, whose 'self-conceit' had worried Dalton, told his son: 'Now that you are five years old, I hope you will always try to be obedient and do at once what you are told, as you will find it will come much easier to you the sooner you begin.'

John Wheeler-Bennett wrote the official biography of the future George VI and made revelations about his childhood which 'have led a number of commentators to suggest that George's early upbringing was bound to induce nervous disorders which would remain with him in later life', according to later biographer Patrick Howarth. Howarth dismissed these ideas as impertinent, but seems to have ignored the role that three doctors played in George's life. The first was Sir Frederick Treves, who is now best known for his care of the 'Elephant Man', the second was Louis Greig, who first met George when the Prince was thirteen years old and a midshipman – Greig was the ship's doctor – and the third was Maurice Craig, then a leading psychiatrist. George did not just stammer: when frustrated, he was prone to violent outbursts of temper, which worried his family.

By the end of Queen Victoria's reign, she had finally been obliged to let Bertie assume some responsibility. She arranged for his son to set off on an imperial tour to show off the royal family to their colonial subjects; the grandparents were left in charge of the children. Alexandra and Bertie indulged David, George and the others far more than they had ever been before. Bertie allowed the children to skip lessons and played funny games, in which the children chased pats of butter. Mary was distressed by her father-in-law's rather sweet behaviour but dared do nothing about it. Bertie teased his grandchildren by saying that when their parents came back, they

would be black all over because they had been under the tropi-
cal sun. In his own book, *A King's Story*, David recalls being both
frightened and curious about this prediction.

A year before she died, Queen Victoria became godmother to
Louis, Princess Victoria's son. In her recollections, the Princess said
her son caused his great-grandmother some trouble a few months
later as 'he waved his little arms so violently, he knocked her
spectacles off'. The Queen did not reprimand her last godson.

The royal family saw the new century in at Sandringham, where
they argued about whether 1900 was the last year of the new century
or the first year of the next.

Queen Victoria finally died in 1901 after sixty-three years on the
throne. Her granddaughter Victoria mourned her, saying, 'She had
taken a special interest in her beloved daughter's children as they
had lost their mother young.' The Queen made Victoria's father,
Louis, one of the executors of her will, showing she had forgiven
him the episode with the disreputable Countess. Princess Victoria
also highlighted a fact that shows the tentacles of the long case
history. There was only one member of the family still alive who
had been present when the Queen had come to the throne, back in
1837. This aunt was herself a niece of George III's wife and was 'now
much appealed to'. She knew all the secrets of the family.

As he assumed the crown, Bertie was determined to avoid a
crucial mistake his mother had made and at once gave George
access to all state papers. It was a sign of respect and his son appre-
ciated that, but his father's respect did not change George's attitude
towards his own children.

Derby was not the only courtier to worry about George and
Mary's less-than-loving attitude as parents. Lord Esher sent Mary a
copy of Gosse's *Father and Son*, a famous memoir of the often difficult relationship Gosse had with his father. In a deferential society,
it must have taken some courage to suggest to the future King and
Queen that they needed to change the way they treated their children. One of George's private secretaries, Alec Hardinge, was also
very aware of the problem. He said, 'they trample on their young'

and was baffled by this because George, 'who was such a kind man, was such a brute to his children'. The royals were still seen as Hanoverians and George V's librarian, Owen Morshead, told Harold Nicolson that 'The House of Hanover like ducks produces bad parents.' George and Mary's ducklings were in trouble.

Bad parenting often makes children anxious. In 1900, a year after Freud published his seminal *The Interpretation of Dreams*, young David had a series of anxiety dreams. Then, when his third son Henry was born, George noted that David asked funny questions: 'I told him the baby had flown in at the window during the night and he at once asked where his wings were and I said they had been cut off.' David claimed that he had a vision of his baby brother, whose wings bled after being snipped off, and this image had distressed him for some weeks. Freud would have interpreted David's account simply: the boy was unconsciously afraid that his intimidating father meant to castrate him.

Eventually, David wrote *A King's Story*, a memoir in which one of the key themes is his relationship with his father. He loves him, he fears him, he wants him to understand that they are not alike and he never quite manages to do so. David even used the language of psychoanalysis and, at one point, admitted that he was in 'unconscious rebellion' against his father. He said of his parents: 'If anything can be said to have come between us, it was the relentless formality of their lives, never wholly relaxed.' David accused his parents of many shortcomings. His father was obsessed with punctuality and never lost the habit of checking the barometer first thing in the morning. Royal duties meant that his parents were rarely present and, 'for better or worse, royalty is excluded from the more settled forms of domesticity'.

David was given a servant, Frederick Finch. Once, when the Prince kicked up a fuss, Lalla Bill stormed in to Finch and said, 'That boy is impossible! If you don't give him a thrashing, I will.' Finch marched the Prince off to the bedroom and, 'while I kicked and yelled, applied a large hand to that part of the anatomy which nature has conveniently provided for the harassment of young boys'.

David shouted that he would tell Papa what he had done. After being 'summoned' to see his mother, David was not 'embraced or mollified' as he expected to be. After all, Finch was just a serv-ant. Instead, he was told that he had behaved badly and was sent to apologise to Finch. David claimed he could not remember the incident, but added that the servant was 'a man of probity' so he accepted his version. Finch stayed with him for years, becoming his valet later on.

When David was eight, his father introduced him to Mr Hansell, who was to be his tutor. In the past, the royals had chosen teachers with care but Hansell was just a very ordinary local schoolmaster, who really never managed to control his royal pupils.

Ironically, David noted Sandringham, where he spent most of his childhood, 'had most of the ingredients for a boyhood idyll'. They could ride on bicycles, play energetic games of golf and, eventually, shoot all the game they wanted, but they always had to be in by 7 p.m. The question of when David and his brother George learned to shoot also suggests their father did not have much faith in them. Often, the sons of aristocrats went hunting with their fathers and uncles from a young age. The future George V, however, only taught his sons how to handle a gun when they were thirteen years old. Perhaps he did not trust the boys to shoot properly when they were younger.

David told Charles Murphy, who helped him write *A King's Story*, that what he remembered most about his childhood was 'the miserableness I had to keep to myself'. He often felt his father 'preferred children in the abstract' and agreed with the view that his naval training had 'caused him to look on his own children much as he regarded noisy midshipmen when he was captain of a cruiser – as young nuisances in constant need of correction'. He dreaded being summoned to his father's study, which he thought of as the Captain's cabin. Though sometimes it was to admire a precious new stamp, more often than not, 'we would be called to account for some alleged act of misbehaviour.' David came in for 'a good deal of scolding' because he had been late, looked dirty, made too much noise or wriggled in church. He concluded: 'the mere circumstances of my father's position interposed an impalpable barrier that inhibited the closer continuing intimacy of conventional family life.' This sentence is very stiff, reflecting perhaps his father's stiffness towards him.

'Remember who you are,' his father kept on reminding him. 'That injunction was dinned into my ears many, many times. But who exactly was I?' David observed. His experience taught him that he had the same interests as other people, 'and that however hard I tried, my capacity was not appreciably above the standards demanded by the fiercely competitive world outside the palace walls'. Admittedly, his father insisted he should not think they were better than other people, but even then David had to partially retract what first appeared to be a compliment; he added that 'by people he [his father] meant children of the well-born'.

It has been suggested that David's mother was different when away from her husband. There is evidence that her son would not have agreed. According to her daughter, Angela, David told his mistress, Freda Dudley Ward, she was lucky to have had a loving mother.

Even before he was ten, David was beginning to display some of the character traits that would make his father disapprove of him. The astute Duchess of Fife noted that he 'seems to have no aversion to girls. He was so from the first. I have a vivid and pleasing recollection of the only time I saw him this year, when he *flirted* with the nice Lady Collins.'

Princess Alice – Victoria's exotic great-granddaughter

The royal family had not been that concerned by the wars of the 1860s and 1870s when children found they were on different sides. All those wars, however, had been relatively minor. This would change after 1910. The events of that decade prompt an unanswerable question: if Kaiser Wilhelm had not felt embittered about his English mother, would he have tried to stop Germany declaring war on Britain?

By 1910, Princess Victoria's husband, Louis of Battenberg, was an admiral in the British Navy. Victoria was unusual in many ways. When she and Louis moved to London as his naval career demanded, they lived in a small flat in St Ermin's Mansions in Westminster and then took an unexceptional house in Eccleston Square. Edward VII had no idea that they had a limited income and could not understand why they chose to live in a square where 'only pianists lived'. They were allowed, however, a key which let them into the gardens of Buckingham Palace. Victoria sent her children to local dancing classes and Alice attended a small private school. Victoria did not rely on nannies much and was very close to her children; she made them feel valued, which does not mean she was uncritical.

Victoria was worried when in 1902 her eldest daughter Alice fell in love with Prince Andrew of Greece and Denmark. They were too young, she felt. She swallowed her doubts, however, and the couple married a year later at Darmstadt. After the civil ceremony, there were two religious ones as Andrew was Greek Orthodox and Alice was Lutheran. We have seen that Leopold chose to be King of the Belgians rather than of the Greeks. Rejected, the Greeks turned to minor Danish nobility, who descended from the multi-titled Prince Christian of Schleswig-Holstein-Sonderburg-Glücksburg. The Greeks never quite accepted their new monarchs, who tended to look down on their subjects, though. It did not help that King George I of the Hellenes spoke Greek with an accent that was abominable, just as George I's English accent had been.

Unlike his father and his four brothers, Andrew at least spoke Greek well and decided to enter the Greek army. Alice too learned Greek and, after a few years, was completely fluent – a real achievement since she was deaf and had to lip-read. Princess Marie Bonaparte visited Athens in 1907 and described Alice as 'a beautiful blonde English woman with ample flesh, smiles a lot and says little since she is deaf'.

The marriage between Alice and Andrew began well; they had two daughters. After they had been married five years, Alice visited Russia for a royal wedding. It would mark a turning point in her life. Her aunt, the Grand Duchess Elizabeth, was setting up a religious order of nurses and, to prepare herself for a more spiritual life, began giving away all her possessions. Most of Ella's relatives treated her as an eccentric, but Alice did not. Her aunt's religious fervour made a great impression on her.

When he came to the throne in 1910, George V faced personal pressures. His youngest son, John, has been largely forgotten, though Stephen Poliakoff made a film about him. John's fate affected the royal family more than they cared to admit. In 1909, when he was four years old, he had an epileptic seizure. It frightened the family, who decided not to let him attend his father's Coronation.

Prince John's epilepsy became very difficult to cope with and his parents sent him to live at Wood Farm on the Sandringham estate. There, he was looked after by Lalla Bill, who had wanted to thrash David, and also cared for by a coachman from Windsor Castle (Thomas Haverly took John on outings and sometimes to the 'big house' at Sandringham). In between fits, John seems to have been normal, as photos show him riding a bicycle. Once he had been eased out from the royal circle, he was the first royal child since Prince William in 1694 to have a close friend who was not an aristocrat. At Wood Farm, he spent much time with Winifred Thomas, a Yorkshire girl who suffered from chronic asthma and had been sent to the country, where the air was much cleaner. The two sick children went on walks together and worked on a small garden John had been given to look after. When John was very ill, Winifred sat by his bed, as Lalla Bill read to both of them.

When she was older, Winifred remembered John was excited when her father, who was a sergeant in the army, came to Wood Farm; John was delighted to meet 'a real, live soldier'. This makes it clear that neither of his brothers who were serving in the forces ever bothered to visit Wood Farm. David himself mentions John only once and noted that his parents only went to visit him at most twice a year. To be fair to Mary of Teck, Winifred remembered her as a loving and interested mother, who spent much time with her son but she may have been being tactful about the woman who was then her Queen. Nothing seemed to help John, however, and his seizures became more severe and more frequent. Of Mary's children, one stammered and was clearly pathologically nervous and one had epilepsy. The royal family seems to have turned to neurologists and psychiatrists for help.

Fashionable analysis

Today, mental illness is still surrounded by a certain stigma but there have been periods when it has been less so and one of these was around 1914. Freud had become famous and nearly everyone he treated was well-off, well connected and functioning well. He was influencing European culture and that influence became even stronger when it became clear how many soldiers suffered from the horrors of the trenches and developed shell shock. The military, whether British, American or German, had little sympathy for the victims, but some doctors realised that many of those who could no longer fight were not cowards. The Germans had a hospital at Pasewalk that dealt with soldiers who broke down; Hitler was treated there when he suffered from hysterical blindness in 1917. There were also asylums in Scotland, like Craiglockhart, which housed many well-educated patients. As early as 1916, a French psychiatrist, Léri, published a book on shell shock. Even comic authors such as P. G. Wodehouse wrote about psychiatrists in their books, though anyone treated by his creations was likely to go madder than Hamlet ever did. In these conditions to seek or even just to discuss help was not considered such a disgrace.

Much has been made of the fact that George V bullied his second son but for some of the war at least the King was impressed by him. Like his father, George joined the Navy. His fellow officers nicknamed him 'Mr Johnson' but they were not deferential because George was a Prince. The King had been a midshipman himself so he knew how to sympathise when his son fell out of a hammock 'with the help of someone else' and got a black eye. 'I should do the same to the other fellow if I got the chance,' his father suggested. To his delight, the Prince was mentioned in dispatches for his bravery as a turret officer during the Battle of Jutland in 1916. The

King wrote in his diary that he hoped that God 'will protect dear Bertie's life'.

Then, however, there was a major drama. George suffered a duodenal ulcer. Louis Greig, who had become something of a mentor, recommended an operation to remove the ulcer as it was causing the Prince so much pain and that pain was making him very depressed. Treves and a number of other doctors were nervous. It was only after months of debate and indecision that the King allowed them to perform the operation his son wanted and needed. By then, the King had been very impressed by Greig and arranged for him to become attached to the Prince's staff. The two men became close friends – and Greig was, in fact, giving the Prince a kind of perpetual therapy. The King even invited Greig to a family Christmas in 1916, which obliged Greig to apologise to his wife for not spending the holiday with her.

The problems David faced during the war were psychological too, but less debilitating. They highlighted the question he had raised, 'Who am I?' He was not allowed to fight at the front line and it took him a long time to become reconciled to this. 'Manifestly, I was being kept so to speak on ice against the day my father died,' he wrote. As he witnessed the slaughter, David bristled at being so protected. This provoked a row with his father. George V nagged him about it being 'very silly of you not doing what I told you to do at Easter' – he had failed to wear all the decorations he was entitled to wear. He tried to explain to his father that he was very aware of the many brave officers who had not been decorated when they had risked their lives. As he was not allowed to do so, it felt a little insulting to wear medals he had not earned. 'Oh, not to be a Prince!' he moaned. His stickler father was not persuaded.

The Battenberg saga

Princess Alice's daughter, Victoria, had married Louis of Hesse, whose family name was Battenberg. By 1914, Louis had risen to be the First Sea Lord but his name was floridly German. Victoria wrote later, and bitterly, that the British government saw him as a

'Jonah' because he was German. After forty-six years in the Navy, Louis was angry but he 'decided to jump overboard' before he was made to resign. One of those who agitated against him was Winston Churchill, who was First Lord of the Admiralty. Churchill insisted the 74-year-old Lord Fisher come out of retirement to take over. Meanwhile, George V did nothing to support Louis.

Victoria complained that the King 'is a nobody' and 'few men trusted the government'. She did not think much of Fisher either, who had once told her: 'I love hating.' He had the bad manners, she noted, of sometimes cutting in when one of his midshipmen was dancing with a pretty woman and taking over. Victoria distrusted Churchill, too, because he had once borrowed a book from her and never bothered to return it. She did not forgive the many insults to her husband – nor did his children.

Princess Victoria was, in some ways, as methodical as the first cousin she despised: George V. She was interested in science and kept meticulous records of the books she had read, which covered a wide range of interests. Unlike George, however, she was fascinated by new ideas and even studied some socialist philosophy. She taught her children herself instead of relying on a tutor. Her younger son, Louis, said that she was:

> a walking encyclopedia. All through her life she stored up knowledge on all sorts of subjects, and she had the great gift of being able to make it all interesting when she taught it to me. She was completely methodical; we had time-tables for each subject, and I had to do preparation, and so forth. She taught me to enjoy working hard, and to be thorough. She was outspoken and open-minded to a degree quite unusual in members of the royal family.

In December 1916, David wrote a more accommodating letter to his father. Trench life was dull. For most men, a tour of duty consisted of two days in a ditch, followed by two days in a dirty French cottage. 'What must be the effect on their brains?' he told his father. He wondered why some of them did not go mad. Seven months later, he wrote to his father that he was thankful to be sitting in comfort in the HQ of the 14th Corps: 'One does appreciate this comfort when one has been forward and seen what it's like in the line now. The nearest thing possible to hell, whatever that is.'

Since 1714, the royal family had been German. Now Germany was the enemy. The King and his children bore the titles Prince and Princess of Saxe-Coburg and Gotha and Duke and Duchess of Saxony; even Queen Mary was a descendant of the German Dukes of Württemberg. Public opinion was hostile towards what seemed to be the foreign royals. H. G. Wells wrote of England's 'alien and uninspiring court' and suggested the monarchy had had its day. The King responded furiously: 'I may be uninspiring, but I'll be damned if I'm alien!' In July 1917, he issued a proclamation changing the name of the royal family from the Germanic House of Saxe-Coburg and Gotha to the über-English House of Windsor. George insisted all his British relatives should give up their German titles and assume far more English-sounding surnames. It was his secretary who suggested they should be called 'Windsor'.

In response to the change of name, Victoria's grandson, Kaiser Wilhelm, joked that he was looking forward to seeing Shakespeare's excellent comedy *The Merry Wives of Saxe-Coburg-Gotha* when he came to England after the war.

Louis Battenberg, who was still smarting from having to resign as First Sea Lord, managed to negotiate that he should be made Marquess of Milford Haven and took a sneaky, clever revenge. While the King renamed his family Windsor, the Battenbergs merely dropped the 'berg' part of their name. In German, 'berg' means mountain or mount, so the Battenbergs became the 'Mountbattens'.

Being obliged to drop the family name proved another blow to the already depressed Louis Battenberg. He also faced financial problems and had to sell his homes in both Britain and Germany. In 1921 he complained of feeling unwell and his wife persuaded him to rest in a room they had booked in the annexe of the Royal Military and Naval Club. Victoria called a doctor, who prescribed some medication. It is typical that she did not send a servant but went out to fill the prescription at a nearby pharmacist's. When she came back, her husband was dead. It made her very bitter. This compounded the tragedy she had faced in 1918 when she learned that the Bolsheviks had killed her beloved sister, Ella, even though she had taken to doing good works for the poor.

Alice's mother comforted herself in thinking Ella's faith would have made her meet death without fear. But Alice would be devastated. Victoria said: 'The misery poor Alicky will have suffered will not have touched Ella's soul.' When Ella's body was found, she was holding a cross of cypress wood. Alice herself faced death: she had to shelter in the palace cellars when the French bombed Athens (1916–17). During the chaos, the King of Greece found himself homeless and a Jewish property magnate, Haimaki Cohen, gave him a house for his family. The King was grateful and told Cohen he only had to ask for help should he need it. Alice would remember that promise. In June 1917, she and other members of the Greek royal family were forced into exile, the first of many dislocations.

George V, who had done nothing to help Louis Battenberg, was worried that the Russian Revolution would provoke even more hostility towards the royals, so he also did nothing to help his cousin the Tsar in his hour of need and refused to grant him asylum. The irony is that Lenin was a pragmatist and would probably have been quite prepared to let the Tsar sail out of St Petersburg on a British warship.

Six days before the end of the war, David wrote to his father that 'there seems to be a regular epidemic of revolution and abdications' which threatened monarchies, but he thought the British one by far the 'most solid'. After agreeing with his father's view that the survival of the monarchy required keeping 'in the closest possible touch with the people', he promised always to keep that in mind and signed himself 'your most devoted son'. He *was* devoted but was also, as his father saw it, delinquent, especially in his love life. The whole family now had to cope with a tragedy they may well have been half hoping for.

In the early hours of 18 January 1919, Queen Mary wrote in her diary:

Lalla Bill telephoned from Wood Farm, Wolferton, that our poor darling Johnnie had died suddenly after one of his attacks. The news gave me a great shock, though for the little boy's restless soul, death came as a great release. I brought the news to George & we motored down to Wood Farm. Found poor Lalla very resigned but heartbroken. Little Johnnie looked very peaceful lying there. For him it is a great release as his malady was becoming worse as he grew older and he has thus been spared much suffering. I cannot say how grateful we feel to God for having taken him in such a peaceful way, he just slept quietly, no pain, no struggle, just peace for the poor little troubled spirit, which had been a great anxiety for us for many years ever since he was four.

The words are eloquent, but George and Mary had excluded their sick son and left him very much to the servants. When John was buried on 21 January 1919, the Queen wrote: 'We thanked all Johnnie's servants, who have been so good and faithful to him.' Some days later she added, 'Miss the dear child very much indeed.' She told George, 'The first break in the family circle is hard to bear but people have been so kind & sympathetic & this has helped us much.' The Queen gave Winifred Thomas a number of John's books, with the inscription: 'In memory of our dear little Prince'.

In *The King's Story*, David mentions his epileptic brother only in relation to his death. After the war, David resumed what his father saw as his distressing fast and frivolous life. It was some consolation that the stammering son seemed capable of something that had not occurred to a senior royal since Victoria met Albert: falling madly in love.

9

THE QUEEN MOTHER AND WOODROW WILSON

In spite of his neurotic troubles and his duodenal ulcer, Prince George had had a decent war, though he only saw active service for less than two years. In February 1918, he became Officer in Charge of Boys at the Royal Naval Air Services training establishment at Cranwell. He was the first member of the royal family to be certified as a fully qualified pilot, which must have pleased his father, given his minor obsession with wings. When George tried to get permission to fly solo, Lt Col Birley, who was the head of the RAF Medical Services, was asked to assess him. Birley concluded the Prince had too many psychological problems to be in the air on his own. It was clear that he needed help, more help than even the ever-present Louis Greig could give.

The cycle of reaction now recurred. George V, who had been pushed into marriage with Mary of Teck by Queen Victoria, decided to allow his own sons freedom to marry. In 1920, George met Lady Elizabeth Bowes-Lyon, the youngest daughter of the Earl and Countess of Strathmore and Kinghorne, for the first time since they were children. She came from a distinguished Scottish family and could count Robert the Bruce among her ancestors, as well as the butler's great-grandson, Henry VII. Technically, however, she was a commoner and had been brought up outside court circles.

Elizabeth Bowes-Lyons had a rather free childhood in Scotland. She saw a great deal of her parents and her mother breastfed all her children, which was still rare among the upper classes. Elizabeth's father adored her. She and her youngest brother, David, were known as 'the two Benjamins' and smoked illicit cigarettes in the Flea House, the attic of a ruined building, which was their 'blissful retreat'. Their nurse couldn't find them there and they amassed 'a regular store of forbidden delicacies acquired by devious means: beer, oranges, sugar, sweets, slabs of Chocolat Menier, matches and packets of Woodbines'. The children smoked on the stairs, and from a turret once poured cold water on unsuspecting guests. They also painted the lower rungs of a ladder with white paint without, of course, telling the painter, standing several rungs above. When his white footprints covered the whole lawn, they loved it. They were spoilt rotten, it could be said.

Elizabeth did not go to school but had a series of governesses. During World War I, she became an auxiliary nurse and treated wounded soldiers. She was part of a very active social circle and 'dated', as we would put it now, a number of dashing young men. George fell in love with her but she did not return his feelings. He proposed to her; she was flattered but she did not accept. The remarkable thing was how well he handled her rejection, given his many neurotic problems. It seems unlikely he did that without help.

George was very depressed by Elizabeth's rejection, as he told John Davidson, the Prime Minister's private secretary, but he did not give up. He proposed another time and, again, she asked him to forgive her, but she could not accept. The King and Queen were quite happy for him to marry Elizabeth, but less so when they realised he was pursuing a young woman who just wanted him to be 'a wonderful friend'. It was undignified for the King's son to chase after a girl who did not want him. For perhaps the only time in his life, George deceived his parents and promised to give up trying to persuade Elizabeth to become his wife. He was far too much in love with her, however, to do that.

The reason that has been usually given for Elizabeth's hesitation is that she realised, if she married George, she would become part of the royal family and her life would be very much constrained. There was more to it, however: she was also aware of George's many problems and she had many other suitors who neither stammered nor lost their temper. She said later that she had been very tempted to marry one of them, James Stuart.

But George was persistent and he proposed yet again. Elizabeth's mother made a comment that reveals the Prince was seen at the very least as extremely needy. He would be 'made or marred' by his choice of wife. Biographers have failed to explain how George, who was shy and lacking in self-confidence, managed both to keep his temper in check when he was rejected and summon up the strength to continue his pursuit. One explanation is that he had been in some sort of therapy, as many upper-class men and women were at the time.

By 1920, few British psychiatrists had been knighted. One of those few was James Crichton-Browne, who had the peculiar job of looking after usually rich patients, who were wards of Chancery. Another high-society psychiatrist was Maurice Craig, who, before the 1914 war, was often consulted when young people came back from skiing in Switzerland. Craig noted 'a few weeks of winter sports' left them 'in a highly exhausted state'. Lionel Logue, who is presented in *The King's Speech* as the therapist who saved George VI, never received a knighthood, but Craig did.

Craig wrote *Nerve Exhaustion*, in which he discussed the problems of shell shock, as well as the best ways to treat children prone to violent outbursts of temper and who stammered. 'The writer attaches great importance to any hyper sensitivity that a child may be born with or accentuated as a result or illness, zymotic disease,' he said, adding that 'fear and dread are the most powerful influences on the child's mind.' He also suggested as therapeutic techniques breathing in a more relaxed way, which we know the future George VI practised. As I have argued, one of the curious results of Freud's growing fame and the awareness of shell shock was that many upper-class individuals saw analysts. William Bullitt, the first American ambassador to the Soviet Union, was one of Freud's patients, as was Princess Marie Bonaparte. For Prince George to seek help in these circumstances would not be so strange, especially as his parents consulted nerve doctors for his brother John. Maurice Craig,

unlike Treves, Greig or Logue, has been airbrushed out of Prince
George's history.

George accepted Elizabeth's many rejections between 1921 and
1923 with good grace. If he had lost his temper, as he was apt to do
when frustrated, then she would have been put off but somehow
he managed to control himself. Elizabeth finally changed her mind
after an odd episode where newspapers reported that she was going
to marry George's brother, David. Once she told George she would
marry him, her fears that life would never be normal again were
immediately realised as reporters surrounded her home but she
had been touched by his kindness over the years when she had
refused him.

Elizabeth and George were married in April 1923. A year after
they returned from a five-month tour of Africa, Elizabeth had her
first child, the current Queen. Four years later, in 1930, she gave
birth to a second daughter, Margaret.

The family moved to a fine, but not especially spacious house at
145 Piccadilly. The house next door, 144 Piccadilly, hit the headlines
in 1969. It was the scene of a famous squat and the aim of the squat-
ters was to prevent the building from being pulled down to make
way for a luxury hotel (they failed). The house at 145 Piccadilly
was far less grand and it was there that Queen Elizabeth II spent
her childhood.

Before describing what we know about the current Queen's early
years, I want to look briefly at the childhood of President Woodrow
Wilson, who had brought America into World War I and contributed so much to the defeat of Kaiser Wilhelm. Freud wrote more
about Wilson's early years than those of any of his other patients.
His book (*Woodrow Wilson*, only published in 1967) emphasises the
problems that a difficult childhood can cause. It is also relevant as
there is a link between its completion and the royal family.

The President and his father
The idea of writing about Wilson came about because one of Freud's
other patients, William Bullitt, had worked for the President, as

had Freud's nephew Edward Bernays. Freud insisted they find out as much as possible about Woodrow Wilson's childhood. Bernays and Bullitt had access to many intimate details; it was history, written by formidably privileged insiders.

Wilson was in the grip of powerful unconscious forces, Freud and Bullitt argued. He would not have agreed to the French and British demands during the negotiations for the Treaty of Versailles after World War I had he been analysed. As he had never been treated, the wily monsters Lloyd George and Clemenceau ran rings round him.

Woodrow Wilson's father, Joseph Ruggles Wilson, was a Presbyterian minister who had high hopes for his son, even when Woodrow was just four months old and, presumably, in nappies. 'That baby is dignified enough to be Moderator of the General Assembly,' his father boasted. Wilson's father was physically very affectionate: he liked to chase his son in the garden, catch him and give him a great hug. Even as adults, the two men kissed whenever they met. But the relationship was inevitably unequal – the son was the passive one and that passivity would later haunt him. Freud and Bullitt had no doubt that Wilson's love for his father went too far: 'He not only expresses his love and admiration for his father but also removes his father by incorporating his father in himself as if by an act of cannibalism. Thenceforth he is himself the great admired father.' American Presidents have been accused of many things, but only Wilson has been accused of cannibalism, I believe.

Wilson only rebelled against his father once: he did not go into the Ministry but into academia. After a minor breakdown, he went to teach politics at Princeton. In 1895, Wilson's father came to live with his son. The result: Woodrow Wilson broke down, this time completely. The reasons were purely Oedipal, argued Freud and Bullitt. Wilson could not allow himself to express any hostility to his father, but, in his unexplored unconscious, he was a boy with an unresolved Oedipal complex, who wanted to 'annihilate the Reverend Joseph Ruggles Wilson'.

Despite these problems, Wilson became the President of

Princeton in June 1902. Eight months later, his father died. Freud and Bullitt sneered, 'After his father's death his [Woodrow's] addiction to speech making which was already excessive grew to fantastic proportions.' One of the pleasures of the book is its bitchy tone. They carped: 'The Reverend Joseph Ruggles Wilson, who incidentally is not to be recommended as a model for fathers, had made his son love him so deeply and submissively that the flood of passivity he had aroused could be satisfied by no other man or activity.'

When the 1914 broke out, Wilson proclaimed the neutrality of the United States. His adviser, Colonel House, wrote on 10 November 1915 that Wilson must use all his skills and the resources of America to achieve a lasting peace. House added: 'This is the part I think that you are destined to play in this world tragedy and it is the noblest part that has ever come to a son of man.' Freud and Bullitt commented that Woodrow Wilson in his unanalysed unconscious seized on the phrase 'son of man'. He longed to be the bringer of peace on earth because he identified with God and his feminine side identified with Christ.

When the President came to Paris in March 1919, he was seen as a saviour but wilted when faced by Clemenceau and Lloyd George. Confronted by strong men, 'the deep underlying femininity of his nature began to control him and he discovered he did not want to fight them with force. He wanted to preach sermons to them.'

Clemenceau and Lloyd George repeatedly exploited the President's vulnerability, but the unanalysed President lacked the insight to see this. Wilson even told his aides that the problem was that Clemenceau had 'a feminine mind'. In fact, nothing 'less feminine than Clemenceau's refusal to be swept off his feet by Wilson's oratory could be imagined', Freud and Bullitt sniped. Instead of using the power of America to impose a fair peace, the President compromised and let the French and British impose drastic conditions on the defeated Germans. Not surprisingly, Wilson's failure of nerve triggered another 'nervous' collapse. When he recovered, he referred to the Treaty as a '99 per cent insurance against war'. Few predictions have turned out to be so wrong.

The writing of the psychobiography had verve, wit and urgency. After years of wrangling, Freud and Bullitt agreed the final text in the garden of Marie Bonaparte's house. A few years earlier, Philip had played in that garden when his mother, Alice, had to be put in an asylum. There are indeed connections between Freud and the British royal family.

Secrecy and the problems of the present

Princess Alice's son, Prince Philip, is still alive. So is the Queen. Dealing with the living requires more tact than dealing with the long dead. As I quoted R. D. Laing at the start of this book, every mother and every father has had his own experiences of being parented so it is not just unkind to be judgemental, but also fool-ish. In families of schizophrenics, Laing said, there was sometimes a desperate need to keep up appearances. For the royal family, this has been an important motivation.

After the 'dissipations' of Prince Eddy, Prince George's need for endless medical help, Prince John's epilepsy, the madness of Princess Alice and the abdication of King Edward VIII in 1936, the royal family became convinced of the need to protect its privacy. No current royal has written as honestly about their childhood as Queen Victoria did. In 1950, Marion Crawford, the Queen's devoted governess, said there was 'a royal conspiracy of silence on so many uncomfortable things'. But what was uncomfortable and unmentionable seventy-five years ago is familiar now.

Since Queen Elizabeth II came to the throne, the royal family has coped with many stresses that are similar to those faced by ordinary families. Princess Margaret, Prince Charles, Princess Anne and Prince Andrew have all divorced. Princess Margaret also had a much-publicised affair with Roddy Llewellyn. I met him at his house in the Cotswolds during the recent phone-hacking scandal when he felt sure that his phone too had been hacked back in the 1970s. One of the few things he said about his affair with Princess Margaret was that they had somehow managed to have about two years before the press found out and started to pursue

them. Llewellyn was furious when one tabloid led on the fact that
'Margaret's toy boy' was on the dole during a week when he was, in
fact, working hard to get an exhibit ready for the Chelsea Flower
Show. He had been very upset when his brother Dai had sold some
of the secrets of the affair, but, by the 1970s, any lover of the royals
was fair game for the press.

The royal family has also had to cope with crises peculiar to their
position. Unlike Queen Victoria, Elizabeth II has not been the
target of any assassination attempts but, in 1982, she did find an
intruder in her bedroom in Buckingham Palace. There was also
an attempt to kidnap Princess Anne in 1974, and a very amateur-
ish attempt on Prince Charles's life on Australia Day in 1994. In
1979, the IRA planted a bomb on a small boat belonging to Lord
Mountbatten, the son of the First Sea Lord who had 'jumped overboard' and resigned. Prince Philip saw Mountbatten as something
of a father; Prince Charles regarded him as an honorary grandfather. Mountbatten was murdered; Princess Diana was not, at least
according to the inquiry begun by the French in 1997, a finding
endorsed by Lord Stevens after he retired as Commissioner of the
Metropolitan Police. Many believe the French inquiry left many
questions unanswered.

When Princess Diana died after the Mercedes in which she was
travelling crashed in the Alma Tunnel on 31 August 1997, spurious
maturity ruled. The Princes William and Harry were persuaded on
the very morning of her death to appear in public. They went to
church for the usual Sunday service to make the point publicly that
everything was still normal. We cannot understand the reaction
of the Queen to these traumas without understanding her own
childhood – and the way she mothered her children.

10

'CRAWFIE' AND THE LITTLE PRINCESSES

The majority of the most acute insights we have into the current Queen's childhood come from her governess, Marion Crawford, who only retired in 1948, when her charge was twenty-two years old. In the introduction to a new edition of *The Little Princesses*, A. N. Wilson argues Crawford was the 'most important Royal writer' of recent times, though literary circles tend to be snobbish about her. 'She was much more like a camera than an authorial intelligence,' Wilson added, which implies she was a total amateur as a writer.

The circumstances surrounding the publication of the book were bizarre. Crawford did not tout her memoir to publishers. Soon after she retired, the American publishers Bruce and Beatrice Gould contacted Buckingham Palace and the Foreign and Commonwealth Office; they wanted positive stories about the royal family. The Palace dismissed the idea but the British government was keen to boost the country's image. An appealing portrait of royal family life would be ideal and the Foreign Office suggested Marion Crawford should write something. The Goulds offered Crawford the then fantastic sum of $85,000 for her story. Despite the fee, Crawford asked that the contract state the approval of the royal family would be sought for any material published. However, the contract allowed the Goulds to publish, even if the Palace refused.

Crawford's account appeared in *Woman's Own* in the UK and in the *Ladies' Home Journal* in the United States. To the intense displeasure of Queen Elizabeth II, *The Little Princesses* became a bestseller. She was quoted as saying: 'We can only think that our late and completely trusted governess has gone off her head, because she promised in writing that she would not publish.'

Crawford was the first servant to cash in on the private lives of the royals and she suffered for it. The royal family never spoke to her again and did not even send the routine Christmas card. Remarkably and hypocritically, however, the King and Queen received the Goulds, who published the work, at Buckingham Palace.

When Crawford retired to Aberdeen, she knew the royal family regularly drove past her front door on their way to Balmoral, but they never stopped to see her. When she died in 1988, neither the Queen, the Queen Mother nor Princess Margaret sent a wreath. The lack of courtesy is startling.

Marion Crawford became the royal governess because she did well in a summer job. She was studying child psychology at Edinburgh's Moray House Institute and, in 1926, went to work as the governess for Lord Elgin's children. Lady Elgin recommended her to the then Duchess of York, who was looking for someone to teach Princess Elizabeth and her two-year-old sister. When Crawford joined the household, no one imagined the Duke of York, Elizabeth's father, would one day be King.

Marion Crawford met the then Duchess (who we, of course, think of as the Queen Mother) and they agreed that she should come down to London for a month to see if they liked her, and if she liked them. Crawford went back to Scotland to collect clothes, as she imagined she would need a succession of smart frocks in her new job. That detail reveals she was seen as a cut above the nurses and nannies who wore uniforms. Mrs Knight, the children's nurse, always wore a white cap, too. Crawford was lucky her mother was a good dressmaker as otherwise her wardrobe would have cost a fortune. In reality, however, life at 145 Piccadilly was rather quiet and did not require much haute couture.

Marion Crawford described the household as 'homelike and unpretentious'. The nurseries were on the top floor and very much the centre of all activities. She was given a bedroom next to Elizabeth's.

Crawford was an astute observer but, as with all memoirs, it is impossible to be sure how accurate every detail and every word of every conversation she gives may be, especially as some of them took place twenty or even twenty-five years before she wrote them. She never deals with this issue and occasionally the wording of the conversations she reports does not seem convincing. The account Crawford gives of the atmosphere in the family feels, however, utterly convincing.

At once, Crawford was struck by the differences between 'Lilibet', as Princess Elizabeth was called, and her sister, Margaret. Even at the age of six, Lilibet was reserved and controlled; her sister far less so. Crawford gives one nice example. The Princesses' father was often in the house for lunch and would spoon out some coffee sugar for his daughters. Although Lilibet loved the sugar, she carefully sorted her lumps out on the table and 'then ate it very daintily and methodically'. Margaret, on the other hand, kept 'the whole lot in her small hot hand and pushed it into her mouth'. Lilibet seemed special: 'I had met many children,' Crawford wrote, 'but never one with so much character at so young an age.'

Life at 145 Piccadilly was relatively informal so nothing had prepared the young teacher for meeting the King and Queen. One day, it was announced that George V and Queen Mary would visit the house. Crawford was nervous, fearing the King would disapprove of her. However, her relationship with the Duchess was good and she told her of her anxieties. The Duchess laughed that there had been some idea that 'someone older would have been a better choice, but the Duke and I don't think so – we want our children to have a happy childhood, which they can always look back on.' Crawford then had a panic over etiquette: she had not learned to curtsy and was terrified she might topple over as she tried to do so. She just about managed to keep her balance when Queen Mary and the King came over to her. Crawford wanted to blurt out, 'Please, will I do?', but managed to restrain herself. Queen Mary smiled at her and the King just 'grunted and prodded the ground with his stick'. He then made a remark which reveals his obsession with order: 'For goodness sake, teach Margaret and Lilibet to write a decent hand, that's all I ask. Not one of my children can write properly.'

When George V fell ill in 1929, the family worried, especially as David had recently fallen badly when steeple chasing. He was banned from that activity and for once accepted his father's decision.

Lilibet was already obsessed with horses and Crawford revealed that her first love was Owen the groom. The Duke once laughed when someone asked what Lilibet thought of something and told them they should ask Owen – he would know.

The girls had a collection of thirty toy horses, all on wheels. 'That's where we stable them,' Lilibet told her new governess. Each horse had its own immaculate saddle and bridle; the girls polished them and followed the routine of a top-class stable. Every night, each saddle was removed and the toy horses fed and watered. One of Lilibet's favourite games involved putting a harness of red reins with bells attached on her teacher. Lilibet would then 'ride' 'Crawfie' – the nickname they used for Crawford – as they went off delivering groceries. 'I would be gentled, patted, given my nosebag and jerked to a standstill. Meanwhile Lilibet delivered imaginary groceries at imaginary houses and held long intimate conversations with her imaginary customers.'

Lilibet already knew how horses behaved and told Crawford that, as a horse, she had to 'pretend to be impatient. Paw the ground a bit.' The dutiful teacher dutifully pawed. Lilibet loved cold mornings because then her pretend horse breathed out clouds of air, 'just like a proper horse'. Sometimes the roles would be reversed and Lilibet would prance around, being the horse, whinnying and sidling up to Crawford in the best equine manner.

From the top of the house, they could see Hyde Park, where the horses trotted up and down Rotten Row. The girls loved looking at the brewers' dray horses as they did the rounds. Lilibet did not expect to become Queen, but said that, if ever she did, she would make a law giving horses Sunday off because 'horses should have a rest too. And I shan't let anyone dock their pony's tail.'

The house at 145 Piccadilly had a few surprising domestic issues. Crawford once found a mouse sitting on her towel. Luckily, the postman arrived. Crawford gave him her poker and asked him to kill it. The postie duly obliged.

There was no schoolroom and so the Princesses did their lessons in a boudoir belonging to the Duchess. Despite the informality, lessons always started at nine in the morning. Crawford did not bring in any specialists to help her until the girls were much older; she felt perfectly competent to teach them English, history, mathematics and to encourage them to read. She had been teaching the Princesses for four years when, in 1936, George V was close to death. His son David wrote: 'All was still as we – his wife and children – stood together by my father's bedside waiting for life to be extinguished.' The moment the King was dead, David's mother and brother surprised him: they took his hand and kissed it, a correct show of homage to the new King. David was embarrassed but, in his memoir, he does not admit that he was overwhelmed with sorrow and anxiety. He and his father had never resolved their relationship. David started to cry on his mother's shoulder. Mary of Teck was also embarrassed and felt it was vital for the new King to set an example; his dead father would have wanted that. She curtsied to her blubbering son and addressed him as 'Your Majesty'.

The Establishment, and especially the Archbishop of Canterbury, was appalled when David, soon to be crowned Edward VIII, wanted to marry the American Wallis Simpson, who was soon to be divorced for the second time. Within months, Edward was left in no doubt that he must choose between marrying the woman he loved and carrying on as King. The orthodox view is that his younger brother had always been nervous of having to assume the throne, but some recent research suggests George remained on surprisingly friendly terms with the Machiavellian Archbishop of Canterbury Cosmo Lang. Lang was plotting Edward VIII's downfall.

In the autumn of 1936, the atmosphere at 145 Piccadilly became tense. Then the Duchess sent for Crawford. She held out her hand and said: 'I'm afraid there are going to be great changes in our lives.' They discussed how to break the news to the children. It seems quite astonishing that it was left up to Crawford, rather than to their parents, to inform Lilibet and Margaret that their father was about to become King. This is one of the few points in the memoir where it feels as if Crawfie might be exaggerating her role. When she told the Princesses that they were moving to Buckingham Palace, the girls 'looked at me in horror'. According to her, Lilibet said: 'What, forever?' and Margaret added: 'But I have only just learned to write York.'

On 12 December 1936, the day after Edward VIII signed the royal assent to his own instrument of abdication, George's daughters gave their father a 'final hug as he went off' in the uniform of the Admiral of the Fleet. Hugging was very normal in their lives. Crawford explained to the girls that they would have to curtsy to their father when he came back for lunch because by then he would be the King. 'And now you mean we must do it to Papa and Mummy,' Lilibet said, 'and Margaret too.'

When the King came home, his daughters curtsied to him gracefully. 'Nothing brought the change in his condition to him as clearly as this did,' Crawford pointed out. The King was taken aback for a moment and then kissed his girls 'warmly'. After that, they went in to have lunch, which Crawford described as 'hilarious'. No one in the family ever spoke of their uncle David again. 'The Royal conspiracy of silence had closed about him as it did about so many other uncomfortable things,' she added in one of the few trenchant criticisms in her book.

The girls would have to behave impeccably at their father's 1937 Coronation. Princess Elizabeth would find that easy, but Margaret was only six years old and Crawford was worried as to how well she would cope. On the day, crowds gathered outside; the children were up early and excited as there was a lot of 'laughter and squealing'. The King had decided that his daughters needed to be comfortable and arranged for very light coronets to be made for them. Before setting out, the Princesses paraded before Crawford. 'Do you like my slippers?' Lilibet asked and lifted her skirt to show off her silver sandals. Crawford noted that she was wearing short socks 'that revealed a length of honest brown leg'. The older sister behaved much as older sisters often do and worried that Margaret would disgrace them all by falling asleep in the middle of the ceremony. 'After all she is very young for a Coronation, isn't she?' Lilibet noted.

When they returned, Crawford asked Lilibet how Margaret had coped. She said that her sister had been wonderful and that she had only had to nudge her once or twice when she made too much noise with her prayer book. The two girls were exhausted, but had to rally for an hour while pictures were taken of them. 'We aren't supposed to be human,' Crawford records their mother saying, rather sadly.

Having the stamina to cope with a Coronation was not exactly a serious problem compared to those the young Prince Philip was facing.

11

PRINCE PHILIP'S TURBULENT CHILDHOOD

After the end of the 1914 war, the Greek royal family returned to Athens. The marriage of Victoria's great-granddaughter, Princess Alice, and Prince Andrew was still happy. They had four daughters, and a son, Prince Philip, was born in a modest family house, Mon Repos, in Corfu on 10 June 1921. Princess Alice was an attentive mother, which had more of an impact on her son than most commentators have suggested. Winnicott would have approved of her: she slept in the nursery with her son when his nanny was away and his sisters admitted they wanted to squash their spoilt little brother. As a small child, Philip was deeply loved.

Philip's father, Andrew, resumed his military career but became a victim of the tangles of Balkan politics. Court-martialled in 1922 for losing a battle against the Turks, Andrew only escaped the death sentence because George V intervened. He sent a cruiser, the HMS *Calypso*, to remove Alice and her children and a diplomat to plead for Andrew's life. The King felt he could do more to help Andrew, a Prince of insignificant Greece, than he had done with either Louis Battenberg or the Tsar.

Once he left Greece, Prince Philip's father set up house in Paris, but he did not provide a home or much security for his children. Alice, who had seen her beloved aunt Ella murdered by the Bolsheviks in 1918 and her father forced to resign from the British Navy, now became increasingly religious. Philip was seven when on 20 October 1928 his mother entered the Greek Orthodox Church. She was still wholly committed to Andrew and translated his defence of his actions during the Greco-Turkish War into English. Soon afterwards, however, she began claiming that she was receiving divine messages, and that she had healing powers. Her eldest daughters became increasingly concerned for her welfare. Andrew came to London and discussed his wife's problems with Thomas Ross, who ran the hospital that had been financed by Edwina Mountbatten's grandfather, Ernest Cassel, and organised with the help of Sir Maurice Craig. Alice's mother, Princess Victoria, got a second opinion and wrote to her friend Nona Kerr that both doctors suggested 'internment. Andrew and I feel it is the only right thing to do. Both for Alice and her family. How hard it has been to come to this decision and what we feel about it you know. This Easter will be a miserable one.'

Alice was sent to the Tegel Clinic in Berlin, which was run by Dr Ernst Simmel, a friend of Freud's. Freud suggested using X-rays on Alice's ovaries to speed up her menopause as he believed the religious fervour had a sexual root. He may have been correct as there were rumours that Alice had fallen in love with a mysterious young man. Her daughters, however, thought their mother was suffering from the delusion that Christ was appearing to her. Simmel did not help her much and so Alice was sent to another friend of Freud's, Dr Ludwig Binswanger's sanatorium in Kreuzlingen, Switzerland. Binswanger and Freud were close. Freud complained to him of his fellow analysts, 'What a gang!'

Andrew could not cope with yet another stress, that of his wife being incarcerated by psychiatrists. After a few months, he left for the south of France, leaving his children to be brought up by various members of the family.

When his mother was put in hospital, Philip was just eight years old. For the next five years, he heard nothing from her, and very little from his father. Philip would be shuttled between France, England and Germany, and some of his family did not welcome him. In 1930, when he went to Kensington Palace, Queen Victoria's daughter Princess Beatrice (then in her seventies) sniped that the Palace was no place for the young. As one of three surviving children of the widow of Windsor, Beatrice had authority in the family and Philip had to leave to live with his mother's younger brother, Georgie Mountbatten, the Marquess of Milford Haven. The boy with a religious mother was now in the care of other members of his family whose morals would have outraged not just the widow of Windsor, but the whole town.

Georgie had married Nada, the great-granddaughter of the Russian poet Pushkin. She was bisexual and her lovers included the heiress Gloria Vanderbilt. A little infidelity among friends did not mean that Georgie and Nada did not love each other, though. Unconventional parents too, they adored their son, David, who was two years older than Philip; the two teenagers became great friends. In a splendid show of defiance of convention, when David was seventeen, his parents sent him to live in a brothel in Paris. Perhaps not surprisingly, he became famous for his collection of pornography and catalogues, which included titles such as *Sparkling Tales of Fun and Flagellation*. Georgie's sister-in-law, Edwina Mountbatten, had many lovers, including the first Indian Prime Minister, Nehru, while her husband, Louis Mountbatten, had a close and perhaps erotic relationship with his secretary, who it has been alleged was a KGB spy. Mountbatten's biographer, Philip Ziegler, denies the two men were lovers, but others who have studied Mountbatten disagree. Mountbatten did say that he and Edwina spent their lives getting into other people's beds, Ziegler also reported.

Philip's Parisian relatives were magnificently outrageous. In Paris, he lived with his uncle, Prince George of the Hellenes, and his wife, Princess Marie Bonaparte. The Princess was Napoleon's great-grandniece. Her mother died a month after Marie was born and she was brought up by her grandmother, a monstrous snob who would not permit a descendant of Napoleon to mix with ordinary children.

Princess Marie's first lover was her father's secretary, who then blackmailed her. She eventually married Prince George of the Hellenes in 1907. On their wedding night, 'Big George' told his new wife that he knew the act was distasteful but their loins had to do the necessary and provide heirs for Greece. The frustrated Princess took many lovers, one of whom was the Prime Minister of France. Her husband did not mind as he suffered from an unusual erotic fixation himself: he was in love with his uncle Waldemar. In her search for sexual fulfilment, Princess Marie had a bizarre operation to have her clitoris moved closer to her vagina. Later, she went to meet Freud, hoping he could cure her of frigidity as none of her many lovers had managed to do so. Freud suggested that she had witnessed 'the primal scene' in the form of her nurse making love with her uncle and this inhibited her. The Princess hared off in her Rolls-Royce, questioned the nurse and found that Freud had guessed correctly. From that moment on, she became totally devoted to him and their relationship became a platonic love affair. Freud gave the Princess analytic sessions which lasted two hours, a privilege granted to no other client. She even asked him if she might not overcome her sexual problems by committing incest with her son. A bad idea, Freud suggested, as he was quite conservative. In Milford Haven, Philip was in a Bohemian bisexual milieu; in Paris, among sexually curious psychoanalysts.

The way children respond to trauma depends on their intelligence but also on personality and good and bad fortune in a way that psychologists have not yet managed to fully understand. Freud would probably argue that what gave Philip the ability to cope was that, before she fell ill, his mother had loved him and held him lovingly. That was well in the past, however. In Kreuzlingen, Philip's mother talked not just with Christ but also with other religious luminaries after she read *Les Grands Initiés*, which promised secret spiritual knowledge to those who followed a strict regime of prayer, fasting and meditation. Alice, however, always insisted she was sane. Her psychiatrists who, like Freud, were mostly convinced atheists were not impressed.

Philip was also lucky in his grandmother, Princess Victoria. He told an early biographer, Basil Boothroyd: 'I liked my grandmother very much and she was always helpful. She was very good with children; she took the practical approach to them. She treated them in the right way – the right combination of the rational and the emotional.' The latter remark is, of course, both measured and insightful. In later interviews, Prince Philip has been far more brusque. He told Fiona Bruce of the BBC when she tried to get him to discuss his childhood: 'It's simply what happened. The family broke up. My mother was ill, my sisters were married, my father was in the south of France – I just had to get on with it. You do. One does.'

The young Philip was not just abandoned, but was also aware of the conflicting attitudes in his family – his religious mother who was now in an asylum, his absent father and his Bohemian relatives. It is surprising that Louis Mountbatten and Marie Bonaparte never had an affair since they had affairs with virtually everyone else they shared a drink with.

The unconventional life led by the Mountbattens did not make them uncaring, though. Louis Mountbatten felt that Philip needed a respectable education and sent him to Cheam, an old and reputable preparatory school. In the summers, Philip often went to visit relatives in Germany, but his mother was too ill to see him and his father does not seem to have been very interested.

In 1933, when he was twelve years old, Philip was sent to an experimental school in Salem in Germany. It was run by Kurt Hahn, a teacher who believed the young were in danger from 'fivefold decay'. According to him, they were not fit enough physically, they were not self-disciplined, they were not compassionate, they did not show initiative and they lacked many skills. Hahn admitted he had developed his ideas by studying the great thinkers of the past. He may not have been original, but he was certainly eccentric. He claimed, for example, that doing the high jump helped make children more decisive and was especially helpful to those who stammered and had a 'refined intellect'.

Like some Jews, at first Hahn did not want to see the threat Hitler presented. He did so only in 1933, when the Führer condoned the murder of a Communist party leader. Hahn wrote to all the parents of the children at Salem, demanding they break with the Nazis. The local police put him in jail, but one of his former pupils was the private secretary of the British Prime Minister Ramsay MacDonald. The British persuaded the Nazis to release Hahn, who fled at once across the Channel. Philip was a pupil at Salem during this fraught period.

Hahn then received backing to create a new Salem at Gordonstoun in Scotland. Philip was among the group of pupils who helped put up some of the buildings. The regime was Spartan but Philip was resilient – he did 'get on' with it. He also did well in becoming captain of cricket and he liked sailing. As he did not get seasick, he was given the job of cooking when Hahn took pupils on expeditions to the Hebrides and the Shetlands. One of his school friends revealed that Philip was not afraid of doing dirty work.

In the holidays, Philip often went back to the Mountbattens and, while with them, he got an early experience of high-society controversy. Gloria Vanderbilt, Nada's lover, was involved in a custody battle for her ten-year-old daughter. *The New York Daily News* reported that Gloria was 'a cocktail crazed dancing mother, a devotee of sex erotica and the mistress of a German Prince'. It hinted she was a lesbian when not in bed with her German and concluded, 'it was a blistering tale no skin lotion could soothe.' Nada wanted to fly to New York to help her lover, but George V, who was forceful even when old, persuaded her against that. The last thing the royal family needed was for the wife of one of Queen Victoria's descendants to make lurid headlines all over the world.

When Philip was in his early teens, his mother tried to escape from the asylum. She was watched more carefully after that, but, slowly, Alice did get better. In 1934, she was well enough to leave the asylum but she did not come back to see, let alone look after, her son. Instead, she cut herself off from the whole family, apart from her mother Victoria, and, for a number of years, travelled incognito around the Continent. Just before this happened, Philip attended the wedding of the Duke of Kent, one of George V's other sons. Marie Bonaparte was also one of the guests. Philip's biographer, William Eade, suggests she may not have told her relatives that she was going on to lecture at the British Psychoanalytic Society on her favourite topic, female sexuality. I doubt it. Bonaparte did not hesitate to shock her royal relatives.

The wedding of the Kents was important for another reason. One of the bridesmaids was George and Elizabeth's elder daughter, who was eight years old. It was the first time that the future Queen of England met her future husband.

After the abdication

Following the abdication of 1936, David's brother became King and his family had to adjust to their new role. George VI still found time to play with his children and the family's life did not entirely change. Crawford said they all found solace on the weekends when they went to Royal Lodge in Windsor, where court etiquette was forgotten. 'We were just a family again,' she wrote. Phrases like that may well have intensely annoyed the royal family: trusted as she was, Crawford was only a servant. She went on to describe the way the parents, the children, the butler, the chauffeur and herself put on old clothes and mucked about at Royal Lodge. The King had an assortment of tree-cutting implements that fascinated his daughters. He loved hacking away at trees and making bonfires and roped everyone in to work tirelessly. Gladstone had written a good deal about how cutting down trees helped him relax when he was Prime Minister; it was much the same with the new King.

One of the many telling observations Crawford made brings out how much the King loved his daughters. He placed two rocking horses outside his study and Crawford wondered if he had put them there specifically for his horse-mad girls to use, so that he could hear them playing while he worked.

She also records a number of differences between the girls. Margaret liked practical jokes; Lilibet did not. Crawford enjoyed such jokes and sometimes conspired with Margaret. They once hid the gardener's broom in the bushes so that the man spent some time wondering why it was not where it should be: in his cupboard. Crawford was also sharp in pointing out the isolation of the royal family. The King and Queen wanted their children to

be 'members of the community. Just how hard this is to achieve
if you live in a palace is hard to explain. A glass curtain seems to
come down between you and the outside world.' Crawford used
the phrase 'glass curtain' over thirty years before the first use of the
now familiar 'glass ceiling' in an American magazine piece about
'The Up-and-Comers'.

Not long after she had left the asylum, Alice had to face another
tragedy. In 1937, her daughter Cecilie, her son-in-law and two of her
grandchildren were killed in an air accident at Ostend. Cecilie was
pregnant and the stillborn child was found in the wreckage. Alice
and her husband met for the first time in six years at the funeral.
Their son Philip was there and it seems to have been the last time
he saw his parents together. Lord Louis Mountbatten came too, as
did Hermann Goering. The Nazis kept on hoping that the British
royal family would ally themselves to their cause.

Cecilie's youngest child was not on the plane and was adopted
by her uncle, but the little girl only survived her parents and older
brothers by nineteen months. Soon after, Alice's brother, George
Mountbatten, died of bone cancer. Princess Victoria's granddaughter,
Lady Pamela Hicks, remembered her grandmother weeping bitterly.

After these tragedies, Alice stayed in contact with her family
but, a few months later, she went back to Greece alone. She took
a modest two-bedroom flat in central Athens and was totally
committed to religion and to working with the poor. The family
did not understand her behaviour.

A joyful reunion

As tensions grew in Europe, the royals had to show the flag abroad.
Early in 1939, George VI and Elizabeth went to visit Canada and
the United States and were away for months. Crawford highlighted
not the separation, which was the only lengthy separation from
their parents, but the 'joyful reunion'. When their parents returned,
it 'was a great event in the children's lives'. The girls took the train
to Southampton, reading comics all the way, and then boarded a
destroyer to sail into the Channel to meet their parents on the *Empress*

of Britain. Once the destroyer reached the *Empress of Britain*, the girls, Crawford and Mrs Knight – no doubt in her white cap – had to climb down a ladder onto a barge. The King and Queen were waiting with 'great eagerness', as their daughters climbed another ladder up to them. 'The little girls could hardly walk up the ladder quickly enough but when they reached the top they rushed to Mummie and Papa. They kissed them and hugged them again and again. Everybody else kept out of the way,' Crawford added. Margaret had lost weight while her parents were away and demanded they notice that she was quite a good shape now, 'not like a football as I used to be'.

Fifteen years later, Prince Charles, then much younger than his mother and aunt had been when reunited with their parents, received a very formal handshake from the Queen.

Once the war started, the Queen told Crawford that the possibility of moving to Canada had been raised, but she had to be with her children and there was no way she could leave the King. The royal family did not claim special privileges and did not eat more lavishly than their subjects while rationing was in force so they all got one egg a week and looked forward to it. Back then, the royals were making do in a way royals had not done for centuries. They still managed to have fun, however, as the Princesses put on a pantomime: Margaret played Cinderella, while Lilibet was the principal boy. Margaret dolled herself up in a white wig, which made everyone laugh.

The King knew his daughter would one day succeed him and decided Crawford needed help. He arranged for Elizabeth to visit Eton to be taught by an expert in constitutional history. It was also important for the Princesses to mix with ordinary children. Crawford claims it was her idea that there should be a Girl Guide troop at Buckingham Palace. Lilibet was old enough, but Margaret was too young. The increasingly assertive Lilibet remained undaunted. She told her sister: 'Pull up your skirts, Margaret, and show Miss Synge [later Commissioner for the Girl Guides] your legs! You can't say those aren't a very fine pair of hiking legs.' Lilibet was persuasive. Miss Synge agreed that two Brownies could join the Palace troop and Margaret was allowed to become a Brownie herself.

The experiment was a great success. When they went hiking, the girls did their share of the dirty work. Crawford remembered Lilibet 'looking ruefully at a large cauldron full of greasy dishes, into which she had to plunge her arms to do the washing up'. The Princesses did not shirk or malinger: 'They were more than willing to pull their weight.' They mixed more with normal children than any other royal children had ever done since William, Duke of Gloucester.

The Blitz has been the subject of many books, but the effect that the war had on British children has been less studied than one might expect. Crawford evokes the Blackout and the fears it provoked well. The first night that the Princesses had to live through the Blackout, they needed much reassurance as they saw 'apartments were muffled in dust sheets' while pictures were sent off to storage. 'All night ghostly figures flitted around,' and the task of blacking out a palace proved never ending. One old retainer told Crawford: 'By the time we've blacked out all the windows here, it's morning again, miss.'

The Princesses were in the Castle when Windsor was bombed. Crawford and the staff hurried to get them into an air-raid shelter, but Lilibet called, 'We're dressing, Crawfie; we must dress!' 'Nonsense, you are not to dress! Put a coat over your nightclothes at once,' Crawford replied. Finally, Lilibet came to the shelter. The scene offers a nice example of Lilibet's anxiety that everything should be just so; her grandfather had been very similar. She would get out of her bed several times a night to check that her shoes were straight and her clothes 'arranged just so. We soon laughed her out of this.'

As the sisters grew up, Crawford noted there was much less friction between them than is usual between female siblings. She thought this was due to 'Lilibet's unusually lovely nature. All her feeling for her pretty sister was motherly and protective. She hated Margaret to be left out; she hated her antics to be misunderstood.' The mischievous Margaret often made her family laugh, but sometimes at the wrong time. When posing for an official photograph, Lilibet occasionally nudged Margaret or gave her a 'sisterly look that has said plainer than any words "Margaret, please behave"' or made it obvious this was not the right time to laugh. As a teenager, Margaret became interested in clothes (which Lilibet never was) and started sketching designs.

Like thousands of others, the royal family sent their children to live in the country, where they would be less vulnerable to bombing. With their governess in tow, the Princesses went off to Sandringham. The Queen told Crawford to carry on as usual, as far as that was possible.

The huge majority of British men and women felt a sense of duty during the war and Crawford was no different: she wanted to marry, but delayed her plans because she felt that she would be deserting the royal family. In one of her few moments of self-aggrandisement, Crawford wrote that the King and Queen 'carried such crushing responsibilities' and that she knew they would have 'considerable peace of mind so long as I remained with the Princesses. So duty won the battle.'

Prince Philip and his mother

The war also changed the lives of Philip and his mother. After leaving Gordonstoun, Philip entered the Navy, where he passed the examinations easily. He distinguished himself when his ship was bombed and a number of shipmates felt he had saved their lives. His mother, meanwhile, was in Athens, which the Axis powers had occupied. Her family was divided in its loyalties. While her son was in the Royal Navy, Alice's sons-in-law fought for the Nazis. One of her cousins was also the German ambassador in Greece. Alice devoted herself to good causes, just as she had done in the 1914 war but this time more subversively. As well as working for the Red Cross and organising soup kitchens, she played on her royal status to fly to Sweden. She said that she was visiting her sister, Princess Louise, although in fact she used the trips to bring back medical supplies (she was helped by the fact that the Fascist powers presumed she was pro-German, as one of her sons-in-law was a member of the SS). Alice did not hide her true feelings when a German general asked her: 'Is there anything I can do for you?' 'You can take your troops out of my country!' she replied. But she was a Princess, and so she was not arrested.

Alice took an even greater risk then. Until late 1943, she had done nothing to help the few Jews who had not been deported and were still in Greece. But then the widow of Haimaki Cohen, who had housed Andrew's father after the flood, some twenty-five years earlier, turned to her for help. Alice hid Rachel Cohen and two of her children so they were not sent to the death camps.

Meanwhile, Philip was moving in very different circles. In Christmas 1943, 'having nowhere particular to go', he went to Windsor Castle with David Milford Haven, lately resident in a brothel. Philip had travelled around the world and already had at least two romantic relationships; Lilibet was a child by comparison.

Crawford noticed how Philip had changed from a rather bump-tious boy to 'a grave and charming man'. He looked like a Viking, she thought, 'weather-beaten and strained and his manners left nothing to be desired'. In his company, Elizabeth had 'a sparkle about her eyes none of us had ever seen before'. On Boxing Day, they all danced till one in the morning. As her father had done in 1920, Elizabeth had fallen in love. After Christmas, she and Philip wrote to one another and she placed a photograph of him in the little private sitting room she had been given.

Louis Mountbatten began to sense an opportunity, especially after the death of the Duke of Kent, the King's younger brother. The Duke had fulfilled engagements on behalf of the King. Rather as if he were running an employment agency, Mountbatten touted the idea that Philip could now fill in for the Duke of Kent. As a preliminary, Philip would give up his Greek citizenship. It seems possible that Mountbatten was also seeking to make a point: the Battenbergs had been sacrificed in the 1914 war. Now the Windsors needed them.

Mountbatten pushed his scheme too far, though, when he

suggested that, as Philip and Elizabeth were getting on well, they should marry. The King wrote to him a few weeks later to say that he had been thinking it over and 'I have come to the conclusion that we are going too fast.' Ben Pimlott, in his biography of Elizabeth II, suggests it is quite implausible that the King would accept help from his young and distant cousin who belonged to the Greek royal family, which had not exactly covered itself in glory. It was less than twenty-five years since they had given up the Saxe-Coburg-Gotha name; they did not need a Greek suffix now.

The behaviour of Alice in Athens may also have worried George VI. When the city was liberated in October 1944, Harold Macmillan found her 'living in humble, not to say somewhat squalid conditions'. The two did not communicate well as Macmillan had not realised she was deaf (he also had a beard at the time, which made it hard for her to lip-read). In a letter to Philip, his mother admitted that, in the week before Greece had been liberated, she had had no food except bread and butter, and had not eaten meat for several months. By early December, the situation in Athens grew worse as Communist guerrillas were fighting the British for control of the capital. To the dismay of the British, Alice insisted on walking the streets, distributing rations to children and breaking the curfew. When told that she might have been shot by a stray bullet, she replied: 'They tell me that you don't hear the shot that kills you and in any case I am deaf, so why worry about that?'

Religious though she was, Alice still seems to have wanted the glittering match for her son. Mountbatten warned her not to mention a word of his plan when she visited the King and Queen in England. For once, Alice did as her family requested.

In his pursuit of Elizabeth, Philip was as pressing as George VI had been in pursuit of her mother. In June 1946, Philip apologised to the King for brazenly inviting himself to the Palace, but added, 'nothing ventured nothing gained.' He did gain, because Elizabeth's parents liked him enough to invite him a few weeks later to Balmoral to shoot. It was there that the couple 'began to think about it seriously and even talk about it', Philip said. Crawford was sure they would marry. 'Where Lilibet gives her love and affection she gives it once and for all,' she wrote. The King and Queen were still hesitant: their daughter was so young, Philip's family so problematic and Mountbatten so keen on the marriage. In the end, the great-great-grandson of Queen Victoria and Prince Albert married their great-great-granddaughter.

The Little Princesses ends with the birth of Prince Charles in 1948. 'Lilibet has become Mummie,' Crawford noted wryly. Princess Margaret joked that she had become 'Charley's aunt – probably my proudest title of all'.

In 1948, Crawford left royal service to marry a bank manager. She was made a Commander of the Royal Victorian Order. Some writers have suggested that she was offended not to have received a more senior honour and wrote her book in a fit of pique and revenge. One would have to be perverse to believe this. Though occasionally critical, *The Little Princesses* is a loving tribute to two girls and their parents. In the end, the governess had better manners than the royals. They ignored her totally after the book came out. In her will, the ever-loyal Crawford bequeathed a collection of the pictures she had taken to the Queen.

12

PRINCE CHARLES – AND SEPARATION ANXIETY

The marriage of Philip and Elizabeth took place in 1947. Alice was invited, but not her three surviving daughters, whose sons had fought for the Nazis – Britain was still hostile to her recent enemy.

After Princess Elizabeth gave birth to their first child – Prince Charles – in 1948, the boy nestled by his mother for an hour or so and was then moved to the nursery. He was circumcised, even though he was not Jewish. In 1950, she gave birth to a daughter. Charles and Anne would see far less of their parents than Elizabeth and Margaret had done of theirs. Nevertheless, the Queen had absorbed a great deal from her own childhood; she and Margaret hugged, and were hugged by their parents often. Touching, as Winnicott observed, is important. Elizabeth was not remote and liked to give Charles and Anne their baths, something the white-capped Mrs Knight had usually done at 145 Piccadilly.

In 1949, the family moved to Clarence House at a time when George VI's health was causing some concern: his perpetual smoking was affecting his lungs. His daughter started to take on some of her father's duties. One of Charles's first biographers, G. F. Wakeford, noted: 'the Prince learned early in life the inevitability of separation' and went on, in a splendid display of psychological naïveté, to add, 'Charles was still young enough not to feel the absence of his mother too keenly.' Wakeford obviously hadn't even read newspapers such as *The Times* attentively, or he would have learned of groundbreaking research by Harlow and by John Bowlby, a psychoanalyst at London's Tavistock Institute. The work showed that both human and monkey infants cried bitterly when their mothers left them and sometimes hurt themselves in their distress. In his study of forty-four juvenile thieves, Bowlby also established that most of them had been separated from their mothers when they were young.

Of course, Charles did not turn into a juvenile thief, but too much of his childhood was spent away from his parents. There were good reasons of state for this, but a toddler could hardly be expected to understand the need to show the flag round the world, as the royals had been doing for generations. His parents missed his second birthday because his father was serving at sea and his mother had to help her own father. The King's poor health forced Philip and Elizabeth to delay their departure for two weeks in October 1951 as her father had to have an operation to remove his left lung after the discovery of a malignant tumour. When she finally left, Elizabeth took a sealed envelope with her. It contained documents that she would have to sign if George VI died. As a result, Charles spent yet another birthday, his third, without his parents.

Almost as soon as his mother returned from America after a four-month-long absence, she began planning a tour of the Empire and Commonwealth, which would again take her away from her son. There are suggestions that she was not happy that she had to put her duties first, but she had no choice and it is likely her husband saw no need to mollycoddle Charles; after all Philip had had to grapple with far more serious problems than whether his parents would light the candles on his birthday cake. At Christmas, Elizabeth took Charles to visit Father Christmas at Harrods, but most psychologists would suggest what Charles really wanted for Christmas was his parents.

Charles saw much of Queen Elizabeth, the Queen Mother, but very little of his other grandmother as Alice stayed in Greece. In January 1949, she fulfilled her ambition and founded a nursing order of Greek Orthodox nuns: the Christian Sisterhood of Martha and Mary. She modelled it on the order her aunt, the martyred Ella, had established forty years earlier. Alice devoted much energy to raising funds for her mission and travelled to America twice for this, as well as to Sweden and India. 'What can you say of a nun who smokes and plays canasta?' pondered an amused Princess Victoria (she herself had smoked since the age of sixteen).

Princess Victoria died in 1950. Before she did, Queen Victoria's granddaughter, who had lost one child and tried to help another through her 'madness', told her son, Louis Mountbatten:

> What will live in history is the good work done by the individual & that has nothing to do with rank or title. I never thought I would be known only as your mother. You're so well known now and no one knows about me, and I don't want them to.

A bereaved daughter

Soon after Christmas, Charles and Anne were once again left alone by their parents. In January 1952, a frail George VI waved his daughter and her husband off at London Airport as they flew to Africa. While they were in Kenya at a hunting lodge, the ailing King died. Back home, the two children spent most of the day in the nursery. Charles sensed something was wrong and asked to be taken to see his granny. The Queen Mother took him on her knee and assured him that 'Mummy and Papa will be home soon.' She comforted him, admitting later that he comforted her, too.

Four days later, when Charles's mother came home, she had tremendous new responsibilities. She herself was only twenty-five years old but her father had made her aware that she had to be extremely conscientious. Whatever controversies there might have been about the private lives of the royals, no one disputes that Elizabeth has been a hardworking Queen, who only faced one moment when the survival of the monarchy was even remotely in question: after the death of Diana.

Charles seemed too young to sit through the whole of his mother's Coronation ceremony but he did attend part of it. Alice came from Greece and there is a wonderfully dramatic picture of her, walking in her nun's habit down the aisle of Westminster Abbey. Marie

Bonaparte spent much of the ceremony flirting with François Mitterrand, later the President of France, but by then Princess Marie was over sixty and too old for the priapic President so they just talked. The contradictions in Philip's background are striking.

Following this, the Queen and Prince Philip moved into Buckingham Palace. They were obviously worried about how the change would affect their son and tried hard to make the nursery seem as much like Clarence House as possible. Charles brought his box of toy soldiers, his cuckoo clock and his 10ft-high mock Tudor doll's house. His mother's study was out of bounds, however. Once when he walked by her door, Charles asked her to come and play with him. 'If only I could,' she said.

In an age of deference, everyone deferred to the royal family as a matter of course but the children also had to defer to adults. The Queen and Prince Philip also did not want their children spoilt – they insisted the Palace staff call their son 'Charles' without any flummery. He was once punished when he spoke to a detective without saying 'Mr' to him. When he misbehaved, Philip smacked him and the nannies were told not to be inhibited if Charles was naughty. Philip once spanked him when he stuck his tongue out at the crowd watching the royal family being driven down the Mall. When a footman rushed to close a door left open by Charles, Philip told him to leave it. 'The boy's got hands,' he said. When Charles threw some snowballs at a soldier in Sandringham, Philip told the man to pelt his son back. Compared to the way James I and George IV were treated, the princely bottom was thwacked rarely and mildly, but times had changed.

Charles did not enjoy a normal childhood, though. It was not just the many and long separations. When he was three, he got a car, a chauffeur of his own and his first own personal footman. At the start of this book, I quoted his father who questioned: 'What is a normal upbringing?' Prince Philip was not being either insensitive or ironic, which he often is; the best footman is not a father, as Queen Charlotte suggested in the 1780s.

Privilege was not the only problem: there was enormous press interest in Charles, which only increased when his parents decided to send him to a real school (revolutionary for a royal). In 1957, a week before his eighth birthday, he was sent to Hill House in Knightsbridge. Through her private secretary, the Queen appealed to editors to spare her son 'the embarrassment of constant publicity'. They were more respectful then than now, but the appeal still did not entirely succeed.

In his splendid *How to be an Alien*, the Hungarian humorist George Mikes, who had taken refuge from the Nazis in Britain, poked fun at postwar society. The true Brit did not just have a stiff upper lip but also never cried. Sadly, no one read this book to Prince Charles. In 1956, when the Queen and Prince Philip went on another politically necessary foreign tour, the boy was allowed to see his parents off at Heathrow, but cameras caught him crying. When his parents flew back, Charles was made to stay at Buckingham Palace and watch their homecoming on television: it would not do for the future King to be seen blubbering, sniffling or showing emotion. Prince Charles was learning that, if he displayed his feelings, he would suffer. A few months later, his father left for a four-month world tour, the highlight of which was to open the 1956 Olympic Games in Melbourne.

After Hill House, Charles followed in his father's footsteps to Cheam. Philip introduced the headmaster to his wife by saying, 'This is my late headmaster, who used to cane me.' The Revd. Harold Taylor later wrote that the Queen smiled and responded: 'I hope you gave it to him good and proper.' Cheam trained boys for Eton and the great public schools, but Prince Philip wanted his son to follow him to Gordonstoun because he thought Charles needed to be toughened up.

Philip personally flew his son to see the school. The event was filmed and Charles behaved impeccably, shaking hands at all the appropriate times (obviously, he felt under pressure to do as his parents wished). Gordonstoun gave Philip the stability he desperately needed in the 1930s, but he had one key advantage over his son: no one knew, or cared, who he was because at the time he was not well known; his fellow pupils did not see him as being 'different'. Charles was the future King and he was teased and sometimes bullied. The inspirational, if eccentric, Hahn was also no longer in charge. The school did not suit Charles so well as it had done his father; when he attended school in Australia for a brief time, he liked it better. The Queen and Prince Philip wanted to give him experience of a school other than in Britain; it also showed the flag in Oz.

The 1960s saw a great change in sexual mores. One did not have to be Bohemian or a member of the Bloomsbury set to experiment. The Mountbattens had led raffish lives so it is hardly surprising that Louis thought that, after he left school, Prince Charles should sow his wild oats – and, as one of the most eligible bachelors on the planet, he did not find it hard to attract girls. The press made much of his affair in Australia with a girl he met on a beach, but, when I made *The Madness of Prince Charles*, I discovered that Charles did not always get his girls himself. I was introduced to Luis Basualdo, a top-class Argentinian polo player who had been the son-in-law of Lord Cowdray. Luis gave me an amusing history of his friendship with Charles and some interesting insights.

By the time I met him in his New York apartment, Luis was a handsome man in his late fifties. His hair was slicked back and he enjoyed recalling his friendship with the Prince. He described two different periods in Charles's life in some detail. The first was around 1967–8. The Prince was at Cambridge, studying properly for a proper degree, although Lord Butler, the Master of his College, was often annoyed when the Palace insisted Charles take time off from his studies to perform some minor public duty. Luis said that he and Charles were part of a polo-playing group that included Camilla Shand and her future husband, Andrew Parker Bowles. Parker Bowles was 'very witty'. Charles, however, was shy and not confident with girls. Luis said that, as he was three years older, he gave him advice on how to handle the opposite sex: he told him to be tough and frankly encouraged him to use his position to attract girls. It worked – girls threw themselves at the future King of England.

Luis told me that personally he liked younger girls, but Charles did not at all. He sometimes introduced him to stunning seventeen-year-olds only to find that the Prince wasn't interested. Luis smiled at me and spread his arms, which he brought together to hug himself: mothers hug. He said that he thought Charles was always looking for lovers who mothered him and he shrugged after making that observation.

The valet's perspective

While still at Cambridge, Charles acquired something few undergraduates have: a personal valet. Stephen Barry, who became Charles's 'Jeeves' in 1970, wrote a book far less astute than Crawford's, but it still provides many interesting details. He found Charles friendly, 'but he was always Royal' and distant. Barry learned never to sit in his presence unless specifically asked to. He had to wake him at 7.50 a.m. Breakfast was nearly always the same, as the Prince liked oats.

Barry provides nice facts about Charles's relationship with his mother. If they were both in Buckingham Palace, they would nearly always have dinner together. Charles always visited his mother in her apartments, she never came to his. He often told Barry that the Queen was very wise. When Barry first went to work for him, Charles sometimes said: 'We will see what happens when I'm in charge', but later he heard that refrain far less often.

Prince Philip deferred to the Queen in public, but he made many key family decisions. He often used to tell his son off for being slow and being distracted. Barry adds: 'Then you could hear his father calling, "Charles — come *along*!" He is always trying to speed him up.'

'Coming, Poppa,' the Prince would say, according to Barry.

Unlike Luis, Barry said nothing about girlfriends. The two polo players kept in touch after Charles left Cambridge and went into the Navy. Luis was now married. He told me that he often fixed Charles up with girls and let the Prince take them back to an attic room in the house belonging to his father-in-law. He played practical jokes, often locking Charles, and whoever the girl was that night, in the room. It was merry, but not that innocent. One of the girls with whom Charles had a fling was also seeing another polo player, who played for England – and also, Luis claimed, Sarah Ferguson's father, who had a major position in national polo life. All good fun, he smiled, and very much in the spirit of the decadence of the Mountbatten set of thirty years earlier. The girls 'knew the game,' Luis added.

Classic psychoanalytic theory suggests that men who play around are fundamentally hostile towards women and this is often the result of a difficult relationship with their mothers. A Freudian would claim that Luis was being a little naïve: Charles was not looking for the love and hugs he felt he had never had but taking his revenge on his mother's entire sex. His wife would bear the brunt of this.

In the course of my research, I also made a second discovery involving the living and the recently dead, which needs to be handled with tact. It concerns post-natal depression – and its victim was not Princess Diana, but a more senior member of the royal family who was treated with ECT by Dr Denis Leigh. Leigh became well known in the 1970s when he was one of many leading psychiatrists to criticise the way the Soviets detained dissidents in mental hospitals. He worked at the Maudsley Hospital in London and eventually chaired the World Psychiatric Association. The ECT episode matters because it should have made the Queen more sympathetic when Diana suffered from post-natal depression.

13

PRINCESS DIANA AS A MOTHER

When Charles and Diana married in 1981, the press asked if a Spencer was good enough to marry a Windsor. Her father countered that the more appropriate question was whether a Windsor, recently a Saxe-Coburg-Gotha with Greek trimmings, was good enough to marry a Spencer. Charles himself joked that Diana was rather more English than he was, which is perfectly true.

Diana's father, Johnnie Spencer, was a 32-year-old ex-army officer when he met Frances Roche, whose family held the Fermoy baronetcy; he was also heir to the Spencer name and their wonderful house at Althorp. If Spencer was dinosaur-dyed nobility, the Fermoys were new blood on the block that had made their money in 'trade', manufacturing paint. Frances's mother, Ruth Fermoy, had fought her way into the aristocracy. There is no riche like a nouveau riche and, perhaps, there is no grandee as grand as one whose earlier generations were not grand at all. Ruth Fermoy sometimes behaved in ways that recall Marie Bonaparte's snobbish grandmother back in the 1890s. Fermoy was a stickler for convention, especially once she had achieved the distinction of being appointed a Lady of the Bedchamber to the Queen Mother. Ruth was delighted when Spencer, who could trace his genes back to John of Gaunt, proposed to her daughter. She was equally delighted when the witnesses to the marriage included the Queen and Prince Philip.

Spencer had not impressed much in the army. His commanding officer said he was very nice, but very stupid. After leaving, Spencer tried to get work so that he would not have to rely on an allowance from his father. The old boys' network was supposed to work for 'chaps' like him, but, when he asked an old school friend to introduce him to the bankers and stockbrokers Hoare & Son, the friend refused. Spencer had never been any good at maths, he reminded him, which might prove a handicap for a banker. In fact, Spencer did nothing much but look after Althorp when his father died.

The Spencers were happy at first. Frances gave birth to two daughters but her husband and her mother were desperate for a male heir. Frances's third child was male but died within hours. The death certificate noted the child 'died from extensive malformations'. Her husband and mother did not let her see her dead child. Frances minded terribly: it was, she felt, as if the baby she had been carrying for nine months had never existed. Her husband and her mother then behaved more like Henry VIII than people of the 1960s. If Frances wasn't producing healthy boy babies, something must be wrong with her insides; they sent her to have gynaecological tests. The ordeal was humiliating.

Despite this, Frances became pregnant again, but she lost the baby. Later, when she revealed the problems in her own marriage, Diana said this obsession with a male heir affected her. She was supposed to be a boy and felt she had disappointed her family, which did nothing for her self-esteem. 'I was hopeless,' she often said.

Diana was born in 1961. Pressure to provide a male heir was not the only pressure in her parents' marriage: Frances was beginning to find Johnnie Spencer dull, as just about everyone had done for most of his life. When she finally gave him the longed-for male heir, the marriage did not improve. Frances said, in the last three years of their relationship, she and Johnnie drifted apart and neither of them seemed able to do anything about it.

Memories of early childhood are not necessarily accurate, but Diana remembered often seeing her mother cry and said that her father never explained why. In retrospect, she realised that her parents were always 'sorting themselves out' but, in fact, failing to do so.

The unhappy Frances spent more and more time in London. During one of her visits, she met Peter Shand Kydd, heir to a wallpaper fortune and also the brother-in-law of Lord Lucan, a man whose dissipations rivalled those of Edward VII's first son, Eddy. Kydd's marriage was also in trouble, but he did not begin an affair with Frances. In a far more innocent way than among the Mountbattens in the 1930s, the two couples became friends; they all got on well and went on a skiing trip together in 1967 to Courchevel. But, on the slopes and après-ski, Frances and Peter realised that they were strongly attracted to each other and they did something about it after the holiday; being rich has its uses when it comes to adultery. The couple did not have to use hotels – Shand Kydd rented a flat in Belgravia, where he and Frances could meet. In September, someone told Spencer his wife was being unfaithful to him. He was furious and sued for divorce on the grounds of adultery. Frances admitted that, but alleged that he had been guilty of cruelty. The divorce became venomous and there was a betrayal for which there are few modern precedents: Spencer persuaded Ruth Fermoy to take the extraordinary step of giving evidence against her own daughter. It may be that a woman whose family had made its money out of paint could not bear to see her daughter give herself to a man whose family had made its fortune out of wallpaper.

In the 1960s, divorce was still seen as a disgrace. The records of the case have remained secret, but Frances claimed that her mother alleged her personality was so flawed that she could never be a good parent. Following this, the court gave Spencer custody of the children. This was an extremely unusual decision at the time, especially as Spencer had been a typical upper-class father and knew more about baccarat than bringing up children. For Diana, the divorce was traumatic. 'The biggest disruption was when Mummy decided to leg it,' she said.

Diana's father approached being the main carer for his children by making life fun for them. He built an outdoor swimming pool and, of course, hired nannies. The nannies had to cope with very unhappy and confused children. Diana and her siblings would stick pins in chairs so the nannies would sit on them and they would sometimes throw the nannies' clothes out of the window, especially if these young women 'were seen as a threat', Diana said. The last phrase suggests the children hoped their parents would get together again, which of course was even less likely to happen if their father flounced off with the help.

Diana was eight years old when the divorce proceedings started. She was told a judge was going to come and see her at her school – a very unusual proceeding – to ask which of her parents she wanted to live with. In the event, no judge ever came to talk to her. In the chaos, Diana took refuge in pets and started a menagerie. She also became very protective of her younger brother, Charles, who became the first child she looked after.

One aspect of Diana's childhood suggests that she already had a slight rebellious streak. Eight-year-old girls whose ancestors included mistresses of Charles II were supposed to be mad about horses. Diana did not show the least interest in riding, though – her passions were tap dancing and ballet.

After the divorce, Diana's mother tried to keep in contact with her children, but, like many divorced couples, Frances and her ex-husband were angry and bitter. In 1971, Spencer hired a new nanny, Mary Clarke, who had more patience with the children than her predecessors. Frances found it very painful to see another woman bringing up her children. One incident made matters worse – and again it involved skiing. Frances and Peter were allowed to take the children to Switzerland. When Mary Clarke met them at King's Cross to deliver the offspring, Diana was holding her arm. According to Frances, she soon discovered that her daughter had broken it and neither her father nor the nanny had noticed. It must be said that they rushed to the slopes rather than to the nearest casualty, but, when the children were handed back, Mary Clarke noticed that: 'To my surprise I saw Diana's arm in a sling.'

The incident gave Frances hope; she saw a chance of getting her children back and instructed solicitors to sue for custody because they were obviously at risk if no one had noticed her daughter had a broken arm. One evening, Spencer asked Mary Clarke to come into his study and, with some embarrassment, read her his ex-wife's statement. Clarke claims she was shocked by the venom of Frances's accusations. At the custody hearing, the nanny defended her competence. 'I wanted no share of the despair of the mother or the jubilation of the father,' she has said. Clarke convinced the judge and Spencer kept his children, though their mother still saw them.

It would be hard to imagine family relations could get any more difficult but they did when Spencer fell in love with Raine, daughter of the romantic novelist Barbara Cartland. In 1972, I filmed Barbara Cartland for a documentary on pin-up girls and was amazed by her snobbery. Cartland would not let the cameras roll until we hired the Queen's make-up lady for her. It cannot be easy to have been her daughter. Raine was certainly not easy with her own stepchildren. She was outrageously rude when she first met them and, in a fine display of manners, belched loudly. Diana laughed, which marked the start of a long and hostile relationship between the two of them.

Diana did not shine academically; she left school with one O-level. She then took a flat at Coleherne Court in Kensington, which she shared with two girl friends. Diana said that she always had the feeling that she was destined to 'marry someone in the public eye'. Although she had boyfriends, there was no scurrying back to their beds in some attic – she always kept them at bay. She became an early example of what Ann Barr and Peter York characterised as a 'Sloane Ranger', but unlike Sarah Ferguson, who later became her sister-in-law, Diana had no lovers.

Diana may have left school with hardly any qualifications but she had learned the lessons of her own traumatic childhood well. She was emotionally intelligent in her dealings with children and that probably started when she protected her younger brother during the trauma of their parents' divorce. The work that Diana did in the brief period before she became engaged to Charles could almost have been designed to help her be a good mother. Many of her informal, part-time jobs after she left school involved looking after young children. In this, she was imitating what many fine child psychologists who had had disturbed childhoods did themselves. Anna Freud became a famous child therapist – Freud himself felt she was too close to him, though he had personally analysed her, something that would now be considered outrageous. When he was ten, John B. Watson, who wrote the bestseller *Psychological Care of Infant and Child*, saw his father leave home and move in with a Native American woman. Penny Junor has recently argued Diana was not such a good mother, but, in a number of her books, Junor has always sided with Charles. She has produced little persuasive evidence that Diana failed her sons.

Many people Diana worked for, as a nanny or a teacher of small children, were struck by her rapport with her charges, and her skill. She knew how to play with them and care for them. As a teenager, the Queen Mother had worked with wounded soldiers during the 1914 war and that influenced her attitudes. In a similar way, Diana was changed by her experiences in looking after small children. When she became a mother, she used both her natural talent and what she had learned; no other royal parent had had as much experience of hands-on childcare, with the possible exception of the child-rearing diva, Queen Charlotte.

The irony is that Charles and Diana should have folded each other into a happy marriage. Both had had difficult childhoods, which left them needy, but it was not to be.

Charles – the most eligible man in the world
After Cambridge, Charles joined the Navy as his father had done and was eventually given command of a minesweeper. With Camilla Shand, he was indecisive. By the time Charles realised he wanted to marry her, she had already decided to marry Andrew Parker Bowles after his relationship with Princess Anne ended. It would have been a major break with tradition for the heir to marry a woman who had had other lovers; permissiveness stopped at the palace gates. By

the mid-1980s, when Sarah Ferguson married Prince Andrew, some experience for the wife of a Prince was acceptable, as Ann Barr noted in an acute piece in *The Observer*, but Ferguson's children had no chance of ever coming close to the throne.

As we have seen, there was considerable psychiatric history in the royal family and Charles, whose grandmother had spent years in an asylum, had enough humility and insight to look for help. Unfortunately, however, he had got to know Laurens van der Post, who became a major influence on him. Van der Post was a Jungian disciple. Unlike Freud, who for all his many flaws enjoyed a stable and relatively happy marriage, Jung was a sexual adventurer. He had an affair with one of his patients, Sabina Spielrein, and eventually settled into a ménage à trois. Van der Post never managed to stay faithful to his wife for long; given Charles's all too understandable conflicts about women, he was perhaps not the wisest person to choose as a mentor. He was also a serial liar; his biographer, J. D. F. Jones, complained of this publicly and the book has the waspish title *Storyteller*.

In 1977, Charles flew to Kenya with van der Post and the two men disappeared for two weeks. In homage to Jung, together they travelled into an area where, in the 1920s, Jung had lived for nine months – a time when he met a number of witch doctors, meetings he claimed were vital for his spiritual development. Charles came back much more confident, especially in his ideas about alternative medicine.

Charles's problems with women and marriage were not helped by the attitude of his 'honorary grandfather', Louis Mountbatten. Mountbatten again tried to engineer a royal marriage, this time between Charles and his real granddaughter, Amanda Knatchbull. Prince Philip also wanted to see his son settle down but Charles, perhaps feeling somewhat railroaded, at least had the sense to delay making any decision.

On 27 August 1979, Mountbatten went lobster potting and tuna fishing in the *Shadow V*, which was moored in the harbour at Mullaghmore in the Republic of Ireland. During the night, an IRA man had attached a radio-controlled 23kg (50lb) bomb to the boat. Soon after Mountbatten came aboard, the bomb was detonated. He was pulled alive from the water by local fishermen, but died before they got him to shore. Lady Brabourne, the 83-year-old mother-in-law of Mountbatten's daughter, was seriously injured and died the next day. Two teenagers were also killed, including one of Lord Mountbatten's grandsons. On the same day, the IRA also killed eighteen British soldiers in an ambush at Warrenpoint.

Charles was devastated. 'He just looked at me and said very quietly, "What was the point?"' his valet, Stephen Barry, recalled. Later, he also told Barry how helpless he felt. The man who had been nagging him to marry had been murdered; Charles needed consolation and perhaps needed to honour the old man. It seems plausible that at this point he decided perhaps his elders were right and he should find a wife. He finally proposed to Amanda Knatchbull but she refused him. It has been claimed the violent deaths made her feel she did not want to be a member of the royal family. When he met Diana, he was still recovering from the shock of Mountbatten's death. She spoke at some length to the biographer Andrew Morton about how she tried to comfort Charles when they first started courting because he was grieving so much. He was needy, but clumsy. The girls Luis had introduced did indeed 'know the game' and part of the game was being quick and willing. 'He was all over me – I thought men were not supposed to be so obvious,' Diana remembered, but of course she had had no serious boyfriends. 'I couldn't handle it emotionally – I was very screwed up,' she said.

Whatever his feelings for Diana were, Charles seemed quite unable to separate from Camilla, but he was in a hurry. Twenty-eight days after he had what might be described as his first 'date' with Diana, he proposed to her. The woman he was going to marry included among her ancestors a mistress of Charles II; the woman he loved was the great-granddaughter of Alice Keppel, the mistress of his great-great-grandfather, Edward VII. When the happy couple were interviewed after becoming engaged, Diana said of course she loved Charles. His diffident comment, 'Whatever love might be', suggests he was very confused and, besides, it was hardly gallant. Eleanor of Aquitaine would have smacked him, but Diana was too awed, just as Mary of Teck had been. After all, her husband-to-be would one day be King.

In the end, Charles married Diana feeling he had been pushed into marriage – and with the wrong woman. Before long, he took it out on her, too. The 'hopeless' Diana constantly made excuses for him when they got engaged. Before the wedding, she left to see her mother in Australia. She was away for three weeks and her fiancé neither rang her nor returned her phone calls during that time. Whatever love is, it is not that: this seems more like anger.

The marriage of the century

Before the wedding, Diana realised the hold that Camilla had on her future husband. It must have terrified her, given the shambles of her own parents' divorce. Her brother later said that it was only when he got married that he realised the impact his parents' divorce had had on him. Diana denied the rumour that she had ever seriously contemplated not going through with the marriage, however: she was in love with Charles.

The amateur Jungian and the Sloane Ranger were married in 1981. While she was saying her vows, Diana reversed the order of Charles's names, putting Philip in front of Charles. Freud would have had fun analysing the true meaning of that slip. Did Diana's unconscious have doubts?

'I had tremendous hopes, which were slashed by day two,' Diana later admitted to Andrew Morton. By then, they were honeymooning on the Royal yacht, *Britannia*. No one had the sense to suggest that it might not be ideal for two relative strangers to start married life with a hundred sailors for company. Charles also seems to have had his mind more on reading than most new husbands. He arrived with seven books by the insufferable van der Post and proceeded to read them all. 'My dreams were appalling,' Diana said. She dreamed of her rival Camilla. Soon after the honeymoon, Diana noticed that Charles was happiest alone with his thoughts – then he did not have to perform or conform.

'Charles was in awe of his mother and intimidated by his father,' said Diana, before adding that her husband 'longs to be patted on his head by his father'.

I have suggested that in some ways Charles and Diana were an excellent emotional match – both had been left needy after difficult childhoods and soon they discovered one telling bond: neither of them could bear to sleep in total darkness. John B. Watson had the same problem and was sure this was the result of his traumatic childhood, when his father walked out.

When she became pregnant, Diana suffered from terrible morning sickness. In January 1982, when she was some four months pregnant, she flung herself down the stairs of Buckingham Palace and landed in a heap at the bottom. Charles accused his wife of crying wolf and got ready to go riding.

The Queen Mother was one of those who saw Diana and was appalled, especially perhaps because she had the wisdom to see that, if Diana was so unhappy during pregnancy, she was likely to suffer from post-natal depression. She herself had seen the damage that could do in her own family.

Charles turned for help not to his father – who had, after all, grown up among therapists – but to the obsequious van der Post. He told him to send Diana to a Jungian analyst. 'All the psychologists and analysts you could dream of were trying to sort me out,' she said later. For a husband to choose his wife's analyst is, of course, an act of control which no good therapist would be party to.

The world was waiting for an heir and the young couple did not disappoint. When Diana gave birth to Prince William on 21 June 1982, Charles came out cradling the baby – a touching photo. But there is also a photograph of William and the family taken a few days later at the Palace with van der Post in the back row. He continued to play an unhelpful part. Having had endless nannies, Diana insisted on being far more of a hands-on mother than most aristocrats. William did have a nanny, but his mother insisted that he would not 'be hidden upstairs with a governess'. Though she adored her son, Diana suffered severe post-natal depression.

Eventually, Diana saw Maurice Lipsedge, a psychiatrist who was not pushed on her by van der Post. Lipsedge had made his name by showing that immigrants tended to be hospitalised more than one might expect for mental illness. Diana said that, when she first went to see him, he asked: 'How many times have you tried to do yourself in?'

'Once a week.'

Lipsedge promised, perhaps a little rashly, that she would be in much better shape within six months. She stayed on as his patient for rather longer but he helped.

The marriage recovered enough for Diana to accompany Charles on a six-week tour of Australia and New Zealand. The 1983 tour had a very political purpose – to jolly the Australians into not voting to turn themselves into a Republic. Malcolm Fraser, the Australian Prime Minister, suggested to Diana that she might like William to come along too. It seems likely that Fraser let the Queen know his views. Diana plucked up the courage to ask her if William could accompany her and Charles. Perhaps because she was well aware of the damage that had been caused when she and Philip had left a very young Charles alone for long periods, the Queen agreed. It was a break with royal precedent, and very wise too.

The couple and their baby were a great success in Australia. Everyone expected the media to lose interest in Diana after the marriage, but the opposite happened. What she said, what she wore, even how she did her hair commanded headlines and much television time. Charles, who had been used to being in the limelight, was jealous, although he usually joked about it. The 'hopeless girl' had become a star, but no one in the royal family praised her any more than Albert and Victoria had praised Bertie after his triumphant tour of America in 1860.

After Australia, the marriage recovered again. It was important for the succession to be assured, as it would be if Charles and Diana had another child. She became pregnant once more, but the date for Harry's birth had to be carefully negotiated in light of his father's commitments, she claimed. 'We had found a date when Charles could get off his polo pony for me to give birth,' Diana said wasp-ishly later. Charles has never denied that particular swipe. When Harry was born, Diana stated that Charles had said that he was 'so disappointed. I thought it would be a girl.'

A year after Harry was born, the first reports suggesting a marriage in crisis appeared and, by 1987, *The People* wrote of a 'blaz-ing row' between Diana and Charles. But it was worse than that for the couple moved into separate bedrooms; soon they were leading separate lives. Diana, who had had issues with eating before, started to suffer from bulimia.

Around 1985, when she stopped seeing Lipsedge, Diana was treated by the psychotherapist Susie Orbach, author of *Fat is a Feminist Issue*. Photographers lurked outside Orbach's house to snap the Princess. *The Daily Mail* pointed out that Orbach, whose father had been a Labour MP, was left wing and 'hated the traditional family'. Orbach now lives with the novelist Jeanette Winterson. I knew Orbach from my childhood and tried to persuade her, after Diana died, to discuss a little of what had happened in the therapeutic sessions. Orbach told me that she would not ever reveal a scintilla.

Diana's aims as a mother made sense in light of her own history. Of her sons she said: 'I want to bring them up with security and not to anticipate things because they will be disappointed.' She added: 'I hug my children to death.' It seems likely that they needed comfort because few children remain unaffected when their parents' marriage is failing.

Diana had experiences other Princesses had never had and did things they had never done. For example, she often went shopping with her children and tried to persuade the boys not to eat things that were bad for them; she also tried to 'choose health foods for the boys' tea'. Diana made sure that neither of her sons was assigned a personal footman, as Charles had been when he was three. She herself bought their clothes and added, 'I have to buy two of everything otherwise they squabble.' She also read to them the same books that millions of parents read to their children –

Winnie the Pooh, *Babar The Elephant* and many others that she had loved during her own childhood. Diana's friend and former flatmate, Carolyn Bartholomew, admired the fact that Diana and Charles were aware of the differences between William and Harry and were 'proud of William's self-confidence and independence and are equally proud of Harry's thoughtfulness and gentle nature'.

Therapy made Diana willing to talk publicly about her own problems, which marked a sharp break with royal precedent. She opened a number of conferences on eating disorders and described the feelings she had had as a child as 'guilt, self-revulsion and low personal self-esteem, creating a compulsion to dissolve like Disprin and disappear'.

Diana was a loyal supporter of the work of Broadmoor, Britain's oldest asylum for the criminally insane, which houses some of the country's most dangerous men and women. Ronnie Kray was a patient for ten years and the Yorkshire Ripper, Peter Sutcliffe, has been there for over twenty-five years. Diana visited the hospital many times, often without it becoming public knowledge. To the terror of Alan Franey, then the hospital's general manager, she insisted on talking to patients on her own. Franey told me she had considerable rapport with them. The experience of her parents' divorce had perhaps shaped, and sharpened, her emotional intelligence.

The body of Princess Alice

While the Queen and Prince Philip were trying to cope with their son's disintegrating marriage, they faced a reminder of Philip's troubled past. His mother had come to England in 1967, when the Colonels staged a coup in Greece. Alice said she wished to be buried in Gethsemane on the Mount of Olives in Jerusalem, near to her literally sainted aunt, Ella. When her daughter complained that it would be too far away for them to visit her grave, Alice jested: 'Nonsense, there's a perfectly good bus service!' Nineteen years after she died in 1969, Alice's body was still in Windsor, though. Transporting a body is not hard so long as you can pay

£4,000 and you can contact efficient funeral directors, which is hardly beyond the royals. Alice did not have her wishes honoured, however, until 3 August 1988.

When she was buried, the Israeli authorities' memory was jogged but, again, rather slowly. Six years later, Alice's two surviving children – Prince Philip and Princess George of Hanover – went to Yad Vashem, the Holocaust Memorial in Jerusalem, to witness a ceremony honouring her as one 'Righteous among the Gentiles' for having hidden the Cohens. Prince Philip said: 'I suspect that it never occurred to her that her action was in any way special. She was a person with a deep religious faith, and she would have considered it to be a perfectly natural human reaction to help fellow beings in distress.'

The publication of Andrew Morton's book *Diana: Her True Story* made it clear her marriage was beyond saving – partly, as Diana saw it, because of the influence of the courtiers who protected Charles, and because of Charles's relationship with Camilla. Seven months after the book appeared, the Prime Minister, John Major, told the House of Commons that the couple were to separate. By then, no one was surprised. The Queen said that 1992 was her *annus horribilis*, echoing Hugh Dalton, the son of Canon Dalton, who had said that 1947 was an *annus horrendus* for the British people.

When Diana and Charles separated, public sympathy was largely on her side, just as it had been with Caroline against George IV. In 1994, Anna Pasternak's *Princess in Love* revealed Diana's affair with James Hewitt, an army officer who was also not a bad polo player. It was only after Hewitt that she became involved with men who were radically different from Charles, such as the heart surgeon Hasnat Khan. Despite this, Diana somehow remained untouched. She did not forewarn the Queen or the Palace of her famous television interview with Martin Bashir on BBC's *Panorama* in November 1995. In it, she gave a stunning performance, being both verbally and emotionally assured. She had committed adultery, but was that surprising as there had been three people in the marriage, making it rather crowded? She also criticised the royal family for not supporting her and wondered if Charles really wanted 'the top job'.

Diana projected the picture she intended: that of a woman who had been betrayed and had discovered herself with the help of therapy. Although the mother of a future king, she herself would never be Queen, but she said that she hoped to be 'a Queen in people's hearts'. The huge audience concluded that Charles was to blame for the failure of the marriage. She, not he, came across as the doting parent. The divorce negotiations were bitter – one unnecessary humiliation was stripping Diana of her title as Her Royal Highness.

The day the divorce was finalised, Diana went to open the new premises for the Ballet Rambert. I had by then written a book on body language and GMTV asked me to observe and comment on the Princess's body language. Never before had I been a member of the royal press pack. I was astounded. There were perhaps 300 reporters, photographers and cameramen all scrabbling to get the best angles. Many came with ladders on which to stand. For any person to be something of a 'good-enough parent' in such circum-stances was quite an achievement. Anthony Holden, the author of two generous biographies of Prince Charles, told me he had to contrast Diana's courtesy with her husband's rudeness: Charles had never thanked him for his work, but, after Holden wrote a piece in support of Diana, she arranged to meet him at her favourite restaurant. The Princes were also there. Holden was charmed by her, and by them.

No one knew at the time that Diana was deeply in love with the heart surgeon Hasnat Khan. She went to Pakistan to see his family but they rebuffed her because they did not want their son to marry a divorced woman. A few weeks after the relationship broke up, the owner of Harrods, Mohamed al-Fayed, invited Diana and the Princes to spend some time on his yacht in St Tropez. She accepted partly because he could provide security for herself and her chil-dren. By then, Diana was saying she wanted to live abroad: 'Any sane person would have left long ago, but I cannot. I have my sons.'

William was now fifteen years old and his mother was pleased that her children were protective: 'My boys are urging me continually to leave the country; they say it is the only way. They want me to live abroad. I sit in London all the time and I am abused and followed wherever I go. I cannot win.'

In St Tropez, Diana met Dodi al-Fayed. There has been endless speculation as to whether or not it was a serious affair for her. The Princes had always been due to return before the end of the holiday to join their father in Scotland, and they did so. After they left, Diana and Dodi flew to Sardinia and on to Paris, where they booked into the bridal suite at the Ritz, owned by al-Fayed. The intriguing question of where they were going at 10 p.m. when the Mercedes belonging to the Ritz crashed in the Alma Tunnel has never been finally resolved. The way back to the apartment owned by al-Fayed was not through the Alma Tunnel. It has been suggested that they were on their way to a business meeting as someone was offering Dodi a share in a new nightclub and he wanted to show off his new girlfriend. The matter of where Henri Paul, the driver of the Mercedes, was between 7 p.m. and 10 p.m. has also never been resolved. At 10 p.m. Paul was called back to the Ritz to drive the couple. He was said to be drunk, but I found video evidence that, sixty minutes before taking Diana and Dodi to their unknown destination, he managed to squat on his haunches and tie his shoelaces. Such perfect balance is hard to manage if one is drunk.

Those like David Aaronovitch who argue that there was no conspiracy have never explained where Diana and Dodi were going on the night of 30 August 1997.

When Diana died, Charles behaved emotionally and with dignity. The Prince of Wales flew to Paris to collect her body and insisted the royal standard be placed on her coffin. He seemed very sad, but then, when she first met him, Diana had been struck by how sad he looked.

At the funeral, Diana's sons walked slowly behind the coffin, very young but very controlled. Since her death, they have consistently talked of their warm memories of their mother. Prince William wishes his mother had met Kate Middleton, the woman he married on 29 April 2011: 'I'm just sad she's never going to get a chance to meet Kate,' he said.

Charles was now a single father – and a single father in an awkward position. His sons knew that he wanted to marry the woman who had caused their mother so much distress. There is no doubt that he tried more than ever before to be a good father but his own childhood had hardly equipped him for the task.

Knowing the truth about contemporary royal relationships is virtually impossible, but, fifteen years after Diana died, it seems that Charles and his sons get on well. We don't yet know what kinds of fathers Charles and Diana's sons will make – nor how much their mother will influence them. Both William and Harry remain devoted to her memory. When, and if, either of her sons has a daughter, it will be surprising if she is not called Diana.

Conclusions

At the end of this long history, one should try to draw modest conclusions at least. Children have to learn about boundaries and one of the problems royal children face is that these boundaries change because their status changes. One of the most poignant moments in Shakespeare is when Prince Hal, who had gone drinking – and probably whoring – with Falstaff, denies him and says: 'I know thee not, old man.' The man who beat the future Edward VIII when he was a little boy eventually became his charge's valet. Princess Margaret often insisted on being called 'Her Royal Highness' in the most informal of situations. Charles was given a footman when he was three and that footman was told to call him by his Christian name. We do not know, however, at what point the footman was ordered to revert to protocol and address the Prince as 'Your Royal Highness'. I would argue that some royal children get confused by such changes – what we are called is central to our sense of identity – and, in the future, they should at least have the confusion explained to them.

In terms of parenting, the evidence since 1066 shows profound

changes have sometimes occurred very quickly under the pressure
of personalities and events. Between 1066 and 1485, princes had to
be taught practical warfare above all else. I have argued that, partly
due to the influence of Margaret Beaufort from 1485 onwards,
royal children had an elite education and were often taught by the
best minds in Europe. After James I's death, the Stuarts were more
interested in pleasure and, to some extent, in religion than in any
kind of scholarship. Education was infinitely less important to the
Hanoverians and, from 1714 to 1837, the relationship between royal
parents and their children became not just unloving but hostile.
Queen Victoria was a victim of this emotional abuse when she was
a girl and she did not behave as her mother had done, yet she
allowed Prince Albert to try to turn their eldest son, Bertie, into
an obedient pedant. Many children would have been crushed by
such expectations, but he proved resilient and reacted against his
draconian upbringing.

Since the end of the nineteenth century, each generation has
reacted against the way it was brought up. There is an exception
to this, though. Once Bertie became King Edward VII, he gave
his son access to all state papers. George V, in turn, gave his son
George access to many papers and even let David – who provoked
so many anxieties – see some of them. We do not know the extent
to which the Queen has done this with Prince Charles but it seems
likely that she has not been so open, once it became clear that
Charles was trying to intervene in political matters far more than
convention allowed.

The long case history also shows how wise it was of George III's
wife to warn against relying too much on royal servants when bringing up children: the most devoted nurse is not quite the same as
one's own parents and children often know it. Princess Diana was
in no sense an absentee mother, though Prince Charles was often
an absentee father – and that persisted to some extent even after
the death of Diana. Even good-enough parenting needs parents to
devote much time to their children; Diana complained Charles was
too often distracted.

Some radical suggestions are perhaps worth making in terms of the future. The present government is making great play of 'parenting classes'. It would be a magnificent symbol for Prince William and his wife Kate to attend such classes when they have children; it would show that everyone has something to learn when it comes to bringing up children. A second radical suggestion concerns schooling. Prince Charles and Diana sent their sons to Eton, as Charles clearly had little fondness for Gordonstoun. The Provost of Eton is now Lord Waldegrave, a descendant of the doctor who attended a number of Stuart births in the 1680s. Today's Waldegrave is a very clever man as he is a Fellow of All Souls, but Eton remains elitist and now attracts a growing number of pupils from very rich families in Russia and the Far East. Since royal children started to go to school, it has been assumed they must attend an elite public school. It might benefit both the children and the monarchy if the next generation spent a little time in an ordinary state primary school. Small children are less conscious of status and so Princes and Princesses might be able to mix with ordinary children more or less normally, at least as small children.

The philosopher John Locke and, over two hundred years later, the psychologist John B. Watson argued that parents need to talk to their children about problems at the end of every day and on as equal a footing as possible. That remains sensible advice – for every parent.

At the end of this book, it seems fitting to return to Froeze's Ten Commandments for Parents, which are now over fifty years old. Having studied ten centuries of royal parenting and, I hope, learning from the experience, I now take the liberty of revising them:

See your child as the most precious responsibility entrusted to you.
Do not try to mould your child in your own image.
Children need space to develop physically and playfully. Let them have it.
Get to know and respect your child's personality.
Do not push your child too hard.
Do not use force against your child.

Encourage your child to be confident even if sometimes they are
bound to annoy you.
Protect your child.
Do not lie to your child and do not tempt the child to lie to you.
Most important of all,
Enjoy your child.

One of the sad truths is that, all too often, for all the reasons explored
in this book, royal parents have not enjoyed their children as much
as they could have done, or as much as they *should* have done.
When Prince William and Catherine, Duchess of Cambridge have
a child, I hope they will enjoy him or her. Diana would certainly
want her son to hug, play and lark about with her grandchildren.

BIBLIOGRAPHY, LETTERS AND OTHER SOURCES

Many biographies of the kings and queens of England have examined their childhoods with less of a psychological perspective than one might expect. Writing this book has made me more familiar with the long and varied tradition of royal biographies, which range from the gossipy to the soberly academic. Some monarchs, like Elizabeth I, have been written and re-written about; others, such as James I, attracted far fewer biographers. I have found the following useful and often entertaining.

Ashley, Maurice, *The Life and Times of William I* (London: Weidenfeld & Nicolson, 1973).

Bradbury, Jim, *Stephen and Matilda: The Civil War of 1139–53* (Stroud: Sutton, 2005).

Doherty, P. C., *Isabella and the Strange Death of Edward II* (London: Constable & Robinson, 2004).

Flori, Jean, *Richard the Lionheart: King and Knight* (Greenwood: Praeger Publishers Inc, 2007).

Mortimer, Ian, *The Perfect King: The Life of Edward III, Father of the English Nation* (London: Vintage, 2008).

Warren W. L., *King John* (New Haven: Yale University Press, 1997).

As well as these biographies, *She-Wolves: The Women Who Ruled England Before Elizabeth* by Helen Castor (London: Faber & Faber, 2011) offers an insight into the powerful medieval women who had enormous influence. *Winter King: The Dawn of Tudor*

England by Thomas Penn (London: Penguin, 2011) is an excellent recent work on Henry VII; David Starkey has written splendidly on both Henry VIII and the young Henry. *The Six Wives of Henry VIII* by Alison Weir (London: Vintage, 2007) offers a good account of that half dozen, as does David Starkey again. *Mary Tudor: England's First Queen* by Anna Whitelock (London: Bloomsbury, 2010) provides a sober account of a troubled girl, who became a troubled Queen.

Two good biographies of Elizabeth I are by J. N. Neale and by the more modern champion of the Tudors, David Starkey. The long rivalry between the Virgin Queen and Mary, Queen of Scots is well charted in Jane Dunn's *Elizabeth & Mary: Cousins, Rivals, Queens* (London: Harper Perennial, 2004). Like Elizabeth, Mary, Queen of Scots has been lucky in her biographers, who include Lady Antonia Fraser and John Guy. The title of his book has a Mills & Boon touch – *My Heart is my Own* (London: Harper Perennial, 2004).

James I, the best writer ever to occupy the throne, offers considerable insight into his own personality. The classic biography by Carla and H. Steeholm, *The Wisest Fool in Christendom*, was published back in 1938. More recent biographies have tended to be rather short. The reason for the neglect of the scholarly King who gave us the King James Bible eludes me. Richard Cust's *Charles I* (London: Longmans, 2007) covers the latest research on James's stubborn son, who has had much more study devoted to him than his father did. The essentially Marxist Christopher Hill offers a measured but admiring account of Oliver Cromwell in *God's Englishman: Oliver Cromwell and the English Revolution* (London: Penguin, 1999), while Lady Antonia Fraser, though no Marxist, evidently also admires much about him in *Cromwell, Our Chief of Men* (London: Phoenix, 2008). Curiously, there is no proper biography of Richard Cromwell, Oliver's son who ruled briefly, fled the Kingdom, returned after some twenty years and settled down to the life of a country gentleman. Antonia Fraser's *King Charles II* (London: Phoenix, 2002) remains an excellent account of the monarch who was not merely 'merry' but also a great survivor.

The relationship of the House of Orange to the English throne merits a case history of its own as the Oranges were always trying to marry first the Stuarts, then the Hanoverians, and then Victoria's children. There seems to be no book on this relationship.

Edward Gregg provides a decent account of Queen Anne (New Haven: Yale University Press, 2001), though he is much less detailed on her obstetric tragedies than Jack Dewhurst in his *Royal Confinements* (London: Weidenfeld & Nicolson, 1980).

J. H. Plumb's *England in the Eighteenth Century* (London: Penguin, 1951) provides a good account of the four Georges. Frederick, George II's eldest son who became Prince of Wales, never made it to the throne. Sir George Young's *Poor Fred* (Oxford: Oxford University Press, 1937) traces his tragicomic career. The most useful biography of George II is Andrew Thompson's *George II* (New Haven: Yale University Press, 2011).

As a psychologist, I am curious that the question of whether George III was mad or whether he was suffering from porphyra or arsenic poisoning during two periods of his reign is still not quite resolved. Alan Bennett's witty play *The Madness of George III* pokes fun at the pretensions of the royal doctors but modern experts differ as much as the eighteenth-century physicians. Nesta Pain's book, *George III At Home* (London: Methuen, 1975), makes clear how domestic he and Queen Charlotte were. Some forty years ago, J. H. Plumb, that doyen of eighteenth-century historians, published a nice pamphlet, *New Light on the Tyrant George III*, after giving a talk in America – and asked the good folk of Cincinnati to revise their view of the allegedly despotic King who, of course, never visited America. Jeremy Black has published a biography that embraces the latest research (*George III: America's Last King*, New Haven: Yale University Press, 2006).

On George IV, J. B. Priestley's *The Prince of Pleasure and His Regency, 1811–20* (London: William Heinemann Ltd, 1969) is both partisan and surprisingly sweet, given that George IV maddened (I choose the word advisedly) his father and runs Henry VIII a close second in the royal narcissism stakes.

There have been many fine biographies of Queen Victoria, including Elizabeth Longford's *Queen Victoria* (Stroud: The History Press, 2009), Cecil Woodham-Smith's *Queen Victoria: Her Life and Times*, 1819–61 (London: Hamish Hamilton, 1972) and Christopher Hibbert's *Queen Victoria: A Personal History* (London: HarperCollins, 2001).

Sir Philip Magnus's biography of Gladstone (London: John Murray, 1954) did not have access to the Grand Old Man's diaries, in which he detailed his many encounters with prostitutes. In his *King Edward the Seventh* (London: John Murray, 1964), Magnus was also a shade reserved.

Philip Ziegler has written good biographies of King William IV, the sailor King (London: Fontana Books, 1973) and of the less amiable Edward VIII (Stroud: Sutton Publishing, 2001). Kenneth Rose's biography of George V (London: Weidenfeld & Nicolson, 2000) gives a sound, if traditional account. Edward VIII wrote his own – *A King's Story* – long after he had abdicated. *Hidden Agenda: How the Duke of Windsor Betrayed the Allies* (London: Macmillan, 2000) by Martin Allen also offers a good account of his career.

William Shawcross's authorised biography of Elizabeth, the Queen Mother (London: Pan, 2010) manages to be both entertaining and tactful. There is no proper biography of the current Queen as too many sources have to be careful and certain topics remain off limits while she and Prince Philip are alive.

The literature on Charles, Diana and Camilla will one day be the subject of a PhD as it illustrates how hard it is for authors to remain unbiased when dealing with current historical figures. My own book, *Diana: Death of a Goddess* (London: Arrow, 2005), has been seen as more hostile to the Prince, while Penny Junor in *Charles: Victim or Villain?* (London: Harper Collins, 1999) and Caroline Graham in *Camilla: The King's Mistress* (London: John Blake, 1995) are clearly more hostile towards the Princess.

Among many useful sources, the excellent series of the letters of monarchs, covering from Queen Elizabeth I onwards (Kila, MT: Kessinger, 2007), have been key. The diaries of Queen Victoria, which were heavily edited by her daughter, Princess Beatrice, provided invaluable material, though Princess Beatrice did not allow anything to be published of which her formidable mother might have disapproved. *The Dictionary of National Biography* has proved valuable, though by its nature the entries tend not to push a particular thesis.

References

Addison, Joseph, 1713, *Remarks Upon Cato*, B. Lintott.

Adler, Hermann, 1892, *The Nation's Laments*, Westheimer & Lee.

Albert, Victor and George, Prince of Wales, 1886, *The Cruise of the HMS Bacchante*, Macmillan. (The Princes were said to be the authors, though most of it was written by their tutor, Canon John Dalton.)

Alice, Princess HRH, 1966, *For My Grandchildren*, Evans Brothers.

Allen, Martin, 2000, *Hidden Agenda*, Macmillan.

André Le Chaplain, 1941, *The Art of Courtly Love* (introduction and notes by Parry, John), Columbia University Press.

Aronson, Theo, 1994, *Prince Eddy and the Homosexual Underworld*, John Murray.

Ascham, Roger, 1815, *The English Works of Roger Ascham*, Cochrane.

Baker-Smith, Veronica, 2008, *Royal Discord*, Athena Press.

Barrie, J. M., 1918, *The Admirable Crichton*, Hodder & Stoughton.

Barry, Stephen, 1983, *Royal Service: My Twelve Years as Valet to Prince Charles*, Macmillan.

Bathurst, B., editor, 1925, *Letters of Two Queens*, Robert Holden, London.

Benson, A. C. and Esher, Viscount, (editors) 1908, *The Letters of Queen Victoria*, John Murray.

Bertin, Célia, 1987, *Marie Bonaparte*, Yale University Press.

Bingham, Caroline, 1968, *The Making of a King: The Early Years of James I*, Collins.

Boothroyd, Basil, 1971, *Philip: An Informal Biography*, Longmans.

Bowlby, John, 1988, *A Secure Base*, Routledge.

Bradford, Sarah, 2011, *George VI*, Penguin.

Breslau, Naomi, Lucia V. C. and Alvarado, G. F., 2006, 'Intelligence and Other Predisposing Factors in Exposure to Trauma and Post Traumatic Stress', *Archives of General Psychiatry*, vol. 63, 1238–45.

Buchanan, George, see Ford, P., 1982, *Prince of Poets*, Aberdeen University Press and *Renaissance Scholar*, catalogue of the 1982 exhibition at Glasgow by John Dorken, Stephen Rawles and Nigel Thorp.

Burchill, Julie, 1998, *Diana*, Weidenfeld & Nicolson.

Burney, Fanny, 1987, *Selected Letters and Journals of Fanny Burney*, ed. Hemlow, J., Oxford University Press.

Burrell, Paul, 2007, *The Way We Were: Remembering Diana*, HarperCollins.

Campbell, Beatrix, 1998, *Diana, Princess of Wales: How Sexual Politics Shook the Monarchy*, Women's Press.

Cocks, Geoffrey, 1985, *Psychotherapy in the Third Reich*, Oxford University Press.

Cohen, David, 2005, *Diana: Death of a Goddess*, Arrow.

Cohen, David, 2005, *Kavanagh MP*, Psychology News.

Cohen, David and MacKeith, Stephen, 1993, *The Development of the Imagination*, Routledge.

Cohn, Norman, 1993, *The Pursuit of the Millennium*, Pimlico.

Combe, George, 1838, *Outlines of Phrenology*, Maclachan & Stewart.

Combe, George, 1893, *The Constitution of Man in Relation to the Natural Laws*, Cassell.

Crabitès, Pierre, 1937, *Victoria's Guardian Angel: A Study of Baron Stockmar*, Routledge.

Craig, W. M., 1818, *Memoirs of Her Majesty Sophia Charlotte*, Caxton Press.

Craig, Maurice, 1922, *Nerve Exhaustion*, J & A Churchill.

Crawford, Marion, 1953, *The Little Princesses*, Transworld.

Crosby, Travis L., 1999, *Two Mr Gladstones*, Yale University Press.

Darwin, Charles, 1971, *A Biographical Sketch of an Infant*, Heinemann Medical (originally published in 1832).

Dewhurst, Jack, 1964, *Royal Confinements*, Weidenfeld & Nicolson.

Dimbleby, Jonathan, 1980, *The Prince of Wales*, Little, Brown.

Dodd, Gwilym and Musson, Anthony, 2006, *The Reign of Edward II: New Perspectives*, York Mediaeval Press.

Eade, Philip, 2011, *Young Prince Philip: His Turbulent Early Life*, HarperPress.

Erasmus, 1510c, *On the Education of Children* (available in a 1990 edition from Klinieksieck publishers).

Erasmus, 1510c, *A Handbook on Good Manners for Children* (available from Klinieksieck publishers).

Erikson, Erik H., 1972, *Young Man Luther*, Faber & Faber (originally published 1959).

Esher, Viscount (ed.), 1912, *The Girlhood of Queen Victoria* (two volumes), Murray.

Eysenck, Hans, 1985, *The Decline and Fall of the Freudian Empire*, Viking.

Flori, Jean, 2007, *Richard the Lionheart*, Praeger.

Fortescue, Sir John, 1928, *The Correspondence of George III*, Macmillan.

Foxe, J., 1978, *Foxe's Book of Martyrs* (originally published in 1559), available now from Zondervan.

Fraser, Antonia, 2008, *Cromwell: Our Chief of Men*, Phoenix.

Fraser, Antonia, 2009, *King Charles II*, Phoenix.

Freud, S., *The Interpretation of Dreams*, standard edition, Hogarth Press, vols 4–5 (originally published in 1899).

Freud, S., 'On Narcissism', standard edition, Hogarth Press, vol. 14, pp. 69ff (originally published in 1912).

Freud, S., *Totem and Taboo*, standard edition, vol. 13, pp. 1–161 (originally published 1910).

Freud, S. and Bullitt, W., 1967, *Woodrow Wilson*, W. W. Norton.

Froebel, F., 2009, *The Education of Man*, Dover (originally published in German, c. 1820).

Froeze, L., 1992, *The Rights of the Child and the Changing Image of Childhood*, ed. Veerman, Philip E., Martinus Nijhoff.

Fulford, Roger, 1976, *Darling Child: The Private Correspondence of Queen Victoria and the Crown Princess of Prussia*, Evans Bros.

Goleman, Daniel, 1996, *Emotional Intelligence*, Bloomsbury.

Gordon, Harvey, 2012, *Broadmoor*, Psychology News.

Gosse, Edmund, 1907, *Father and Son: A Study of Two Temperaments*, Heinemann.

Graham, Caroline, 1995, *Camilla: The King's Mistress*, John Blake.

Gregg, Edward, 2001, *Queen Anne*, Yale University Press.

Greig, Geordie, 2011, *The King Maker*, Hodder.

Greville, Charles, (ed. Fulford, R.), 1963 *The Greville Memoirs*, Batsford.

Hague, William, 2004, *William Pitt the Younger*, HarperCollins.

Hague, William, 2009, *William Wilberforce*, HarperPerennial.

Hayter, Alethea, 1968, *Opium and the Romantic Imagination*, Faber & Faber.

Henderson, E., 1898, 'The Present Status of the Konigsmarck Question', *American Historical Review*, vol. 3, p 464–76.

Hervey, Lord, 1963, *Memoirs*, Macmillan.

Hervey, Lord and Frederick, Prince of Wales, 1733, a Play – Captain Bodkin.

Hibbert, Christopher, 2000, *Queen Victoria: A Personal History*, HarperCollins.

Hibbert, Christopher, 2001, *Queen Victoria In Her Letters and Journals*, John Murray.

Hill, Christopher, 1999, *God's Englishman: Oliver Cromwell and the English Revolution*, Penguin.

Holden, Anthony, 1989, *Charles: A Biography*, Fontana.

Holmes, T. H. and Rahe, R., 1967, The Social Readjustment Rating Scale, *Journal of Psychosomatic Research*, 11, 213–8.

Hough, Richard, 1974, *Louis and Victoria: The First Mountbattens*, Hutchinson.

Howarth, Patrick, 1987, *George VI*, Hutchinson.

Irvine, Valerie, 2005, *The King's Wife: George IV and Mrs Fitzherbert*, Hambledon & London.

James I's writings are available in a number of editions but all originally appeared in his lifetime.

A Counterblaste to Tobacco

Basilikon Doron

The True Laws of Free Monarchies

Daemonologie

The Political Works of James I (1918) with an introduction by McIllain, C., published in Cambridge Mass.

The Scottish Text Society produced an edition of James I's minor prose works in 1982.

James, C. L. R., 1986, *Beyond a Boundary*, Hutchinson.

James, Robert Rhodes, 1984, *Albert, Prince Consort: A Biography*, Random House.

Jenkin, Lewis, 1703, *Memoir of William, Duke of Gloucester*, Payne, etc.

Jones, J. D. F., 2001, *Storyteller: The Many Lives of Laurens van der Post*, John Murray.

Jung, C. G., 1965, *Memories, Dreams, Reflections*, Routledge & Kegan Paul.

Junor, Penny, 1999, *Charles: Victim or Villain?*, HarperCollins.

Junor, Penny, 2012, *Prince William: Born to Be King*, Hodder & Stoughton.

Laing, R. D., 1961, *The Divided Self*, Penguin.

Laing, R. D., 1968, *Knots*, Penguin.

Langer, Walter C., 1974, *The Mind of Adolf Hitler*, Pan Books.

Leiningen, Prince Charles, 1841, *A Complete History of the Policy Followed at Kensington under Sir John Conroy's Guidance.*

Lemel, Alix, 2010, *Les 200 Clitoris de Marie Bonaparte*, Fayard.

Léri, André, 1919, *Shell Shock*, University of London Press.

Lewis, David, 2004, *The Man Who Invented Hitler*, Headline.

Lipsedge, Maurice and Littlewood, Ronald, 1987, *Aliens and Alienists*, Routledge.

Locke, J., 2007, *Some Thoughts Concerning Education*, Dover (originally published in 1693).

Locke, J., 2011, *The Educational Writings of John Locke*, Cambridge University Press (originally published in 1705).

Lyttelton Sarah, 1912, *Correspondence of Sarah Spencer, Lady Lyttelton*, John Murray.

Magnus, Philip, 1954, *Gladstone*, John Murray.

Magnus, Philip, 1965, *King Edward the Seventh*, John Murray.

Marx, K. and Engels, F., 2005, *The Communist Manifesto*, Penguin (originally published in 1848).

May, Steven W., 2005, *Elizabeth I: Selected Works*, Simon & Schuster.

Mikes, George., 1946, *How to be an Alien*, Andre Deutsch.

Montaigne, Michel de, 1993, *Essays*, Penguin (originally published in 1580).

Morshead, Owen, 1951, *Windsor Castle*, Phaidon.

Morton, Andrew, 1992, *Diana: Her True Story*, Michael O'Mara.

Mumby, Frank A., 1909, *The Girlhood of Elizabeth*, Constable.

Neale, J., 1974, *Queen Elizabeth I*, Penguin.

Nicolson, Harold (ed. Nicolson, Nigel), 1969, *Diaries and Letters 1886–1968*, Fontana.

Nicolson, Harold, 1952, *King George V*, Constable & Co.

Norton, Elizabeth, 2010, *Margaret Beaufort: Mother of the Tudor Dynasty*, Amberley.

Orbach, Susie, 2006, *Fat is a Feminist Issue*, Arrow.

Parton, J. and Greeley, H., 1868, *Eminent Women of the Age*, Gibbs & Nicol.

Pasternak, Anna, 1994, *Princess in Love*, Bloomsbury.

Pestalozzi, Johan (2010), *How Gertrude Teaches Her Children*, Kessinger (originally published in 1801).

Piaget, J., 2001, *Language and Thought in the Child*, Routledge (originally published in 1926).

Pope-Hennessy, J., 1959, *Queen Mary 1867–1953*, George Allen & Unwin.

Priestley, J. B., 1969, *The Prince of Pleasure*, Heinemann.

Quetelet, A., 1968, *A Treatise on Man and the Development of his Faculties*, Burt Franklin (originally published in 1842).

Rohl, J., 1998, *Young Wilhelm: The Kaiser's Early Life*, Cambridge University Press.

Rose, Kenneth, 1983, *King George V*, Macmillan.

Rousseau, Jean-Jacques, 2007, *Emile, or On Education* (trans. by Bloom, Alan), Basic Books (originally published in 1762).

Rowbotham, Sheila, 2009, *Edward Carpenter: A Life of Liberty and Love*, Verso.

Sacks, Oliver, 1986, *The Man Who Mistook His Wife For a Hat*, Picador.

Salovey, P. and Mayer J. D., 1990, 'Emotional intelligence', *Imagination, Cognition, and Personality*, 9, 185–211.

Schure, Edouard, 1983, *Les Grands Initiés*, Pocket (originally published in 1889).

Shawcross, William, 2009, *Queen Elizabeth, The Queen Mother*, Macmillan.

Skelton John, 1983, *The Complete English Poems*, Penguin.

Skinner, B. F., 1976, *Particulars of My Life*, Basic Books.

Steeholm, Clara and Steeholm, Hardy, 1938, *The Wisest Fool in Christendom*, Michael Joseph.

Steinbeck, John, 1960, *The Short Reign of Pippin IV*, Penguin.

Stockmar, Ernst Alfred Christian, 1872, *The Memoirs of Baron Stockmar*, Longmans, Green & Co.

Strickland, Agnes, 2011, *The Lives of the Queens of England*, Continuum (originally published in 1875).

Sully, James, 1895, *Studies of Childhood*, Longman.

Thompson, Andrew C., 2011, *George II*, Yale University Press.

Tomalin, Claire, 1998, *Mrs Jordan's Profession*, Penguin.

Trapp, Maria Augusta, 1972, *The Story of the Trapp Family Singers*, Creation House.

Treves, Frederick, 2012, *Made in the Trenches*, Forgotten Books (originally published in 1919).

Van der Post, Laurens, 2002, *Jung and the Story of Our Time*, Vintage.

Van der Kiste, John, 2003, *The Children of George V*, Sutton.

Victoria, Princess: unpublished manuscript of her memoirs from among The Mountbatten Papers in the University of Southampton Library.

Victoria, Queen HRH, 1983, *Highland Journals*, Webb & Bower (originally published 1869).

Wakeford, G. F., 1969, *The Heir Apparent*, Robert Hale.

Warwick, Christopher, 2006, *Ella: Princess, Saint and Martyr*, John Wiley & Sons.

Watson, J. B. and Watson, R. R., 1929, *The Psychological Care of the Infant and Child*, Lippincott.

Wharfe, Ken, 2003, *Diana: Closely Guarded Secret*, Michael O'Mara.

Wheeler-Bennett, John W., 1959, *George VI: His Life and Reign*, Macmillan.

White, T. H., 1964, *The Age of Scandal*, Penguin.

William of Malmesbury, (ed. Mynors, R. A. B. et al.), 1997, *Gesta Regum Anglorum,* Clarendon Press (originally published in medieval times).

Windsor, Duke of, 1998, *A King's Story*, Prion (introduction by Philip Ziegler) (the original edition was published by Cassell).

Winnicott, D. W., 1980, *Playing and Reality*, Penguin.

Winnicott, D. W., 1971, *The Child, the Family and the Outside World*, Penguin.

Woodham-Smith, Cecil, 1973, *Queen Victoria: Her Life and Times*, Cardinal.

Wortley Montagu, Lady Mary, 1997, *Selected Letters* (ed. Grundy, Isobel), Penguin.

Young, George, 1937, *Poor Fred: The People's Prince*, Oxford University Press.

Ziegler, Philip, 1973, *King William IV*, Readers Union.

Ziegler, Philip, 1985, *Mountbatten: The Official Biography*, Harper-Collins.

Ziegler, Philip, 1991, *Edward VIII: The Official Biography*, Knopf.

ACKNOWLEDGEMENTS

This book would not have been possible if many years ago David Lloyd at Channel 4 had not commissioned a treatment of a film on the death of Princess Diana. In the end, I made the film for Chris Shaw, then at Five TV. Both encouraged me. I must also record my thanks to Francois Gillery, with whom I collaborated on a film for French TV. As ever, David Carr Brown, who filmed and edited my film was an excellent foil as we pondered the edit (before making that film, I had never ventured into royal territory).

A number of libraries were very helpful – the Wellcome Trust in London, the British Library (though it did not have a copy of the Kensington System), the University of Southampton, which houses the Mountbatten papers, the Bishopsgate Institute and the Royal Society of Medicine. Robert Greenwood, one of the librarians there, gave me a wonderful story but, alas, told me I could not use it. I have honoured his request. Ben Shephard, whose books on psychiatry in World War I have been widely praised, was extremely helpful in providing some ideas.

My agent and friend Sonia Land was very supportive, as was her assistant, Samuel Humphreys.

Jeremy Robson liked the idea from the first and provided stability and useful criticism. Hollie Teague sensibly urged some cuts in the first chapter. At the end of the process Emily Carter read the book with great care and I am most grateful for her hard work. The mistakes remain mine, of course.

INDEX

Boleyn, Anne, mother of Eliza-
beth I, second wife of Henry
VIII 39–42, 44, 45, 47, 48, 54
Boleyn, Mary, mistress of Henry
VIII 39
Bonaparte, Princess Marie 11, 15,
112, 208, 214, 219, 225, 241–4,
256, 261
Boothroyd, Basil 242
Bothwell, Henry 59–60
Bowes-Lyon, David 224
Bowes-Lyon, Elizabeth, later
Queen, later Queen Mother,
mother of Elizabeth II 11, 12, 17,
223–6, 233, 235, 254–5, 266, 270
Bowlby, John 253
Boxwell, Dr 174
Brabourne, Lady 14, 268
breastmilk, wonders of 165–6
Breslau, Naomi 57
Broadmoor Hospital 273
Brock, Mrs 149
Brontë children, imaginary worlds
of 151
Brooks Club 128
Brooks, Peter 6
Bruce, Fiona 243
Bryan, Lady 44–5
Buchanan, George 61–4
Buchanan, James 173
Buckingham, Duke of 32
Basualdo, Luis 258–9
Bullitt, William 8, 225, 226–9
Burchill, Julie 2
Burney, Fanny 125–6
Bute, Earl of 116–18
Butler, Lord 258
Caesar, Julius 54
Cambridge, Duchess of see
Middleton, Kate

Cambridge, Duke of see William,
Prince
Cambridge, Duke of (previous
occupant) 132
Cambridge, Duke of and 'Eddy'
192
Cambridge University 79, 173, 191
Captain Bodkin 110
Carey, Lady 63–4
Carey, Sir Robert 63–4
Caroline of Ansbach, grandmoth-
er of George III, wife of George
II 102–4, 105, 110–14
Caroline of Brunswick, mother
of Princess Charlotte, wife of
George IV 131, 132–4, 136, 138,
142
Carpenter, Edward 186, 192
Cartland, Barbara 265
Cartland, Raine, stepmother of
Princess Diana 265
Casanova, Giacomo 110–11
Cassell, Ernest 11, 240
castration anxiety 211
Catherine of Aragon, mother of
Mary Tudor, wife of Henry
VIII 36–42, 57
Catherine of Braganza, wife of
Charles II 82, 87, 91
Catherine of Valois, mother of
Henry VI, wife of Henry V and
of then Owen Tudor 31–2
Cato 115
Cecil, Sir Robert 57
Cecilie, Princess, daughter of Prin-
cess Alice 14, 246
Chapsky, Countess 191
Chapuys, Eustace 40–42
Charles I, father of Charles II and
James II 61, 64, 73–8